JONATHAN FISHER

～ *Maine Parson* ～

1768–1847

By MARY ELLEN CHASE

The Bible and the Common Reader
Dawn in Lyonesse
A Goodly Fellowship
Mary Peters
Silas Crockett
This England
Windswept
Jonathan Fisher: Maine Parson, 1768-1847

The Rev. Jonathan Fisher, 1824. Copied, 1838

JONATHAN FISHER

~ *Maine Parson* ~

1768-1847

BY

MARY ELLEN CHASE

THE MACMILLAN COMPANY · NEW YORK

1948

This book is dedicated in gratitude
to three persons
who have made its existence possible:

Roland Merrill Howard

Edith Chase Weren

Gaylord Crossette Hall

PREFACE

THIS book has been made by many hands and many minds. I am but its scribe. For several years those who have made it have contributed generously of their time and labor, and only through that time and labor has its completion been possible.

It is based almost entirely upon the "Common Journals," or Diaries, of Jonathan Fisher, which he kept daily for forty-five years of his long life, upon his many notebooks, and upon his countless letters and sermons. All these documents, except certain of the letters, were originally written, or later transcribed, in a shorthand code, which he devised in 1792 when he was a student at Harvard College. Since nearly every source upon which the book is based had to be carefully decoded by the use of a key which the parson thoughtfully left behind him, a vast expenditure of time on this task alone has been inevitable.

Most of the difficult deciphering of this mass of material has been done by my sister, Edith Chase Weren of Pleasantville, N. Y., assisted by Gaylord Crossette Hall of New York City, a great-grandson of Jonathan Fisher. Each has worked literally for years upon this colossal job. The loan of the material itself has been given by Gaylord Hall, who has added to his own collection various papers lent him by several other Fisher descendants, and by Roland Merrill Howard of Bluehill, Maine. To the latter, whose name justly appears first on the dedicatory page, is due the very existence of the greater part of the Fisher material left in the deserted parsonage upon the death of the last member of the Bluehill family. It was Roland Howard who twenty years ago rescued the vast number of these papers, together with Jonathan

Fisher's paintings, his books, and articles of household furnishings made by him, from destruction by theft or fire and himself preserved them. Through later purchase of them from Fisher heirs, he is now their appropriate owner. To this large Howard collection and to the smaller, though important, one of Gaylord Hall, this book owes its being; to Roland Howard it owes also his wide knowledge of Bluehill history and to Gaylord Hall his complete familiarity with his family tree; and to both of these gentlemen its writer owes immeasurable cooperation, courtesy, and unfailing interest.

Others among the Fisher descendants and several other members of my own family have given me indispensable aid. Mrs. G. N. Lauman of Ithaca, N. Y., Mrs. A. F. Steinman of Deposit, N. Y., Mrs. Henry Crowell of Winnetka, Ill., Mrs. Theodore Lyman of Great Barrington, Mass., Mrs. Murray Crossette of San Antonio, Tex., Mr. Aaron Fisher of Westhampton, Mass., and Miss Ethelwynne Hinckley of New York City,—all these must be thanked for the generous loan of books, records, letters, or pictures, composed by or pertaining to their ancestor. The likeness of Jonathan Fisher on the book's jacket and used also as a frontispiece is taken from his self-portrait owned by Samuel Fisher of Litchfield, Conn., a great-grandson, who graciously had a photograph taken of it for this purpose. My sisters, Olive Chase O'Brien of Portland, Maine, Virginia Chase Perkins of Detroit, Mich., and Mildred Chase Hinckley of Bluehill, have worked on various town and church records; my nephew, William Peters Hinckley of Orrington, Maine, has explored family graveyards and deciphered their half-obliterated inscriptions; my nephew, Edward Chase Weren of Cambridge, Mass., has traced and re-lettered the Jonathan Fisher map used as an end-paper. To my brother, Newton Kimball Chase, Assistant Headmaster of the Thacher School in Ojai, Cal., and teacher of American History, I am deeply indebted, not only for weeks spent in copying church records and for research in various Maine libraries, but for much of the background material and even for the original writing of the chapter entitled "Mr. Fisher and His Times." Without his invaluable help, indeed, I could not have written the book. *Jonathan Fisher: Maine Parson* is, therefore, quite clearly not so much my own as it is the work of the Fisher and the Chase families, together with that of Roland Merrill Howard.

In addition, I must express my appreciation to many others. To Clifford Shipton, Custodian of the Harvard University Archives and Librarian of the American Antiquarian Society of Worcester, Mass., who has not only cheerfully answered numberless questions and lent books by Jonathan Fisher, but who has also read my manuscript, chapter by chapter, with a kindly eye to inaccuracies; to Carolyn Jakeman, Robert Haynes, and David McCord, for work done for me in the Harvard Library; to Marion Brown of the Brown University Library, to Rena Durkan of the Memorabilia Room at Amherst College, to Mildred Jaques of the Dedham Historical Society, Dedham, Mass., to Katharine Hodgdon of Milton Academy, Milton, Mass., to Alice Whitney, Recorder of Phillips Academy, Andover, to Helen Johnson, Registrar of Bowdoin College, to Kathryn McCraw, Registrar of Williams College,—all of whom have assisted me in running down helpful historical or genealogical information. To Mrs. Berton Towle of Holden, Mass., for information concerning Joseph Avery and the history of the Holden Congregational Church; to Janet Byrne for her article on Jonathan Fisher as an engraver, entitled "An American Pioneer Amateur" and published in *The Princeton University Library Chronicle*, June, 1945; to Karl Kup, Curator of Prints in the New York Public Library, for his treatment of the parson as engraver in *American Artist*, April, 1947; again to Gaylord Hall for his two biographical sketches of Jonathan Fisher, privately printed in 1945 and 1946; and to the late Fannie Eckstrom Hardy, of Brewer, Maine, whose knowledge of Maine history and folk-lore has been widely recognized and who for several years gave me generously of that knowledge. Acknowledgment must also be made to those W.P.A.

workers, who in 1938 and 1939 made such admirable investiga-
tions of Maine town and village records and who, through the
courtesy of Elizabeth Ring, State Research Editor of the Historical Records Survey, supplied me with copies of their findings.

I am especially grateful to friends in my native village of Bluehill, who have been naturally interested in this book and who
have given me their time and assistance. To Dorris Parker of the
Bluehill Library and her helpers, to Jennie Littlefield, Annie
Clough, Adelaide Pearson, Alice Wescott, Emma Stover, Florence
Morse, Enoch Grindle, Ethel Stover, Dorothy Austin, Lillian
Emerson, Sally Tucker, all of whom have gladly helped me in a
dozen different ways. I am especially indebted to Esther Wood,
herself an authority on early village history, and to the late
Dr. Otis Littlefield, who lent me various important documents
in his possession. I wish also to thank the town officers of Bluehill and the pastors of its two churches, who have generously
allowed me access to records and papers.

To colleagues at Smith College who have given me constant
help I am also grateful. Margaret Johnson, reference librarian
at Smith, has been indispensable both in knowledge and good
humor; Oliver Larkin of the Art Department has given hours of
time and interest to the study and criticism of Jonathan Fisher's
paintings and drawings, of the value of which I was totally ignorant. Henry Elkan, photographer for that Department, has gone
to Bluehill to photograph pictures and manuscripts in the
Howard collection, and I am indebted to his work for several of
the illustrations in the book. Daniel Aaron of the Departments
of English and Government has helped me both by his knowledge of American History and by his perennial interest in Jonathan Fisher. William Christian of the Department of Religion
has suggested valuable books for supplementary reading on
Fisher's period. My housemate, Eleanor Duckett, Professor of
Classical Languages, has not only translated Jonathan Fisher's
Latin dissertations at Harvard, but has constantly buoyed up my
spirits through years of often irritating labor.

Finally, to my secretary, Gladys Nute, and also to Hazel Ourada, who have written hundreds of letters and cheerfully made intelligible my many pages of messy manuscript, I offer incommensurate, but genuine thanks. Truly my statement made at the beginning of this necessarily long preface, that I am but the scribe of this book, is now more than obvious!

Since the book is based almost wholly on original documents, it has seemed unnecessary to include any bibliography. The several works on American social and religious background, which have been either illuminating or complementary, are all carefully named in footnotes. For the same reason few other annotations are made since practically all quotations are drawn from diaries, letters, notebooks, or sermons available only in manuscript form. In several instances I have taken the liberty of combining without notation diary entries and excerpts from letters on the same subjects where one has supplemented or complemented the other.

Mary Ellen Chase

SMITH COLLEGE,
NORTHAMPTON, MASSACHUSETTS.
DECEMBER 26, 1947.

CONTENTS

ILLUSTRATIONS

I N his brief, yet significant and moving, biography, *John Gilley, Maine Farmer and Fisherman,* President Eliot gives as a reason for his book his desire to preserve, even perhaps for but a short time, the memory of a man whose dignity, honesty, and vitality and whose perception and use of life redeemed in no small sense his day and generation. It is almost precisely this same desire which has prompted me to write of the Reverend Jonathan Fisher. A country parson and pastor, in the strictest, most Biblical sense of that ancient word, Jonathan Fisher spent fifty years of the seventy-nine allotted to him, "by Divine Mystery and Grace," in the small seacoast village of Bluehill, Maine. There he settled in 1796; and there, full of years and good works, he died in 1847. A century has not sufficed to dim the memory and, indeed, the wonder of him among the succeeding generations of those who knew him. For he was a Leonardo da Vinci of his own time and place; and his multifarious accomplishments, both mental and manual, must have astounded his contemporaries as they have astounded me during the years given to the reading and the study of his voluminous journals and his countless letters. A mechanical genius from his boyhood, a farmer, a surveyor, an architect and builder, a scientist, an artist, a writer of poetry and prose, a theologian, a linguist, a missionary traveling thousands of miles "on foot like my Master," Jonathan Fisher was one of those rare souls possessed of an almost incredible vitality and a consuming sense of the value and use of life itself. Such qualities, it has seemed to me, deserve, indeed almost demand, preservation for themselves alone.

My book is written also in the hope that the time and the society which it may reveal, even within a relatively small compass, may prove of value to the knowledge of American life and particularly to that of rural New England of the late eighteenth and early nineteenth centuries. Nor is its compass, as a matter of fact, so small and circumscribed. For Father Fisher, as he was known to his flock, perhaps as much from dread as from affection, never mistook his parish for the world outside its boundaries or held its affairs of greater importance than those problems and controversies engaging the more discerning and farsighted of his contemporaries in larger spheres of labor. While he sounded his Calvinistic warnings to the erring minds and sinsick souls of his congregation, he was not unaware of human frailty elsewhere; and although "human depravity" in various forms seems to have been the favorite subject of the more than three thousand sermons, which he neatly left behind him, he kept, like St. Paul, his loins constantly girded against the inroads of that depravity in his State and nation. He was deeply concerned with what he felt to be the unjust and lamentable treatment of the American Indians and with the injustice and sin of slavery; he was an ardent champion of the American Society for the Colonization of Liberia, a voluble opponent of the War of 1812, and a stalwart supporter of the American Temperance Movement, all of which causes he made the subjects of his voice, his pen, and his always lean purse. He was untiring in his care for the training of young men in the ministry, for their manners and their minds as well as for their souls; and both the founding and the perpetuation of the Bangor Theological Seminary owe not a little to his unflagging zeal. Although the children of his parish were terrified at his frequent catechizing of them and doubtless fled his ominous approach whenever possible, he cared deeply for the nurture of their minds as well as for the salvation of their souls, and, for his day, was a startling advocate of the inclusion of the fine arts in the Maine academies and even in the elementary schools, particularly those of music and of painting.

He lies in the Old Burying Ground of Bluehill, beneath a tall granite shaft, which bears an open book, marked with Socrates', and his own, repeated injunction, *Know Thyself*. When I was a child at the close of the last century and went, fifty years after his death, with my playmates for strawberries to that long unused graveyard, seemingly an incomparable place for their nurture, we never ventured to gather them on Father Fisher's grave!

I

BACKGROUND AND BOYHOOD

T HE old town of Dedham, Massachusetts, ten miles from Boston, was the place of Jonathan Fisher's background and, throughout his long life, of his loyal affection. Planted as a colony in 1635 from Massachusetts Bay and incorporated in 1636, it was for many generations the home of the Fisher family. Here shortly after its founding came "in early life" Anthony Fisher from the county of Suffolk, England, and here in the year 1654 was born his son Josiah. Anthony Fisher, we learn from records in the Dedham Historical Society, was clearly a man of importance in the early years of that colony. By the year 1652 his lands included some two hundred acres; he had been twice chosen as Selectman; and he had served as Deputy to the General Court of Massachusetts. He had also distinguished himself "on account of his proud and haughty spirit," which delayed for several years his being "comfortably received" into the Dedham church! And if his son Josiah left no such record of power and personality behind him, he was, according to the Dedham records, at least married four times in eighty-two years—an accomplishment which suggests that resiliency and that abundance of life clearly characteristic of the Fisher stock! One of the many great-grandsons of Josiah was Jonathan, the subject of this book, whose father and grandfather bore the same name as his own.

Dedham was likewise the home of Jonathan's mother, Katharine Avery, the descendant of Dr. William Avery, who, coming to Dedham from Berkshire, England, in 1650, combined the somewhat disparate occupations of a blacksmith and of a physician, and who was known as "a liberal patron of learning," especially

toward the "Colledge at Cambridge." And, finally, Dedham was
the home of Jonathan's wife, Dolly Battle Fisher. His roots,
therefore, were unquestionably there; there he spent his recesses
from Harvard College; and there he returned as often as possible
during the five weeks allowed him annually from his Maine
pastorate.

Jonathan himself, however, was not born in Dedham but in
the village of New Braintree, "near the centre of Massachusetts
proper," and at the home of his grandfather Fisher, with whom
his father and mother lived from the time of their marriage in
1766 until 1773 when they moved with their four young children
to Northampton. The date of his birth, October 7, 1768, was
never allowed to pass unnoticed or, indeed, unchronicled in the
day by day Diaries which he kept for forty-five years. Always it
formed the occasion for thanksgiving to God in prose or in verse
for creation and preservation, and not infrequently for misgivings on the "wretched state of his immortal soul" while the
"ruthless passage of cruel time" brings him hourly closer to his
"blessed reward or everlasting punishment."

With that consuming respect, even passion, for manual labor
which Jonathan Fisher felt all his life and the complete delight which he took therein, it seems odd that in the *Sketches* of
his life, which he began in 1812 at the age of forty-four, he
takes small pains to identify the pursuits or professions of his
immediate forbears. It is only through letters of his mother and
of various other members of his family and through certain of
the many epitaphs which he wrote upon the death of relatives
that clues are given as to their ways and means of life. Since
he frequently worked as a boy during the summer for his grandfather Fisher "in the fields at harvest," it is safe to conclude that
his grandfather and his father, who lived together for ten years,
were farmers, at least to some extent. The epitaph which he
wrote upon the death in Dedham in 1796 of another William
Avery, his maternal grandfather, identifies him as a blacksmith,
like his ancestor, the early patron of learning:

Hard at the anvil threescore years he wrought,
But far above it soared his heavenly thought.
The Church he loved, and forty years or more
The sacred office of a Deacon bore.

His mother's letters, of which we have some forty in number, written mostly from Dedham, in their many references to good and bad crops of hay, corn, potatoes, and "garden sauce," to the loss of fruit through high winds, and to a storm which "blew down the great walnut tree by our cow-yard" would suggest farming as a means of livelihood among members of her family. One of her brothers, Joseph Avery, a graduate of Harvard in 1771, was for many years the Congregational minister in Holden, Massachusetts. Of her four sons, three were clergymen, Samuel and William [1] following their elder brother Jonathan in that profession and settling in New Jersey and New York parishes, and Stephen becoming a farmer in Westhampton, Massachusetts, and later in New York State.

But although few concrete facts can be ascertained as to the Avery and the Fisher means of life, two remain certain beyond the shadow of a doubt: both families were poor and both were pious. Moreover, it is abundantly clear that any lack of material possessions, even of necessities, were as nothing in comparison with the want of a humble and contrite heart irrevocably set upon the blessed hope of salvation. Katharine Avery Fisher's letters to her son Jonathan are concerned before all else with her soul and with his, with the souls of all Fishers and all Averys, as well as with those of Dedham, Conway, Sunderland, Northampton, and "the heathen lands beyond the sea." The anxiety which she quite reasonably feels over making $29 suffice for her needs from May to December in 1818 is little enough in the face of her greater anxiety over the desire of several in the Congregational Society at Dedham for "a pastor of Liberal sentiments," over the deplorable increase of the Baptists there, and over the

[1] Samuel and William Fisher were graduates of Williams College in 1799 and 1805.

growing numbers of "Arians, Socinians, and Arminians" in Massachusetts. Although at seventy-five she suffers from a trying cough, which keeps her from sleep, her bodily health must needs be improved by her rejoicing over "a great awakening in the town of Brookfield" and by the comfortable knowledge that "seventy persons there have attained to a blessed hope."

Katharine Avery Fisher was a woman of parts in any age and place, admirably deserving the title of Honored Mother, by which her son always addressed her. Much of that prodigious vitality which he possessed to such a marked degree quite obviously sprang from her own abundant life. Nor was all her strength and vigor expended upon her preparation for the next world. There was enough and to spare for this one, which, much as she professed to discount its pleasures and pastimes, she thoroughly enjoyed.

Perhaps, indeed, that enjoyment lay in no small measure in her ability to cope with those trials and misfortunes "thoughtfully provided by Divine Goodness" either for "deserved chastisement" or as a wholesome means for her "soul's nurture." Left a widow at the early age of thirty-one with seven children to rear, she had ample cause, indeed, to claim the peculiar thoughtfulness of Divine Goodness! Like her son she took pride in the work of her hands, which supported her throughout her long life. When she was nearly eighty, she wrote of weaving in one summer "20 yds. of checked shirting, 18 yds. of linnen, 20 yds. of heavy Thersy for blankets, and 31 yds. of carpets." In another summer she accomplishes "90 yds. of carpet well-woven" and has her mind set on completing "3 rag floor coverings" before the season is full spent. Small wonder that next to piety toward God and obedience to their parents, she constantly warned her many grandchildren against idleness and sloth, "the weapons of Satan to snare and to delude."

Like her son, she enjoyed the weather, the drama in its extremes always taking precedence over the discomforts; and "two yellow daffodils blowing" in her sister's garden in Dedham presumably helped to mitigate in her imagination "the low state of religion among us." She apparently loved to go on a journey, "by waggon," stagecoach, sleigh, or coastwise vessel, and never missed an opportunity. She had a distinct predilection for the ravages of disease or for disaster in any form, a taste, one suspects, not wholly to be explained by her concern for the immortal souls of those stricken; and this predilection she handed on in full measure to her son, who never missed an opportunity for a death-bed poem and for whom battle, murder, and sudden death in all forms never failed to provide both excitement and easily rationalized pleasure. One can imagine the agreeable gloom enfolding both over a letter written by her to him in October, 1802:

This has been a melancholy week. Wednesday Ira Draper's youngest child was buried. Yesterday poor Mason was executed, and one of Joseph Swan's daughters was buried. The other lies dead, which is all they had except an infant born since the others were taken sick. Today old Mr. Stoddard was buried. He died of the palsy.

Her carefully tabulated lists of the deaths occurring in New York City during the especially "sickly season of 1825," of which she has read in the newspapers, together with the diseases causing dissolution, find countless echoes in Jonathan's Diaries. She begs for more details concerning the deaths and the accidents in her son's parish:

You mentioned the Death of a Mrs. Peters, that was Molly Clay. When you write again, please be a little more particular.

And solemnly as she discourses in practically every letter concerning "a dying world" and "the constant Presence of Death among us," one easily gathers that the scythe of the Grim Reaper actually enlivened her days to no small extent.

She was meticulous concerning the receipt and expenditure of money, of which she had deplorably little, and this carefulness also she handed on to her son, who kept a complete and exact account of every penny spent during nearly sixty years. She is angry over the charge of .79 to convey her "goods from Boston to Dedham," regretful that the costs of repairing her loom are .50, anxious that her son Stephen owes $40 although he owns, to be sure, 25 acres of good land. She would "derely love" to send her grandchildren some little gifts, a peppermint each if she could, but since she is "entirely lacking in any funds, good counsel must suffice for earthly joys."

In a letter written from New Braintree in 1770 at the age of twenty-four to her brother, Joseph Avery, then in his third year at Harvard, she deplores that she has "but a dull brain"; yet there is surely no evidence of such a possession in all her correspondence. All through her life she loved to read and is continually thanking God for His kind preservation of her eyes. One surmises from several early letters that she did not look upon her children as an unmixed blessing since she twice reminds her brother that if he "had a Babe to suckle," he would be "aware of a Difference" in his time for reading and study and that he "cannot easily think how much trouble a young child is." Her later letters, written to her son, refer constantly to her reading which, denied her in earlier years, she is obviously enjoying to the fullest extent. In May, 1818, when she is seventy-two, she is reading Neal's *History of the Puritans,* which she recommends strongly for the library in Bluehill. In this book, she says, she has found a most interesting account of the King James Translation of 1611, from which account she copies at some length, since such valuable information, she fears, may not be in any of the books owned by Jonathan. In 1820 she is reading "Dr. Dwight's Sermons called Theology Explained and Defended in 5 Vols," and from this work also she makes extracts "on the meaning of the word *church,* particularly as it obtains to those baptized in infancy."

Evidently most of her reading was of a religious nature, for she makes no references to books of a lighter sort, and quite as evidently she brought to bear upon it her own intelligence. For

Puritan though she was and carefully nurtured in Calvinistic dogma, she exercised her own mind on theological matters and is neither slow nor fearful about expressing her opinions. For example, in a letter written in 1824 she remonstrates with her son against any impulse to pray for afflictions, salutary though their consequences may conceivably be to their recipients:

I don't think that we should pray for affliction. In the Lord's prayer we pray that we may be Delivered from evil, and Christ in His last prayer prays that the cup might pass from Him. But we ought rather to pray that afflictions may be sanctified for our good, for without they will not profit us.

Like William Hazlitt's mother, her contemporary in eighteenth century England, her "dearest wish was that her son might be a Dissenting Minister," and to realize this wish she was ready and eager to work and to sacrifice. "My mother's desire," wrote Jonathan Fisher in the *Sketches* of his life, "was that I should have a public education, nor was I averse to it provided I could obtain it, but I saw no prospect of ever being able to defray the expense of it. Through my mother's advice and encouraging words, however, I came at length to the determination to pursue my studies, and sometime in my 17th or 18th year, I cannot say which, I was permitted to lay aside other work and follow study constantly." That Katharine Avery Fisher somehow provided whatever money her son did not himself earn during his four years at Harvard College, his letters to her from Cambridge and numerous entries in his college diaries bear sturdy witness. In October, 1789: "I was called upon as a delinquent in the payment of quarter bills for the year. My mother came and brought me $11 to defray them." In April, 1791: "I received of my mother $14.62." In June, 1791: "My mother came to see me. She took my 4th Quarter Bill of $9.62." On several occasions she brings baskets of wood to his room in Massachusetts Hall; again she comes with needed clothing which she has made for him and bears away "my linnen for washing"; and at least three times, seeing no other means of meeting his bills, she borrows funds with which to pay them from the church at Dedham. His careful accounting to her of the probable, or actual, cost of his college books would suggest that she found the money for them. All in all, the portion contributed by her toward his four years as a Harvard undergraduate must have been at least half of the $238 which he records as the actual cash which he paid the college during that period. For upon his graduation in 1792 he gives her a note for $119 which, he states, is the exact amount of his indebtedness to her.

2

In the spring of 1773 Katharine and Jonathan Fisher with four small children moved from New Braintree to the western part of the town of Northampton, there in a sparsely settled region to found a home of their own. Jonathan was at that time in his fifth year. In the *Sketches* of his life he describes the small house, built by his father on Cub Hill, in what is now Westhampton, as "a cottage containing one room and built of hewn logs with a stone chimney." "With food we were well-provided," he writes, "and generally had a competency of clothing though sometimes we were in rags. One winter myself and my brothers and sisters were without shoes, and our bare feet were daily accustomed to the snow. My father's cottage, I trust, however, was the habitation of piety and contentment."

He describes his father as a man "who carried that presence with him which commanded both the fear and the love of his children" and rendered severe chastisement unnecessary, although it was wisely not withheld when deserved. His parents' concern for the souls of their children as well as for their own resulted in such early religious training that by the age of six, or seven, he had committed to heart the Assembly's Catechism and states himself well-versed in the "first principles of Christianity." There being no "preaching of the Gospel" nearer than Northampton, meetings were held each Sunday in the home of one settler or another, to which the Fisher family proceeded in a home-made cart, or sled, "drawn by a well-governed, tractable ox," and in which services his father took a leading part. Not infrequently, he records, missionary pastors were present, and on one occasion a certain Reverend Mr. Kirtland, missionary to the Indians and accompanied by a pious Mohawk, delivered such a discourse on the straight gate and the narrow way that the young Jonathan experienced a painful concern for his future bliss or agony, a concern destined never to leave him for a single day of the many vouchsafed to his earthly pilgrimage.

Since he mentions no school in the neighborhood, he was evidently taught to read by his parents, for he describes himself "most tractable" in learning. Indeed, at six years old the sight of Greek characters in a book of his mother's so excited him by their mystery that he was filled by a desire to master that language and all other "dead tongues," a desire also destined never to forsake him.

The four years in Northampton were brought to a sad and sudden close by the death of his father. Called to service in the autumn of 1776 as a Lieutenant in the War of the Revolution, he died of fever in March of the following year in Morristown, New Jersey. A few weeks later Katharine Avery Fisher with her six children and another soon to be born went to the village of Sunderland, near Hadley, to stay with relatives. Shortly after the birth of her son Samuel her large family was broken up, the various children being scattered about among willing, or unwilling, Averys and Fishers. The lot of Jonathan at the age of nine fell to his uncle, Joseph Avery, Congregational pastor to the church in Holden, Massachusetts, with whom he was to live, and learn, for the next eleven years of his life.

Few laborers in the vineyard at any time have concentrated their energies as did the Reverend Joseph Avery, who three years after his graduation from Harvard in 1771 began his work at Holden. For a full fifty years he lived there and for forty-eight of them in most active service as pastor. The hill upon which his house stood is still known as Avery Hill and the house itself as "the old Avery place." A history of the Holden church, written in 1940, describes him as a man of infinite tact, patience, and wisdom, who kept his church from being "rent in twain" by the rise of doctrinal controversies and who was known far and wide as "the peace-maker." His nephew Jonathan writes that he was a man of mild and agreeable temper, "improved by a liberal education," and that his industry was so unflagging that no member of his family was suffered to grow up in idleness. Toward the disposition of his "Aunt Avery" Jonathan is not so enthusiastic. She was a woman, he says, of decent education and good natural sense, most active, indeed untiring, in all domestic affairs, but of an unhappy and chiding temper and of a manner far from agreeable both toward him and toward her servants, all of whom, without exception, tarried with her but a brief season. One assumes that her small store of happiness was not increased by the entrance of a nine-year-old boy into a growing family of young children.

Jonathan is at pains in his *Sketches* to write fully of his life at Holden, seeing in the pursuits and influences of those formative years most of the making of himself. He learned early to swing an axe skilfully, since much of his uncle's ministerial land was heavily wooded and must be cleared for the farming necessary to supplement a small salary. Within the house, where a less pleasant atmosphere prevailed than in woods and fields, he was baby-tender and kitchen help. "Between the years of 10 and 15," he writes, "I began to exhibit some traces of a mechanical genius and a turn toward mathematics, spending my leisure time in making buttons, brooches, windmills, snares, traps, purling-sticks, and the like, and in solving various questions in mathematics, sometimes with a pin on a smooth board and sometimes on a slate, which led the way afterwards to a small measure of proficiency in sketching and painting." His formal schooling during this time was limited to but four or five weeks in each year, and had it not been for his uncle, who apparently was keenly aware of his intelligence, and for his mother, who, from various places of sojourn among relatives from Conway, Massachusetts, to Dedham, urged study upon him, he would have fared badly in the life of books. The Reverend Joseph Avery, doubtless with the memory of his own years at Harvard comfortably within him, began "on rainy days and in the evenings" to teach his nephew Latin and the rudiments of Greek, together with hearing him recite verbatim much of the Bible and training him in those religious truths and tenets which were his own meat and drink.

At sixteen Jonathan reports himself in a state of dark discouragement, not because of his studies, but because he saw no prospect of traveling along that road toward which they seemingly led. He was discontented with his situation and began to consider, first, a blacksmith's trade, then a cabinet-maker's, and finally that of a clock-maker. "In either of the two last-mentioned," he writes, "I might, no doubt, have succeeded; but God clearly had other employment for me." His uncle, wisely anticipating God's clear intentions, allowed him at seventeen, or eighteen, to lay aside farm and household chores and "to follow study constantly," although Jonathan stole many hours from Greek, Latin, and theology "to make figures in geometry and to study dialing, etc."

But although he was discouraged concerning his earthly future during his adolescence, that discouragement was as nothing in comparison with the despondence suffered during his years at Holden concerning Eternity and the dark state of his immortal soul. At sixteen in anguish over his sins he walks alone at night under the stars. What a wretched atom he is in the light of their glory! What an astonishing wonder that Jesus Christ should condescend to come down from Heaven to save such a worthless worm as he! He tries to pray before sleeping, but Satan, ever vigilant, deflects his thoughts toward an unsolved problem in geometry. A boy of his own age dies "in sin." What deserved torments must he now be suffering? Often he goes into the hayloft, away from the noise of the household, to cast his wretched self upon the mercy of God, but unchaste, vicious thoughts assail him even as he sinks upon his knees.

At eighteen, "on the first day of February, 1787," he writes with his customary accuracy, he began to keep a daily diary of his spiritual state; at the age of forty-four he describes in the *Sketches* this early diary which he continued to keep for some twenty years: "I may observe that much in my spiritual journal has been rather a record of miscarriages and failings than of anything else and of a nature to humble me into the very dust of the earth." Surely the brief entries at the start are touching in their obvious misery. "Slothful in my duty toward God, negligent in my studies." "Went to meeting this day and was filled with wandering and lustful thoughts. I returned without profit in anything." "Have a desire to begin my life anew, but alas! resolution is wanting. O Heavenly Father, I beseech thee to help me." "A propensity to impurity is very predominant within me. Alas! this is not the only sin to which I am addicted. I am regardless also of the rule of temperance in eating." Sometimes he indulges himself in verse:

> But my hard heart is prone to sin.
> What deep pollution reigns within!
> Meanwhile I tread with awful speed
> Those ways which to destruction lead.

Various happenings during his life at Holden only increased his discontent and misery. He writes of a servant-girl in the employ of his "Aunt Avery," who "by her impure and unadvised conversation" with him and "by her wanton behavior" introduced into his mind thoughts which for years were to torment him, and who urged upon him "such familiarity with her" as to add to those monstrous fears assailing his distressed soul. He tells of an early experience with a pack of playing-cards, brought to the house one evening by some neighborhood boys while his aunt and uncle were away from home. Upon their unexpected early return, a frightened attempt to conceal the cards resulted in one being left upon the floor, clearly by the merciful Providence of God. His uncle, who the next morning discovered the pernicious bit of cardboard, spoke to him "in a mild, though solemn manner" concerning the unspeakable evils of gaming, whereupon he determined never again to take such an object into his hand. "Through preventing Goodness I have never done it," he writes in 1812, "and I hope through Grace I never shall. This dropping of a card I have ever considered as a very favorable interposition of Providence which may have prevented my temporal and spiritual ruin." He describes graphically an early fall into the snare of intemperance, confessing as a preface to his story that he has always had "a fondness for the taste of spiritous liquors." Having gone into the woods on horseback after berries with some other boys, he "weakly acceded" upon their return at nightfall to their desire to call at a tavern, where they all drank until they were in a woeful state of complete intoxication, "even delirium." The loss of their berries on their homeward journey late at night, their disgraceful inability to ride their horses, which galloped home without them, the humiliation of many succeeding days of shame—these also contributed to his constant doubt as to the present and the future state of his soul.

In the somber honesty always characteristic of him, together with that tendency toward gloomy introspection from which he never freed himself, he feels it necessary to recall that even in his boyhood at Holden, yea, even as a small child in Westhampton, he became anxiously aware of two besetting sins of his vile nature: the first, a propensity toward impure thoughts; the second, which he terms "a still more besetting sin," "a spirit of slumber." These, he says, have been with him from early consciousness, and to the grave he will take them. Oh, if but the silent Grave could conceal them forever! The first, he can truly account for by the corrupt example of others. "Let a bear, robbed of her whelps, meet a child," he writes, "rather than a

vicious man or a corrupt woman!" The origin of the second he
can lay to no source save Satan Himself. "From early childhood
to this day, by the fireside, when reading, when at prayer, it
has fallen upon me like a strong man armed and made me
feeble as Samson shorn by Delilah. To take snuff, to prick myself with a pin, to pinch myself were all insufficient to keep
me awake."

It is difficult, indeed, to discover many pleasurable hours or
occupations in Jonathan Fisher's account of his eleven years at
Holden. Perhaps those stolen from his studies for work with
his hands gave him, as they were to give him throughout his
life, the greatest satisfaction. One hopes that they also afforded
him some salutary forgetfulness of his spiritual state! He has
little to say of occasional visits spent at New Braintree with
his grandfather Fisher except that he worked at farming, nor
does he allude to sojourns elsewhere. During his last year with
Joseph Avery, in December, 1787, he interrupted his studies to
teach school for three months at Dedham, traveling the forty-
six miles there from Holden on foot and receiving for his labors
the sum of eight dollars a month together with his board. He
writes of his "very great natural diffidence" to open his school
with prayer, of his reason to think that he "succeeded tolerably
well in teaching reading and arithmetic," of his distress over
his "indifferent handwriting," which he had been obliged heretofore "to make exceedingly small through want of paper." In
March, 1788, he returned to Holden to "recommence in great
earnestness" his studies for entrance to Harvard College and to
divert his mind from them only "by the making of bird-cages
and the gathering of wild roses for conserve which would bring
me a little cash for necessary expenses."

On July 19, 1788, he makes with easily imagined excitement
the following entry in his "Temporal Diary": "Having finished
the select Orations of Cicero and the Aeneads of Virgil, having
studied all the three first Evangelists and a part of the book
of Acts in the Greek Testament, and being in good measure

recovered from the whooping-cough, I rode this day to Cambridge and offered myself for admission into the college. After examination I received a certificate of admission from the President and a bond from the steward and at night returned home."

YEARS AT HARVARD COLLEGE

1788-1795

"T HOUGH our exercises are very numerous and some of them greater than I can master, yet at this Seat of the Muses, all things considered, I think I have spent the happiest year that I have spent in my life." Thus on July 4, 1789, toward the close of his first year at Harvard College, writes Jonathan Fisher at twenty, to his uncle, Joseph Avery, at Holden. He writes to express his gratitude "for the kind and diligent attention which you paid to my education and manners," and he supplements his own expression of appreciation by quoting from a satire of Horace on the most excellent virtue of wise parental precept and example.

These formalities dutifully performed, Jonathan continues at some length to acquaint his uncle with his life at Cambridge. "My class at present," he writes, "consists of 34 members, among whom are a number of respectable characters with whom I enjoy the pleasures of friendship." He lives in the eastern corner of Massachusetts Hall, the lower story. He carefully lists his classmates, all of whom, with the exception of Henry Daingerfield from Virginia and Benjamin Trappier from South Carolina, come from Massachusetts and New Hampshire. He takes pains also to list the fines imposed upon thirteen of them for breakages and minor misdemeanors. The two young gentlemen from the South seem early to have incurred the displeasure of the authorities, for both pay relatively large fines and in addition Trappier is "publicly admonished," a prophetic prelude to his suspension in 1790 and his "rustication" in 1791. Jonathan himself, it is hardly necessary to say, is free of fines and of all other disgrace! His "chumb," or chamber-mate, is Bradstreet Story of

Marblehead, "an agreeable youth aged about 16," who was to continue living with him during his four years as an undergraduate. He carefully records the numbers in the other classes: of Sophomores there are 24, of whom one "has been degraded"; of Juniors "there are now about 43," since 5 have during the year been suspended, one of whom, it is interesting to note, is another South Carolina Trappier; of Seniors "there are now about 50," since one "has died of a consumption" and another has been "rusticated." He names "the 4 tutors," although two resign during the year and are replaced. "Let the sons of dissipation say what they will," he asserts, "against the government of the college. I think its several departments are filled with men of worthy, respectable characters; and that there is much greater pleasure in deserving their esteem than in meriting their displeasure."

He describes his studies. "During the three quarters our exercises were alternately four days in the week for one fortnight in Latin, and four days in the week the next fortnight in Greek; on friday in a book called the Art of Speaking, in Pike's arithmetic, and in Hebrew and English grammar; on saturday in Rhetoric and Hebrew grammar. During the present quarter we recite one week in Greek, one in Latin, one in Logic, and one in Guthrie's Geography; on friday we are exercised at speaking, and recite in arithmetic, and in Hebrew and English grammar; on saturday in Millot's elements of History, and Hebrew grammar." His reading in Latin, he says, includes Sallust, Horace, and Livy; in Greek, Homer, and Xenophon's "retreat of the 10,000"; in English he has been through Dr. Lowth's grammar and has now "just begun to make English in Perry's exercises."

He says at the close of his Temporal Diary for 1789 that he "wrote several themes" during the last quarter of his Freshman year; but he evidently did not consider them worth preservation. For the twenty-three which he copied into his notebooks kept at Harvard begin with March 12, 1790, and close with April 16, 1792. This last theme, a somewhat solemn and didactic experiment in blank verse on a line from Young, "We cut our cable, launch into the world," is carefully marked: "Last theme, delivered to the Professor, April 16, 1792."

These themes are of varying lengths, the longest not over some 1500 words. Their subjects are usually quotations from the Classics or from the English poets, Young, Thomson, Watts, Pope. From Horace: *Dulce et decorum est pro patria mori* and *Dum loquimur, fugerit invida aetas, carpe diem;* from Virgil: *Procul, O procul, este profani* and *Non ignara mali, miseris succurrere disco;* from the poets, to name but a few titles, *A little learning is a dangerous thing, To err is human, How happy is the holy hermit's lot, Virtue alone has majesty in death.*

Mr. Eliphalet Pearson (A.B. 1773), the Hancock Professor of Hebrew and the stoutest of Calvinists, was clearly Jonathan's tutor also in the writing of English, according to the rule established at Harvard well before Jonathan's day that, besides one's special subject, one taught English as well.[1] Letters from absent classmates ask him to convey to them Mr. Pearson's theme assignments; and once in his Diary he identifies the professor to whom he carries his theme as Mr. Pearson. In letters to his friends he refers occasionally to Pearson, describing in December, 1792, the "Pearsonic dignity, moderation, and emphasis" with which Eliphalet assisted at the installation of a new professor. According to Samuel Eliot Morison, Pearson was "a dominant personality in the college" and was known by the students as "The Elephant," "as a pun on his name and a tribute to his bulk."

Perhaps Mr. Pearson's horror of Arminianism and of the inroads of Unitarianism, which in 1806 was to cause him to resign his chair in Hebrew and send him to found the Andover Theological Seminary, was fortunate for Jonathan, most of whose rather somber and always serious themes managed, whatever the subject, to convey his own staunch and unyielding orthodoxy. His tutor, although to our regret Jonathan records no Pearsonic

[1] This information, with much other interesting material concerning the history of Harvard, has been gained from Samuel Eliot Morison's *Three Centuries of Harvard*. Harvard University Press, 1936.

criticisms of his literary flights, became early accustomed to conclusions in blank verse, in couplets, or in quatrains; and in his
pupil's Senior year received from his pen several themes entirely
in verse, one of 150 lines in couplets entitled "Rich Autumn"
and distinctly reminiscent of Thomson's *Seasons,* and another
far longer in blank verse, this a drama set in a prison and dealing
with the tragic consequences of the love of gold.

Jonathan continued his studies in Hebrew with Mr. Pearson
throughout his four years. Enamoured of that language, as his
later years bear witness, he prefixed all his carefully copied
letters to relatives and friends with their names and addresses
in the Hebrew alphabet, as the only means of identifying them.
He must have made astounding progress in that most difficult of
tongues, if he continued to recite in it only once or twice a week
as his Diary would suggest, for in his Senior year he is translating
several Psalms and the Lamentations of Jeremiah. On May 8,
1792, he begins "to write a little on a Hebrew grammar," the
forerunner of his Lexicon of later years, and a few days later
pays "12 shillings and 9 pence for a Hebrew Lexicon" for himself, a price which, in his financial circumstances, shows a reckless
desire for its possession.

His Classical studies were, of course, pursued throughout his
four years although, from his Diary, one cannot conclude that
they were particularly various. Of Latin authors he mentions
only Sallust, Horace, Livy, and Terence, the last of which was
apparently read continuously during both his Junior and Senior
years. In Greek he seems to have read no other writers save
Homer and Xenophon throughout his four years, although in
addition in his Senior year he "reviewed" the Greek Testament.
Twice he mentions "perusing" both Virgil and Plato, (the *Crito,
Phaedo,* and *Apology*) but this was obviously for pleasure.

His excursions into philosophy seem to have been securely
bounded, for three years at least, by Locke's *Essay on the Human
Understanding,* which in the eighteenth century was also read

exhaustively by the students of Cambridge University, as Laurence Sterne, once at Jesus College there, bears ironical witness. In the field of natural philosophy he read and recited in William Enfield's *History of Philosophy from the Earliest Periods* and in Oliver Goldsmith's *Survey of Experimental Philosophy*. In theology, in which likewise Mr. Pearson was his tutor, he read Hugh Blair's *Sermons*, Butler's *Analogy of Religion*, and George Benson's *Reasonableness of the Christian Religion*. He mentions frequently that he is reading also *The Religious Philosopher* by Bernard Nieuwentijdt, a Dutchman writing in 1718, whose work had been translated in Boston in 1730.

It is, however, abundantly clear that the college "exercise" in which he took the keenest delight was mathematics. The entries in his college Diary have far more comments upon his work in that subject than in any other; and in the *Sketches* of his life, in which he writes of his college days, he says, "The mathematics were particularly pleasing to me." His tutor throughout three of his four years as an undergraduate was the Reverend Samuel Webber (A.B. 1784) who was installed Hollis Professor of Mathematics in 1789 and with whom he studied algebra, plane and spherical geometry, trigonometry, conic sections, heights and distances, dialing, surveying, navigation, and astronomy. Webber, who was a man of liberal religious views and President of Harvard from 1806 to his death in 1810, is described by Samuel Eliot Morison as "perhaps the most colorless President" in the history of Harvard College. That may well have been true, and yet Jonathan Fisher seems to have found him as a tutor and lecturer anything but dull; for in his Senior year he is careful to note that he "attended upon Mr. Webber's public lectures" twice every week. He is careful also to list their subjects. "I attended Mr. Webber's lecture on hydrostatics," he writes on May 16, 1791, toward the close of his Junior year; and through 1791–1792 he apparently never missed Mr. Webber on hydraulics, pneumatics, cold and heat, magnetism, electricity, optics, astronomy, survey-

ing, dialing, the center of magnitude, motion and gravity, mechanical powers (the lever, axle, wheel and pulley), projectile
and central forces, and hydrostatics.

One of the best and most beautiful proofs of Jonathan's genius
in drawing, as well as his love for his science, is a notebook entitled *Mathematics* and made, for the most part, during 1791
and 1792. It is constructed of some fifty sheets of very heavy
paper, 13 by 8 inches, and contains solved problems in various
branches from geometry and trigonometry to navigation. Not
only are the perfectly drawn figures, many of which are colored,
lovely in themselves, but they are often enhanced by page decora-
tions of fruit, flowers, and trees. On one of the pages given to
heights and distances Holden Chapel appears, painted in red in
water-colors; on another on the same subject there stands a green
"elm in the college Yard." The page introducing problems in
navigation shows a mariner's compass enclosed in spirals of
flowers, blue, red, and purple. "I constructed the mariner's compass," he writes on November 11, 1791, "and I drew a flower
about it." This notebook has as its maxim *Labor omnia vincit*,
enclosed in an elaborate scroll, and on its title page within a
border of flowers is the subject of the poem which follows:

Apology for Mathematics.   1791

Some court the muse to lend the harmonious strain,
Cull the sweet flowers from every blooming plain.
Some for their thoughts prefer a different dress,
And free in prose their sentiments express.
These choose to soar, unfettered, unconfined;
Those in soft chains their willing numbers bind.
Some guide the pencil, charm our wond'ring eyes;
Bid the fair landscape rich in beauty rise;
To lifeless matter animation give;
By art illusive make the canvas live.
Some with sweet sounds enchant the listening ear,
Calm rage to rest, and stop the rising tear.
Orpheus! 'twas thine; and Handel! thine to warm
The captive breast, the fetter'd soul to charm.

These noble minds obtain a deathless name,
Are led by genius to immortal fame.
Nor these alone; great Newton! thou shalt stand
High in the rolls of every age and land.
Euclid was thine; o'er him 'twas thine to rise
From measuring earth to mete the expanded skies.

One can hardly believe that the Reverend Mr. Webber did not see his student's notebook since it obviously summarizes his work for his Junior and his Senior year. Moreover, Jonathan was never one to hide his candle under a bushel, this Scriptural injunction according well with the pardonable pride which he always took in the work of his hands. Nor can one believe that upon Mr. Webber's examination of it, its aesthetic as well as its scientific aspects, he failed to experience one of those blessed, and perhaps none too frequent, hours in a teacher's life when he thanks whatever gods there be for his choice of a profession!

2

It was at Harvard and during his vacations spent at Dedham that Jonathan Fisher began to write those countless letters which he left, neatly copied and bound, behind him; and it is through them that we gain added knowledge of his college life. In all he preserved some eighty written during his four years, and he includes besides these several written to him by various relatives and friends. Although a note by a contemporary describes him as "a quiet and peaceful student with a manner eccentric and old even in his college days," he clearly was not unpopular among his fellows, for of his thirty-three class-mates he apparently counted as good friends at least twelve, as his letters to them and theirs to him bear witness.

In his spring and summer vacations of 1789 he seems to have been seized with a mighty urge for writing to his various friends, for several letters then are sent to each of six of them. Willard Peele at Salem, Jacob Abbot at Wilton, N. H., Abiel Abbot at Andover, Levi Hedge at Harwich, John Appleton at Salem, and

Bradstreet Story at Marblehead—all these receive letters, most
of which concern the joys of the seasons, reflections on the "alluring verdure," and descriptions of the flowers in his sisters' garden
at Dedham. Their distinctly lyrical nature is frequently enhanced
by verses on the glories of Nature and the wonder of the Eternal
Plan; and all without exception laud the gift of friendship. He
begs his friend, Abiel Abbot, to be free with him, "plain and
sincere always concerning my imperfections," for such candor is
not only the privilege but the holy duty of true friends. He re-
counts to John Appleton a scientific observation made from the
study of water flowing over a mill-dam. To Willard Peele, who is
stricken with mumps, he gives, with his sympathy, an account of
a Public Exhibition at Harvard, "which gave general satisfaction
to a respectable assembly" and from which Mr. Peele was absent
because of his affliction:

Those in the several departments of government were received,
upon their entrance, with a symphony. Then a Latin oration by
Smith opened the scene. Among other things he anticipated the
future glory of our western territories, particularly of the Ohio.
His oration received the clap of applause, and was succeeded by
a forensic on the question: Whether the safety of the people
were the supreme law? The affirmative was by Moody, and the
negative by Holt. It was well written, persuasive arguments being
advanced on both sides. Then a syllogistic dispute by Harris and
Whiting. An English dialogue by Walton and Whitney. A Greek
oration, well-spoken, by Ward. An English oration by Staniford,
which received a general clap of applause from the audience
and, I believe, equalled the expectations of the chief of those
who were present. A sublime anthem, succeeded by several
pieces of instrumental music, concluded the scene.

He shares with these friends "a few lines on my recess from
Harvard," which from the several copies he makes of them
conceivably afforded him much pride:

> Hail, Seat of Science, lo I leave
>   Thy grateful walls behind.
> I look around, a while I grieve,
>   And sorrows fill my mind.

One year has rolled its circling round
 Since to thy peaceful shade
A kind admittance first I found
 And thee my guardian made.
Some short reflections now demand
 Attention from the Muse;
My feeble muse at their command
 Attempts her power to use.

*   *   *   *

Too much, fair Temple, I confess,
 I've joined the shameless throng
Who here thy sacred walls disgrace
 With poison from their tongue.
For here beneath thy generous light
 Some wretches yet are found
Who court the sable veil of night
 To hide their vicious round.
Here, too, among thy numerous train
 Some constant friends I find,
A sweet relief to every pain
 A pleasure to my mind.

*   *   *   *

Harvard, adieu! I now retire
 Four leagues at least, or more
Forward, where yon fierce meridian fire
 Now burns the valleys o'er.
Kind Heaven, attend my short recess
 Hence to yon rural plain;
There may I spend each hour in peace
 Till I return again.
And when these western realms shall meet
 Thrice ten succeeding morns,
Then may I hail this fair Retreat
 Which Science now adorns.

His letters to his friends continue throughout succeeding holidays, or are written at Cambridge during the absence of one or another of them. In July, 1790, he writes Abiel Abbot at Andover a long letter urging him to abstain from the gammon

board. He himself, he says, during his vacation has been employed with the axe, the plane, saw, and hammer. These exercise the body as well as entertain the mind, but what save ill can
cards, dice, chequers, and the like do to both mind and body?
Mr. Abbot replies within a week with a great friendliness, indeed, but in no uncertain terms, recalling, perhaps, Jonathan's
plea for complete candor. Although he esteems Jonathan's letter
as an expression of his friendship, he is entirely convinced that
the gammon board is well adapted not only for the solace of the
mind, but also for its active and healthful exercise. "When the
mind has been confined a whole day over Mr. Locke's abstruse
reasoning," he writes, "or over the duller demonstrations of
Euclid, it feels itself relieved and exercised by gammon." In
November, 1789, Mr. Levi Hedge suffers from influenza and
describes his sorry state with some liveliness to his friend Fisher.
"Where is now the boasted freedom and independence of America? A Washington could wrest our violated liberties from the
rapacious hands of lawless Britons; but who can save us from the
boisterous attacks of the raging influenza? . . . Let me conclude
with requesting you to obtain my corrected English of Mr.
Pearson, and, *keeping it invisible,* to convey it me enclosed by
letter." His friend Fisher, however, who among all his gifts and
graces could not number much humor, answers with a lengthy,
not to say reproachful, dissertation on the dependence of "our
country" not upon Washington but upon God!—a reply which
must have been like a dash of icy water upon the spirits of Levi.
Moreover, he fails to convey to Mr. Hedge the "invisible" theme
and must have further benumbed him by concluding his didactic
reflections on God versus Washington by a bit of bad verse:

> Let gentle patience waft your pains away!
> Let sweet content your drooping spirits cheer!
> Be calm your thoughts, your mind serene as day,
> May heavenly comfort wipe the falling tear.

During his last two years his letters to his friends take on an

even more serious tone. He is deeply troubled over certain
sinister doubts which have stolen into the perturbed mind of
Jacob Abbot, wrestling in Billerica with the Scriptural claims of
the Antinomians and the Universalists, and writes him eight
pages of strictly Puritan theology in order to set him right once
more. Joseph Sprague of Salem, William Dix of Worcester, and
John Popkin of Boston (who describes himself as "the recluse
of Harvard") exchange with him dissertations dull enough on
the restoratives administered to the fainting soul by various
books of the Bible, on Divine Election, on the awful and mysterious imminence of Death, and on the constant falls from
Grace which they are, alas! experiencing. Their letters, Jonathan
declares, however, are to him as cups of cold water to a thirsty
soul. May they together war manfully against the World, the
Flesh, and the Devil!

His college letters to his mother have to do often with money,
the cost of his books, the meticulous reckoning of his accounts.
Not infrequently he sends her the synopsis of some Cambridge
sermon, and he never fails to tell her, in copious detail, of sudden
deaths in the college community, by drowning in the Charles, by
a quick consumption, an apoplexy, or a violent fever, like that
which caused on May 9, 1790, the solemn death-bed scene of the
Reverend Timothy Hilliard, minister at Cambridge—a scene,
the careful particulars of which doubtless afforded her melancholy pleasure, if *in absentia!* These, of course, draw from him
somber recognition of his own fragile and uncertain existence.
To his sisters, Katharine and Rebecca, three and six years
younger than he, he gives brotherly counsel and advice, urging
them to be diligent in their household tasks, not like the "Miss
Triflers of the World," who with shirts to make for their husbands neglect them the livelong day for vanities in dress and for
idle musings. In one letter he relates to them at length the divine
story of *Paradise Lost* and tells them of his delight in the lesser
English poets and in the discoveries of Newton and Harvey.
They, naturally, he reminds them, cannot like him give time to

reading and to study, and yet he wishes them to cultivate their minds as best they can. To his cousin, Sally Avery, he narrates with some delicacy the full story of the Rape of Lucretia by the base Tarquin, impressing upon her the immaculate virtue of chastity; and to an unidentified Lydia, who is about to enter into marriage, he composes not only a poem on "The Nuptial Hour," but many paragraphs in description of the conduct of "Virago" and "Serena," two hypothetical brides.

Of the affairs of the college he has more to say in his letters to the Reverend Joseph Avery, who, he knows, is deeply interested in his own Alma Mater. He writes of "the Power of Circe which transforms men into beasts," but he is glad to state that the autumn of 1790 has seen less vice in the "Seat of the Muses" than that of 1789. The two chief sins are those of drunkenness and profanity. He himself wants nothing for complete happiness save a virtuous disposition, for he confesses himself not untouched by the "contagion" around him, and he is inwardly most anxious over "that joyful alacrity" with which he too often closes his night prayers. Will his uncle not plead for him in his own less interrupted hours before the throne of Grace? He writes of the resignation of tutors who tarry too short a time for good results, of new appointments, and of the Public Exhibitions, which were held twice each year and at which students elected from the two upper classes gave orations in Latin, Greek, and English and took part in "forensics." He is proud to say that he has argued in one forensic and, in connection with two other students, has twice been selected for "Mathematical Parts." This would naturally be of interest to Joseph Avery since, as a member of the Speaking Club, formed in 1770, he himself had given an oration on "Oppression and Tyranny." Such Public Exhibitions, Jonathan informs his uncle, are too often followed by deplorable disturbances among the students, drunkenness, unseemly shouts, and rioting in the Yard or, alas! at "Taverns."

In April, 1790, he writes that the college has been warned of "a public examination" before the Governing Boards a year from the date of announcement. Apparently the year between these unwelcome tidings and the holding of the examination gave ample time for widespread resentment to be fanned into general fury. The examination was held on the 12th of April, 1791, and a few days later Jonathan sends a full description to his Uncle Joseph in a letter which deserves to be quoted in full:

Dedham, April 22d, 1791.

Reverend and Honored Sir:

I spent the last quarter very agreeably, except some interruptions occasioned by the commotions attending public examination. As fame increases, as it flies, and the truth of distant transactions is often hard to be known, perhaps a short account of these commotions will not be amiss.

About a year ago, a proposal was made for instituting annual public examinations in which all the students were to be examined by a committee of the Corporation and Overseers, in the several branches they had studied. After some debate a law for this institution was enacted; and about the middle of summer published in a code of college laws. After Commencement the students received each of them a copy of these laws. The law respecting examination occasioned much uneasiness in the minds of many of them. Some thought it unjust to impose it upon those who had entered before that law was made; some considered it as an *ex post facto* law, exposing them to disgrace for negligence they had been guilty of before the law was enacted; others thought it impolitic, and that it could not be determined by such an examination who was a good scholar and who was not; that some, who had been brought up to study from their youth and had a talent of discovering readily what they knew, might obtain a reward, though they had been idle at college, and had been persons of very immoral characters; while others, who were but barely fitted, and naturally bashful, though of a good character and diligent in their studies, might appear to disadvantage.

These were the most popular objections; and, the discontent increasing, about the middle of December last, petitions were sent by the upper classes to the Corporation, requesting them to dispense with examinations. These were not granted, but, to pacify the minds of those who were uneasy, the immediate government determined not to examine us farther back than what we had studied since April, 1790; and afterwards, to cut off all reason for complaint, they passed a vote that we should be examined no farther back than we had studied since Commencement, about which time the law was published.

But even this would not avail. The spirit of opposition, though for a while smothered, at length broke out into an open flame. In the evening preceding the examination (April 11th, 1791) a large number of the students embodied, gave several shouts, and were then dispersed. Afterward about 20 squares of glass were broken in the windows of the philosophy chamber. About 4 o'clock next morning a large number went to the top of Massachusetts Hall, sung several songs, gave three huzzas, and descended. Between the hours of 8 and 9 the corporation arrived and were received with shouting and hissing, which, were it not from boys, would have been enough to try the patience of almost anyone. By 9 o'clock the tutors, resident graduates, and upwards of a hundred of the undergraduates were sick with an emetic designedly thrown into the water prepared for breakfast. Diverting would have been the scene, were it not of too serious a nature to be sported with, to see such a number of students, whose minds were raised but just before to the highest pitch, now hanging their heads and puking about the yard.

The governors of the college were men of too much firmness to be daunted by such proceedings, and at 10 o'clock the examination began. Before noon, while the sophomores were under examination, a large piece of brick was thrown with violence into the philosophy chamber, which either hit the chair in which the Governor was sitting or struck very near it. The person who threw it has not been discovered. The students were all immediately assembled in the chamber and a speech, setting forth the nature of the insult, was made by Judge Lowell; he was succeeded by the Lieut. Governor; and a few words were spoken by the Governor; and then the students were dismissed till afternoon. At night the chappel was scented by some drug or other in a manner almost intolerable. The person who scented it was not discovered.

The day following (April 13th) one Henry Jones of Hinsdale, in the sophomore class, threw a stone into the philosophy chamber while the freshmen were under examination; he was detected and the next morning expelled from college; his sentence has been confirmed by the unanimous vote of both the Corporation and Overseers.

April 14th examination was finished. After this the Government proceeded to inquire into the emetic. Several persons brought under oath and the plot on the point of being discovered, William Sullivan of Boston, one of the junior class, confessed that he, in connexion with Justin Ely and Ben. Trappier, both of the junior class, procured and put, or caused to be put into the water a quantity of tartar emetic. The quantity is said to have been 600 grains. Sullivan, who had before sustained a good character and appeared very penitent, was on the morning of the 20th inst. suspended for 9 months. Trappier, having been before suspended, was rusticated. Ely had gone home before the plot was discovered.

This is, I think, as impartial an account as I can give. I hope that during the vacation the storm will subside, and that, while we taste the pleasures of the spring, we may enjoy an agreeable calm.

From your dutiful nephew,
Jon. Fisher.

Jonathan's Diary entry, descriptive of this episode, adds little to his letter except that he himself, having fortunately "eaten milk as usual" escaped the humiliating consequences of the tartar emetic. One is hardly surprised to know that he himself "took no part in these riotous proceedings." Apparently the Corporation and Overseers remained undaunted, for on April 9, 1792, he writes that there were again "great disturbances among the three lower classes on account of the approaching examinations," that "a barn was set on fire and much glass broken." As to the fatal day itself, he is silent.

3

Jonathan's respect, even reverence, for numbers in all their forms, simple and intricate, extended to his personal finances. In a hand-bound account book, which opens on July 19, 1788, (the day he rode from Holden to Cambridge for admission to

Harvard, a journey which cost him for dinner and "horse-baiting" the sum of .30½) and which closes on Aug. 8, 1834, every penny spent is set down. In the *Sketches* of 1812 he explains this strict carefulness in regard to money:

From this day, July 19th, 1788, I began a list of my expenses, noting down the time, the article, and the price. This kind of journal I have continued to the present day, and I have found it in several respects serviceable. It has assisted me in the strict economy which to this day I have found necessary for the support of myself and of the family which it has pleased God to bestow upon me. The journal, by exhibiting the expenses of one year, has enabled me to form some estimate of the money I should need for another year . . . It may also show my children whether I have or have not been extravagant, and in what way they, by prudent management, may subsist and rise from the lowest circumstance to a competency.

From a study of the sums spent during his four undergraduate years at Harvard one gains not a little insight into his own necessities and desires as well as interesting information on the economics of the time. His accounts, until 1793, when the English currency disappears, are in two columns, one in "Lawful money," pounds, shillings, and pence, the other in "Federal money," dollars and cents. His chief expenditures are for paper and for materials for painting and drawing. He buys perhaps too cautiously. On one day he pays .01 for one sheet of paper; on another .04 for 6 sheets; and on yet another .13 for a full quire. Four ounces of white lead cost him .02, India ink .01, 7 Dutch quills .08, a scale and dividers .66, ½ oz. Vermilion .05½, a paper of carmine .11, 1 oz. umber and 4 ozs. English ochre .03 each, a magnetic needle .50, a slate .20 and the accompanying pencil .01½. Whenever he "passes the bridge over the Charles," and he does it frequently, he pays .02; and whenever he satisfies himself with a biscuit on his constant walks, it likewise costs him .02. At Commencement, however, this commodity soars to .06! Twice he is mad enough to purchase one oyster, cost .01, and once two apples for the same price. His numerous entries for candles, of which he usually buys two or three pounds at one time at .09 or .10 a pound, suggest that he kept late hours over his books, as, indeed, he more than once says in his Diary. His books were the largest tax upon his purse: a Xenophon at $1.83, Guthrie's *Geographical Grammar* $2.22, Locke *On the Human Understanding* $3.00, Young's *Night Thoughts* .91, Homer's *Iliad* .33, Enfield's *Philosophy* $3.33, Addison's *Cato* .16, Moore's *Navigation* $1.83, Thomson's *Seasons* .75, Ferguson's *Astronomy* $2.83, and Milton complete at $1.50. One assumes that his mother wove the cloth for the one waistcoat and the two pair of breeches which he enters over four years, for only the cost of cutting and making is recorded and that amounts in all to the incredibly small sum of .75. For a pair of shoes he pays from .50 to $1.50; and for the constant cost of mending them he lists varying amounts from .04 to .12. His garters cost .04, a pair of black worsted hose .91, and the washing of two handkerchiefs .03. Since he mentions several times these handkerchiefs and always by two's, one gathers that his stock was limited! Once he pays .12½ for "several sights at a live catamount." On three occasions he actually buys a ticket to a lottery, price .25, and twice he indulges himself modestly in drink, for a pint of sherry wine .16 and for ½ pint of brandy .05½. For the drawing of a tooth he pays .25; "to Dr. Jennison for itch ointment" .50; and for "the scalding of my bedstead," an item suggestive of further torment, .06.

An agreeable notation is that of a "pocket looking-glass" for .12; and one is glad to see that at his Commencement he apparently throws prudence to the winds and buys "A beaver hat" for $8! Indeed, Commencement in 1792 cost him not a little. There was "$5 to the President for my degree"; and there was also his share of "the entertainment with my chums of some 30 or 40 persons" on the great day itself, July 18, 1792. Thanks to his account books we know what this company had for dinner. They consumed 15 lbs. of bacon at .07 a lb., 1½ bushels of fresh peas at .50 a bushel, and 16 quarts of milk at .03 a quart. The tables and benches for seating them rented for $1.83 and the

hire of cups, saucers, and teaspoons cost .12½. An "entertainment" for them (the nature of which Jonathan does not divulge)
added $1.30 to the total cost.

He apparently kept no itemized accounts of money received,
perhaps because there was so little; and yet he is careful to note
in his Diary whenever any gain is accrued through his labors.
He does not state how much he was paid for the bird-cages, the
"button molds," and the wild rose conserve which he made for
sale during his vacations in Dedham, but he is at pains to say
that he made them "for added spending-money." He does state
explicitly that on several occasions he sold walnuts at .07 a
quart, sometimes for himself and sometimes for his sisters.

During his first and second years at Harvard he worked as a
substitute waiter in the dining-hall, or "Commons," and in this
way helped to lower the cost of his food. On May 16, 1790, he
writes to his friend, Jacob Abbot, the pleasing news that their
petitions for "waiterships" for the following year have been
granted. "We are now chumbs and waiters together, and I hope
our hearts will continue to be united." And on August 18th of
that year he writes in his Diary that he enters upon his "waiter-
ing service," a service which he apparently continued during his
last two years since he speaks of reductions made from his quarter bills. There is likelihood also that he served occasionally in
the college library, for he writes his mother of his pleasure "in a
large french Bible adorned with elegant cuts of Adam and Eve"
which he "perused" while he "waited" there.

His source of largest income, however, small as the sums
earned seem today, came from two terms of school which he
taught in Wilton, New Hampshire, a most agreeable town to him
in spite of the mountains of snow which greeted his weary arrival
in late December, 1790. He spent January and February there in
a school of some "40 to 50 scholars." On February 3rd he writes
a rather moving petition to President Willard and the Board of
Overseers asking that he be allowed to continue his school for
three weeks after the vacation, "a favor, I confess, almost too

great for me to ask, especially considering the tokens of kindness
already shown me. But my embarrassed condition drives me to
use every honest mean I can to procure money to discharge my
bills." His petition was granted, and he received for seven weeks
of teaching $13 plus his board and room which he reports "as
pleasurable as could be wished." During the same months in
1792 he is again at Wilton for another seven weeks' term, this
time receiving $14 together with the present of "a good pair of
boots." Since upon his return to college he mentions in his Diary
letters received from several of his "scholars" at Wilton and
writes of making for one of them "a little book-case" and for
another "a little box," it seems safe to assume that his adventures in teaching afforded satisfactions other than mere pecuniary
gain.

4

Jonathan Fisher's Diary as a Harvard undergraduate does not
record many purely social occasions or suggest that he found his
most pleasant hours in the company of his friends. Only twice,
indeed, throughout his four years does he mention events which
apparently had no other purpose than merely a good time. On
June 7th and 8th, in the year 1790, as "a relaxation from study,"
he joined "many" of his classmates on a two-days' "sail upon the
sea"; and on May 31st of the following year he with twenty-four
other members of the Class of 1792 went on a fishing-party to
Nantasket. He is at some pains to describe this jaunt: "We went,"
he writes, "in the sloop *Sally* of Hingham, Capt. Cushing and
three hands. Cost for the sloop, $6; for provisions $15.15. My
part was defrayed by my classmates." The most satisfactory sentence in the description, however, is that which declares "an
evening spent in jovial mirth at Robin's Tavern on Nantasket."

In a "Foreword addressed to the Reader" of a notebook of
carefully dated poems, written mostly during his years as an
undergraduate, he has a good deal to say concerning the neces-

sity "of those innocent amusements which serve to unbend the mind, over-strained, weakened, and sometimes even deranged through unremitted and intense application." He is wary, however, of the nature of many of these amusements, the fruit of which, he claims, is "either a waste of precious time or, what is worse, a destruction of morals." Although he confesses that he has "too much dallied with such sports" (a confession difficult to believe!) he says that his "principal instruments of relaxation have been the pen, the pencil, and the tools of the mechanic." In other words, he has been at once "the Poet, the Painter, and the Joiner."

He was surely a prolific, if somewhat ponderous, versifier. The forty-five poems which he wrote as an undergraduate and which are almost ominously prophetic of his later vast output are filled with the conventions both of seventeenth century verse and of the so-called Graveyard School, in which he obviously took gloomy delight. The subjects are serious, if not solemn: *The Uncertainty of Life, Solitude, The Death-Bed of the Reverend Timothy Hilliard, The Lonely Grave, Evening Contemplations, To Dorea, on the Death of her Infant.* Nature is constantly extolled, reverenced, or feared through the aid of numberless ejaculations to Aurora, Boreas, Philomel, Eolus, Eurus, the Fancy, and the Eternal Cause; and "sable groves," "sublime shades," "gentle zephyrs," "blushing morns," "forked lightnings," and "chilling blasts" abound. The "fair sex," in the guise of Delias, Celias, and Serenas and addressed as "ye virgin throng, ye blooming fair," is somewhat pompously honored in several effusions; the nuptial hour and Hymen's altar are not neglected; Beauty, Virtue, Vice, Pity, Religion, and Time are all lavishly personified; and the ant, the dove, and "a little mite crawling across my page" give rise both to plaintive reflections and encouragements to virtue. The couplet is the favorite medium, although blank verse and quatrains are not infrequently used. Homeric similes and other epical conventions reflect his study of the Classics and of Milton. In the midst of these flowery wastes a poem in praise of Sir Isaac Newton seems a bit out of place in spite of Jonathan's adoration of him; yet he is careful to locate Newton securely in Paradise, where in his new and beatific vision all the planets appear but as "vanishing bubbles on a gentle breeze."

Although he rarely mentions in his college Diary his writing of poems, one gathers that the composition, or at least the conception, of them took place in the very early morning. In the *Sketches* he says that he rose at four or, at the latest, five o'clock while at Harvard; and that he often took a solitary walk before breakfast at six is clear from several of his letters. His friends must have been aware of his propensity toward versemaking, and not only from his letters to them. In November, 1791, his classmate, Levi Hedge, was his companion on a journey on foot, which Levi calls "the Fisher mode of travelling." Upon arrival at his own destination he writes Jonathan to inquire concerning his safety and well-being. "I mused on the greater length of your tour, but, says I to myself, 'Fisher's Muse always accompanies him to shorten the length of any journey.'" Poor Mr. Hedge goes on to say that his own thoughts alas! never rose above his feet for, "because of the inconvenience of being in fashion," his shoes were at least one size too small for him and gave him torture indescribable all the way to Billerica!

In all Jonathan's poems there is clearly evident the influence of much of his reading. He now and then lists the books which he has enjoyed during given quarters at college. In his Junior and Senior years, when he seems to have had more time for truant reading, he names as his "study fire companions" Young's *Night Thoughts,* Addison's *Cato,* Thomson's *Seasons,* Ossian, Milton complete, all of Shakespeare's Comedies, and *Tristram Shandy.* The last named, it is hardly surprising to note, did not please him; indeed, in one of his early poems he warns his readers against "books like Shandy." The delicious subtleties of Sterne would hardly appeal to a mind like Jonathan's save as an admonition! In addition to his reading of literature he is constantly

"drawing from the library" books on scientific and religious subjects: "Adams on the Microscope and Priestley on Electricity,"
various volumes on Ecclesiastical history, collections of Sermons,
and "several books having to do with Natural History."

He was especially busy during his Junior and Senior years
with pencil and paint-brush; his Diary is filled with entries such
as: "I spent the afternoon chiefly in painting." "I painted flowers
today." Among his subjects were "several views of Harvard College," two at least of which were "Mathematical Parts" for public
exhibitions, "a view of the Lowell house," and one of the Episco-
pal church, "a person in a savage state," "a figure of the lobster
insect," "a view of the Bird of Paradise and one of the Baltimore
Oriole." During the weeks spent in Wilton he drew and painted
any number of "flowers and sprigs." In April, 1791, he begins to
write and to illustrate a "Natural History Book," in which he
composes short descriptions of various beasts and birds together
with watercolors of them. Among these are the fox, the otter, the
wild boar, the pole-cat, and the guinea-pig, of which he says:
"Guinea-pigs seem to have no distinct sentiment but that of
love." He also includes in the same book a rather lengthy "Dictionary of Natural History," which begins with the *acorn,* the
albatross, the *aligator,* and the *antelope* and concludes with the
zebra and the *zorilla.* Between the pages are inserted odd and
extraneous bits of information: "Receipts for those who paint in
water-colors," "how one can make bad butter good," "the best
remedy for a weeping sinew," and "how to secure cabbage plants
from worms."

And always both during vacation and term time his hands are
busy with his tools. In April, 1790, on vacation at Dedham, he
begins a wooden clock upon which he works during every holiday. He constructs a wheel for it and a pendulum; he attempts a
regulator and fails to perfect it; he draws and paints its face. He
makes a pantograph, a theodolite, a "scale," "20 links of a
chain"; he frames "a piece of a glass globe for a burning glass,"
he makes "a staff to put a quadrant on," "a mould for casting an

ink-stand," "a semi-circle for taking the angles of a field," a boot-jack, a sector, and a pair of elliptical compasses.

Indeed, this Poet, Painter, and Joiner finds himself so increasingly occupied in his principal instruments of relaxation from study that he gives barely a line to chronicle his "initiation into the secrets of the Phi Beta Kappa Society" on June 11, 1791.

5

During his years at Harvard he continued to record in his Diary of "Spiritual Concerns" his inward struggles and depressions. His two besetting sins still afford him anguish: his propensity to evil and lustful thoughts and his tendency to fall asleep "even at the most solemn of moments." He records frequently also intemperance in eating, which, he says, clogs the wings of the soul, renders him dull and drowsy and hence an easy prey to Satan. He curses himself as "an Epicurean monster." His heart, which by reason of his lusts resembles "the stagnant lake of Sodom," is filled with vanity and folly, and his wandering thoughts "go to and fro through this vile earth." The foolish conversations which he hears from various of his classmates run continually in his mind while those of serious nature he can "scarce recollect." He is sensible that he is "grievously apostasized from God and in a very dangerous state, a slave to sin, a servant of the Devil." "Unless Divine Grace intervenes," he writes in January, 1789, "I shall be undone forever. And how should a vile wretch such as I hope for pardoning grace? Can I expect that God will hear me when I have so often turned a deaf ear to his calls?"

Such entries continue with little variation. His birthdays present opportunity for even greater despair. On his twenty-first he writes that he is "but a babe in wisdom, unfit to launch forth into the world alone." He feels it his sacred duty to profess his Savior before men, but he is, alas! ashamed to do so. "All within me is cold, lifeless; all is affectation. I lift up my hands, I clasp them, I rub them, I place them upon my breast. But my thoughts, where are they? I am thinking of some young lady, or of a problem in mathematics."

Euclid, indeed, is the veritable ally of Satan, forever lying in wait to snatch his mind away from the consideration of his immortal soul. He goes to bed at night determined to pray in secret; but geometry snares his reflections. "To raise a thought to Heaven is like rolling a stone up a mountain, but to dwell with Euclid is very bliss." He takes a solitary walk in the evening for the express purpose of the contemplation of God; but the geometry of the skies seizes his imagination and will not set it free. When he considers the work of his hands, "looking with vicious pride" upon his drawings, his paintings, his neatly solved problems, he is, in truth, "but a vain and wretched idolater."

Sudden deaths add eloquence to his pages. "The funeral knell has just ceased. Behold that grave! Beneath that new clod lies a youth. Two days have not elapsed since health in all its vigor danced through his veins. Now he is cold as the bed of clay which enwraps him. He was in the prime of life; so am I. He was in his 23rd year; so am I. Too far he ventured into the delusive stream and sunk to sudden death. Why was he taken and I spared? I have often ventured into the same stream and still have been preserved. The stroke is near *me*. It calls me to prepare."

In all this dark night of the soul few entries lighten the gloom. Most of these occur during the month of July, 1790, when he has at last determined to make a public profession of religion, to lay his "hand upon the plow and not to look back." Apparently spurred on to this momentous act by fear and duty, if not by desire, he meditates upon the love of God toward His erring child and describes himself as lost in wonder that Christ should so graciously die for *him*. But once the public profession is made on August 8, 1790, the joy retreats, and the doubts and fears return. On that very day he writes his brother Stephen in Westhampton that he is "too little affected by this solemn and awful transaction." "I have too little sense of the Redeemer's dying love, which ought to melt my soul to tears."

Katharine Avery Fisher

The Parents of Jonathan Fisher

One of Jonathan Fisher's Views of Harvard College

Morbid and unhealthful as such despair seems today, its reality to him was a tragic one, and the tragedy was neither dispelled nor even much alleviated by time, as his later writings in both Diary and letters prove beyond a doubt. There was no psychological knowledge in his day to explain to him that he was temperamentally not one framed to experience that ecstasy, real or imagined, of the saints, or yet of those ordinary mortals who claimed to have mystical and revelatory assurance of the influx of Divine Grace. Such assurance, such illumination, was obviously denied him. Fear and duty impelled him to declare his faith, yet he was rewarded by no inward vision, no indubitable proof of the certainty of salvation for him. In the *Sketches* he makes this assumption doubly clear. In 1815 at the age of forty-seven, writing, with the honesty always characteristic of him, of his spiritual history, he says in reference to his college days: "Sometimes my hopes for a season were raised; then again I was ready to give up all for lost. Thus it has ever been with me. My spiritual journal has been rather a record of miscarriages and failings than of anything else and of a nature, in the review of them, to humble me into the very dust of the earth. I may here add that, although from that day to the present I have experienced seasons of sweet refreshment from the Divine Presence, I have often been much in doubt and have almost altogether given up my hope. When I look back upon my life, it appears to be a sink of iniquity! Oh that at death the silent grave could conceal all! How can I endure to have it all exposed even to my nearest earthly friends, except to magnify the riches of Grace in saving such a sinner—if I may yet hope to be saved."

6

On the day following his graduation from Harvard in July, 1792, Jonathan Fisher at the age of twenty-four "concluded to reside at Cambridge upon the Hopkinton foundation" as a student of divinity. This was a not uncommon practice among the holders of the Bachelor's Degree, especially for those who planned to enter the ministry. They paid board, although no tuition, and received no direct instruction, but rather spent their time in reading theology and philosophy and in attending whatever lectures suited their needs.

Jonathan records rather fully in his Diary his various occupations between September, 1792, when he took up his residence in Hollis Hall, and June, 1795, when he "conveyed his belongings to Dedham and left for good the Seat of the Muses." He was apparently able, at least for the most part, to support himself during these years by preaching on Sunday in several towns, by accepting short sojourns at country pastorates, and by teaching three terms of school. He preaches at Roxbury, Malden, Dedham, Needham, Bedford, Brookline, Waltham, Jamaica Plain, and Boston, receiving $5 for each discourse; in April, 1794, he journeys to Princeton, Mass., where he remains for five weeks and receives $25; in January, 1795, he walks some seventy miles "in very cold weather" to the village of Ashby in northern Massachusetts where he stays "for six Sabbaths at the home of Dr. Carver" and increases his income by $30. In the winter of 1793 he teaches a school at Woburn for eight weeks at $3 a week; in the spring of the same year he receives the same sum for a three-week term at Brookline; and in 1794 from January to April he is again at Brookline with "a little family of 50 scholars," which not only pays him $48, but presents him with the extra sum of $15.04 in appreciation of his work and, for good measure, throws in "a surtout and two pairs of stockings."

His reading during his three years as a graduate student includes Edwards *On the Will,* Paley's *Moral Philosophy,* the Dialogues of Plato, Doddridge's *Sermons,* the *Koran,* and several histories of the Reformation. For his lighter hours he reads his favorites, Young, Thomson, and Milton. He falls in love with Pascal's *Thoughts,* his companion of many later years and an aid in his study of French, which enthusiastic pursuit, begun in 1792, was continued with obvious eagerness, for he writes often of reading French and in 1794 arranged with one, Mr. Nancreed, to give him twenty-two lessons in that language. He continued also his study in mathematics, in spherical trigonometry and navigation, and is especially concerned with surveying, a science later to stand him in good stead.

During his last year he writes "four Dissertations," three in Latin and one in English, all of which he delivers in the college chapel and for which he is given a certificate by the President and the sum of $45 as well. Those in Latin, which he bound neatly and left behind him among his countless papers, are on St. Paul to the Romans concerning "the invisible things of God," to the Corinthians on doing all things "decently and in order," and on the slothful man in *Proverbs* who "hideth his hand in his bosom." The dissertation in English he did not, seemingly, preserve. From his Diary entries he quite clearly "officiated in chapel" on other occasions during the three years, both in Latin and in English, but these uncertificated and unrewarded appearances were, one gathers, of less importance in his mind.

His painting continued to occupy many hours. He makes four views of Harvard College, draws and colors any number of animals and birds, a hyena, a rhinoceros, bears, lions, a bluejay, a red-bird. He paints a study of Adam and Eve and one of David with the head of Goliath. He even attempts the pictorial description of "the diseased hand of a boy." In August, 1793, he begins the first of nearly one hundred and fifty engravings on boxwood, the work on which was to afford him so much pleasure in future years.

His poetic Muse is less voluble than in his undergraduate days although by no means silent. Most of his compositions differ little in subject, treatment, and value from those already described, although he himself obviously thinks highly of a lengthy exercise in blank verse on dueling, since he carefully records in his Diary his hours of labor upon it. This turgid drama consists of long and sententious utterances by two young men, Edward and Henry, one of whom finally convinces the other that Satan alone is lord of so evil and murderous a practice. Equal in dullness is another experiment in blank verse between Sylvanus and Philander, this on the subject of the value of the theatre, which is, at long last, judged valueless, since it deals in but fictitious emotions, encourages displays of fashion, and stirs up lust in youth.

In the autumn of 1792 he was seized by a mighty ambition, which was to cause untold labor and exasperation to his biographers. He determined to invent for his own use "a philosophical alphabet," and in his usual zest for a new project straightway set to work upon that manner of writing which, he claims, will not only save him much costly paper but "may even afford a curious specimen to some few after my death." The latter prophecy has been amply fulfilled! From 1795, when he declares his code at last nearly perfected, although he is still "devising new characters for it," he used it for his Diary and for all his sermons. So enamoured, indeed, was he of his invention that he took pains to transcribe all his Harvard Diaries in this baffling shorthand. Many of his letters written and received after 1794 are likewise copied in code; and all his expense accounts after 1793 are set down either in it or in a kind of phonetic spelling, which he also devised and apparently enjoyed. If the next world is as definite and as literal a place as his imagination conceived it and his always shaky hope of entrance therein has been realized, he may have vastly enjoyed the years of labor expended by others in deciphering these characters of his inventive genius! Toward the close of his life, in one of those exciting hours given to financial liabilities and assets, he reckons that the employment of his shorthand has saved him in the expenditure for paper at least $70 over fifty years. How much more it has cost his diligent researchers into its intricacies would, I am sure, fill him with horrified delight!

In addition to his invention of the code, which he always held in high esteem among his accomplishments, this three-year period was epochal in Jonathan Fisher's life in another way. He quite clearly was at this time on the search for a suitable companion in his chosen profession. His first choice was a certain Miss Betsy Heath of Brookline, with whom he spends many evenings in 1794 and 1795. He has very little to say of this young lady save that he called frequently upon her. It is evident, however, that by November, 1795, his ardor is cooling or, perhaps more truly, is being cooled by Betsy herself. In that same month, quite obviously discouraged in his hopes, he calls for the first time upon Miss Dolly Battle of Dedham. We know nothing concerning the charms of Betsy and little of Dolly save that he describes *her,* rather too literally for kindness, as "the owner of neither external beauty nor riches, but, blessed be God! an *economist* and one who possesses a most amiable temper." The new interest grew rapidly, however, for in late December, 1795, hardly more than a month after his first call, he writes succinctly in his Diary: "I have resigned at her request one who I had in view as a partner for life and have commenced an acquaintance with another whose manner of life may well be more congenial to the place in which God may please to station me."

The place was the frontier village of Bluehill in the Province of Maine, a village in which Jonathan spent the summers of 1794 and 1795 as temporary pastor to the Congregational Society there. He must have impressed the hardy settlers by divers and sundry other assets besides that of sound religion, for in his Diary he writes of various quite secular accomplishments during his two summer sojourns. He surveys land, lays out new roads, does many jobs at carpentry, assists in harvesting crops, draws maps, helps to "raise houses," kills one bear in a trap which he has made, has a successful fight with another, and drives several "from Mr. Christopher Osgood's corn"—these achievements in addition to the writing of epitaphs for tombstones, to countless calls upon the sick, to preaching twice on the Sabbath and once during the week, and to composing deathbed poems and several elegies! Small wonder that the men of Bluehill saw in him a distinct asset, manual as well as spiritual, to their pioneer community and that on October 4, 1795, they proposed that he settle among them. On November 5th, after a month of uneasy decision between Bluehill and Ashby, which also desired his settlement there, he accepted the Bluehill proposal and hence could announce his future plans to Miss Battle, upon the occasion of his fatal first call upon her on November 12, 1795.

That Dolly was a girl both of adventuresome spirit and of quick decision may be gathered from the fact that, by February 4, 1796, she had made up her mind. For on the night of that day her future husband writes briefly and, it must be admitted, in more of a laconic than a sentimental vein: "Spent the evening with Miss Dolly Battle. The question of our future connection settled this evening."

III

BLUEHILL IN 1796

1

I N the Massachusetts Archives of the State Capitol there is a petition dated January 6, 1762, and signed by some three hundred and fifty names, which "humbly prays" that the Governor, his Council, and the General Court of Massachusetts, with His Majesty's approbation, will grant to the signers for immediate settlement a Tract, or Tracts, of "Unappropriated Wilderness Lands and Islands" lying between the St. Croix and the Penobscot Rivers in "that part of this Province called Province of Main." The signers describe themselves as "Persons Brought up to Husbandry and not having lands sufficient for themselves and sons." They came, for the most part, from the region north of Boston and from the towns or neighborhoods of Haverhill, Beverly, Newburyport, and Andover. Their petition, subject to the King's approval, which apparently was never received, and subject also to certain definite conditions, was granted on February 20, 1762; and a decade later some ten families had made homes for themselves along the rocky shores of Bluehill Bay.

The conditions of the grant stipulated that, within six years of the King's approbation, each township should be settled "with sixty good Protestant families" decently housed, that every man should have cleared and cultivated five acres of land on his share, that a suitable Meeting-house should within that time be built, a "Learned Protestant Minister" settled, and a school established. In 1785 the settlers of Bluehill, now numbering some sixty families, were greatly disturbed over a resolve of the General Court to impose a fine of 1000 pounds upon them on the ground that the conditions accompanying the grant had not been fulfilled. They chose one of their number, John Peters, Esq., to represent them before a Committee of the General Court and to state their case. They claim through Mr. Peters that they have been at great expense and labor in laying out their land in "the Wilderness Country" and in trying to procure the King's approbation. They admit they have not a settled ordained minister; nevertheless, they have built a suitable house for Public Worship and for seventeen years they have had "Preaching Every Summer, Except in the time of the late war, and a school-master every winter." The "full examination of the Matter," which they beg of the "Honourable Court," appears to have remitted their fine and left them in peace in their wilderness, although some uneasy memory of this crisis may well have hastened their determination in 1790 to build a meeting-house and to install a settled minister among them.

The naming of their settlement caused some amiable controversy among their number. They first called it New Port, or Newport, Plantation No. 5; then the names of East Boston and of North Andover seemed to have gained adherents. Finally, however, by October, 1788, they have agreed upon Bluehill.[1] In 1789 they incorporated their new town under the Laws of Massachusetts and on March 2nd of that year held their first Town Meeting under its new name.

In some early descriptive sketches, written by the new pastor, he explains the reason for its name. About 1½ miles from the harbor, he says, there rises to the north a hill which is 950 feet above high water mark. The ascent to the rocky summit is quite steep, and from the top one is given "a delightful prospect" of the surrounding land and sea, Mt. Desert Island, Penobscot Bay, the Camden Hills. The fir, spruce, and pine which cover this hill cause it to appear at a distance of a very dark blue color, hence its most natural name.

The broad arm of Bluehill Bay narrows about a mile from

[1] The original spelling of Bluehill was as one word, and it appears thus in town and church records. The tendency of late years, however, although still not in official use, has been to spell it Blue Hill.

the harbor itself into a land-locked, oblong cove, known as Little Bluehill Bay, or the Inner Bay. The earliest settlers built in 1762 their first rude houses outside these Narrows, some two miles from the harbor mouth, at a place which they called the Tide Mills because of the making up of the tide into a rocky stream and, farther, into a pond of brackish water, which they called the Salt Pond. The rush of water here gave them power for the early saw-mills which they built along a narrow neck of land between the pond and the bay outside. Those who came a few years later built their homes along the shores of the harbor itself and on the hills rising above it. Thus Bluehill early possessed two main centers of settlement, the Tide Mills, or Neck section, later to be known as Bluehill Falls, and that of the village proper, the two or three miles intervening by land between them being gradually settled as well.

These first inhabitants of an isolated, rocky section of the Maine coast were men of simple, sturdy background and small means, typical of the thousands from middle class English stock which founded hundreds of small communities such as their own. They were men of thrift and enterprise rather than of large ambitions. The hardships and necessities of pioneer life developed whatever powers of initiative they possessed, and they seized upon every means of livelihood which their environment afforded. They discovered rye, oats, Indian corn, and barley to be their best crops of grain since wheat was frequently injured by blight and mildew. Potatoes never failed them, nor did the usual "garden sauce"; and the land, which Jonathan Fisher declared "too stony for pleasant plowing," excelled in pasturage for cattle and sheep. Lumber was their "staple commodity," and four sizable "mill brooks" provided them with power for its manufacture into staves, logs, and boards. Once they had discovered that the rent of vessels for its shipment was "too dear" and the vessels themselves difficult to procure, they began to construct their own docks and to begin their own ship-building. By 1796, the date of Jonathan Fisher's arrival, their saw-mills numbered seven, and they could boast as well a grist-mill and even a cotton factory.

The larger of the two settlements, that at "the head of the bay," which early became Bluehill Village, had one of the most beautiful situations on the long, indented Maine coastline. To the south and east was the sea, set with spruce-covered islands; to the north, the blue, symmetrical hill. The village itself lay in a small valley with steep roads rising north, northeast, and west to wooded ridges. The village of Penobscot, settled in 1761, lay some seven miles to the northwest, that of Sedgwick, of a slightly later date, about the same distance to the southwest. Skirting the hill on the northeast a rough road led fourteen miles to the settlement on the Union River, later to be known as Ellsworth; and farther toward the northwest, eighteen miles distant, was Buckstown, now Bucksport, on the deep Penobscot, a town founded like Bluehill in 1762 under the same grant and burned by the British in 1779. Castine, whose multi-colored history of French, Dutch and English occupation had begun early in the seventeenth century, was but sixteen miles westward beyond the Bagaduce.

On a map of the township, drawn in 1794 by the young pastor on his first sojourn in his future home, roads, streams, ponds, and hills are carefully marked, together with the specific location of each house and the name of its owner. By this time the first makeshift dwellings had given place to substantial homes, many of them spacious and even beautiful, as those still standing today bear witness. On this map the names of the settlers repeat themselves, Parkers, Hinckleys, Carletons, Woods, Hortons, Dodges, Candages, Holts, and Osgoods, their homes often clustered in one neighborhood.

In his sketches of Bluehill, written at intervals between his arrival and the year 1808, Fisher describes an Indian encampment near the village, which, he says, existed for some years before and after his settlement. These Indians were of the Penobscot tribe and usually consisted of from two to five large families.

They made baskets of grass and reeds, bowls of birchbark, and set traps for fur-bearing animals, among which he names the bear, "very plenty," the wild-cat, raccoon, red fox, mink, "a few sable," the beaver, otter, and "an occasional wolf." Among their number was a certain "Dr. Cook," "very skilful as a physician," who concocted efficacious remedies from cedar twigs for sores and bruises and who understood both French and English and could write and "cipher a little." Dr. Cook, like the others of his race, was much attached to "ardent spirits" and in a state of intoxication fell with a metal pipe in his mouth which pierced his neck and caused his death. With his flair for languages Parson Fisher learned a little of the Penobscot Indian vocabulary, some pages of which he includes among these sketches.

The new meeting-house, provision for which was made at a town-meeting held on April 5, 1790, was apparently in use by the time of Jonathan Fisher's first sojourn. The entire "town" appeared on the first Tuesday in June, 1791, to clear the land for it, and by that date a committee had been appointed to procure materials. The "raising" of the building took place sometime in the autumn of 1792 with an "entertainment at the town's expense." This may well have been an occasion more gay than solemn, since, by a vote of the town, the Selectmen were empowered "to procure one barrel of rum, also molasses and sugar, sufficient for raising the meeting-house"; and it is quite safe to assume that no one able to be present remained at home. By the summer of 1793 the outside was finished and work begun on the interior, which, although in use from this time, was evidently not completed until the spring of 1797 when a sale of forty pews on the lower floor took place "at Public Vendue" and brought a price of from fifty to sixty dollars each. Indeed, work on the inside of the building was still in progress two years later, for the parson records in his Diary in 1799 that he is himself painting the pews and placing numbers upon them.

This first meeting-house stood on the right of the long hill road leading northwest from the village and about three-quarters of a mile from its center. It was fifty feet long and forty wide, built with a porch in front with three pedimented doors, which opened upon similar entrance doors within. Inside, it was modeled in general on the Old South Church of Boston, with square pews, galleries with more seating space, and a high pulpit with a flight of steps leading up to it on either side. A sounding-board was suspended above the pulpit. The outside was painted "a yellow stone color" and the roof "a Spanish brown." Here for more than forty years Jonathan Fisher was to minister to three generations of men and women, many of whom were not infrequently indifferent or even recalcitrant and sometimes blown about by those winds of false doctrine which penetrated even to their distant and isolated shores.

2

The terms of the Reverend Mr. Fisher's settlement in Bluehill in 1796 were carefully drawn up by men as prudent and as practical as he himself. Amended somewhat by the newly appointed parson from their original form, they provided finally for a salary of two hundred dollars in cash, "a barn forty by thirty feet, of thirteen feet and a half stud," finished completely, fifteen cords of hard wood and five acres of cleared land yearly for ten years. After the expiration of ten years Mr. Fisher is to receive two hundred and fifty dollars as salary and thirty cords of hard wood cut and hauled each year. He is to be allowed "to absent himself from the services of the Church five weeks in each and every year."

It is clear from his letters to the church at Ashby during his weeks of painful decision between that town and Bluehill that, left to himself, he would vastly have preferred to minister to Ashby, where he would have been near his family and friends, able "to confer with learned men at Cambridge," and in general far more comfortable than in a far-flung outpost of civilization such as Bluehill. But, in spite of that Free Will with which the Creator endows His creatures, he believes himself irrevocably

called, if not compelled, by God (whose calls to hardship and
sacrifice seem always more clearly ascertainable than those to
ways of pleasantness!) to labor in the far less cultivated vineyard.
He writes the men of Ashby that to deny the Bluehill invitation
would seem to him "like throwing cold water upon a zeal for the
Gospel"; therefore, he must submit to that "insurmountable bar
erected by Providence" against the allurements of their church
and town. His old friend and classmate, Levi Hedge, hinders his
decision and causes him confusion by urging upon him the
claims of Ashby. A wilderness does not attract Levi, who is
equally certain in his own mind that Providence is pointing
Jonathan in a direction quite opposite to that of Bluehill. Abiel
Abbot, on the other hand, who has himself occupied a summer
pulpit in Penobscot, begs Jonathan to resist ease and security
in any Zion, but instead to launch forth bravely across the stormy
wastes to his clearly allotted task. And when one recalls Jonathan's love for the new, the untried, the experimental, his overflowing vitality and his innate inventiveness, one is led to believe
that it was not God alone which made him see in Bluehill certain
adventuresome opportunities to offset the charms of Ashby.

He launched forth on May 31, 1796, in a schooner appropriately named *Industry*. He carried with him a new chest, which
he had made, filled with nails, lime, a new axe, and "other gear"
for building his house, the plans for which he had drawn, and
several times re-drawn, with the approval of Miss Dolly Battle.
On June 2nd, after a passage made miserable by seasickness, the
Industry deposited him in Castine, and on the following day he
reached his temporary lodgings at Col. Nathan Parker's in Bluehill.

His ordination, which he describes in a long letter to Dolly,
was "the most solemn scene" he had ever experienced. It took
place at noon on July 13th and was held under a canopy in an
open field belonging to Mr. Daniel Osgood and at a short distance above the head of the inner bay. The procession, walking
slowly up the hill, was "deeply impressive"; the audience was

"numerous and attentive." Four visiting clergymen, the Reverends Mr. Poor of Penobscot, Mr. Merrill of Sedgwick, Mr. Powers of Deer Island, and Mr. Bradford of Wiscasset, each accompanied by two delegates from his respective flock, conducted the ceremonies. In the bright noon sunlight, for the candidate reports the weather as "very hot," the sermon was preached, the long prayers uttered, the charge given, the right hand of fellowship extended. "Here," writes the new pastor, "I was solemnly separated to the work of the ministry; here I took upon myself the charge of souls."

Solemn as was the occasion, however, and deeply as the new pastor felt his "awful responsibility," the charge of souls quite obviously was not his first consideration during the summer of 1796, if we may trust the entries in his Diary. Although he preached twice every Sunday in the meeting-house, gave a weekly "lecture" every Wednesday, and dutifully prepared his sermons, he clearly spent most daylight hours on the "ministerial lot," a quarter of a mile above the meeting-house, in the clearing and the cultivation of his land and in the construction of his house. On June 8th he sets out a few small pear trees; on the 14th he plants potatoes. The digging and stoning of his cellar proceeds apace; and in early July he is ordering shingles, clapboards, and "5 dozen spruce boards at $5.50 a dozen, also 11 deep joists" at Mr. Daniel Osgood's saw-mill. His parishioners, like those men and women in Exodus whose "hearts stirred them up" and who were "willing for all manner of work," offered their services. From the names of those who labored for him with their sons and their ox-teams there was hardly a man in the parish who did not give some of his time to the building of the parson's home. In his Diary and his account book he lists less than $40 paid for labor during the entire summer, to one, an expert brick-layer, $4 a week and to a certain "Black Bill," evidently a Negro servant in the community, $2.50 a week. And so feverishly did all hands work and with such surpassing good will that on September 1, 1796, he can write with imaginable excitement and pride: "My house was raised today."

Even his reading was neglected during these weeks. He mentions few books, although he gives passing references to "Willison's *The Afflicted Man's Companion*," to William Law's *A Serious Call to a Devout and Holy Life*, and to *Paul and Virginia*, the last of which, much as he abjured novels in any form, may have seemed excusable to him because of his own emotional state. As for the account of his "Spiritual Concerns," it, too, bears out the conclusion that, for once in his life, he was either relatively untroubled by his sins or else found little time to chronicle them. He says succinctly in several brief entries that "worldly cares ensnare him," that "terrestrial concerns intrude into his prayers." He admits that he has neglected to call upon the sick, "being exceedingly driven with business." "For worldly things I have felt active, for the composition of sermons dull." He seems, indeed, far more given to thanking God for sending at long last "rain from Heaven," which diminishes the danger from the forest fires encroaching on his new property, than he does to imploring His forgiveness "for grievous spiritual sloth."

That Dolly Battle was constantly in his thoughts is evident from the frequent references he makes to writing her. The one letter to her which he took time to copy and preserve describes at length his ordination, certain involved and obscure disagreements and prejudices, centering about the Reverend Mr. Merrill of Sedgwick, which threatened to delay it, the effusions of tears which he shed, and the pain in his stomach which distressed him and was due to his general nervous state. He concludes by signing himself: "In a silence that wishes to be broken, your friend till Death."

There is a story still current in Bluehill concerning a neat and pithy remark made by Mr. Fisher on a certain September morning of this busiest of summers. A neighbor, going by the parsonage lot, saw the parson astride his new roof-tree, hammer in hand, and called up to him to inquire how he did. The parson raised himself as high as possible from his precarious perch, brandished his hammer aloft, and called down his reply.

"I am preparing for Battle!" he said.

3

Jonathan Fisher and Dolly Battle were married at seven o'clock on the evening of November 2, 1796. The bridegroom does not say where the wedding took place, but presumably it was held at the Battle home in Dedham. The brevity of his description, if written on the day itself, may be condoned by the exciting nature of the occasion. "At 7 o'clock, a splendid circle being come together, marriage was solemnized between myself and Miss Dolly Battle by the Rev. Mr. Haven, the concluding prayer by the Rev. Mr. Palmer. After a dish of tea and a glass of wine we were entertained by singing suited to the occasion." The poem which concludes this entry is, happily, as brief:

> Hail auspicious day,
> Big with events unknown!
> What joy is this?
> Thou bringest us bliss.
> Oh may it stay
> Till time is gone!

Nor does he fail in the midst of excitement to record the momentous event among his "Spiritual Concerns." "Nov. 2. Through the kind Providence of God I have been permitted this day to take partner for life. I feel myself unworthy of so great a blessing, yet I hope I shall ever be grateful for the favor. I pray God may give me grace to maintain a steady affection for the virgin who has kindly given me her heart." And as a final notation on the gravity of this signal adventure, he gives the following confidence in a letter written two years later to his classmate, J. S. Popkin, who, he hopes, may be contemplating conjugal bliss for himself: "On my own wedding night, after we were retired to our chamber, I read in a low voice the 5th chapter of Ephesians."

With a borrowed horse and chaise the young Fishers drove about for some few days, calling upon relatives, bidding good-bye to friends. The bridegroom, apparently without his partner, saw several of his classmates and "took breakfast in College Hall." Returning to Dedham, he crated his paintings, purchased tools and sundries, packed Mrs. Fisher's goods and his own, and awaited a ship sailing "to the eastward." On November 28th they boarded the schooner *Hancock* of Bluehill and, after two days of lying in Boston harbor awaiting a favorable wind, set sail on December 1st for their desired haven.

A "most violent snowstorm" greeted their arrival in Bluehill after a five days' passage of head winds and "miserable seasickness." The parsonage not yet being ready for occupancy, they lodged at Col. Parker's about a mile above the village center and near the meeting-house. They were given one room for their own and the use of the kitchen and the rest of the house as their needs required. Many evening calls from their parishioners made them welcome, and the wedding gifts brought to them must have eased their minds for a season from the gloomy knowledge of a debt of $400, which the parson anxiously enters in his Diary. Capt. Joseph Wood presented a most promising cow for three years' use; Mr. Robert Johnson, much good beef; Mr. Jonah Holt, a quarter of lamb and a large cheese; Mrs. Nathan Parker, good wool for stockings; Mrs. Joshua Horton, two quarts of molasses; Esq. Peters, a side of pork; the Widow Dodge, twelve pounds of cheese. In grateful return Mr. Fisher set several stubborn clocks going again, made a stove frame for one neighbor, re-bottomed some chairs for another, did his share in "raising" two houses, and helped clear drifted roads throughout the village and the nearby countryside. He made "a stamp for the Public Library," struck off 274 labels, and pasted them upon the books therein.

With equal vigor he set forth upon his spiritual duties. He waded through snowy roads and paths to catechize all the children within a radius of seven miles, drew up a *Confession of Faith* and a *Covenant* for his church, traveled on foot to Sedgwick and thence by boat to Deer Island to arrange with the ministers in those towns for "a day of fasting and prayer in May for the outpouring of the Divine Spirit" upon all three communities, and went, also on foot, fourteen miles to Union River to estimate the state of Grace which that settlement might possess. He found it sadly lacking!

On November 2, 1797, after a spring, summer, and autumn spent in planting and harvesting, in repairing recalcitrant drains, making a kitchen sink, completing a chimney and hearth, and constructing numberless articles of household furniture, he brought Dolly Battle Fisher across the threshold of her new home. The date was the first anniversary of their marriage, a fact which he records in his Diary: "Nov. 2, 1797. This day completes the first year of our marriage state and enters us on the 2nd. Our conjugal felicity, through the grace of God, has been uninterrupted. This day we are removed into our own house. Though in an unfinished state, it is more comfortable than the habitation of many. In the midst of some afflictions, I experience many mercies."

He also describes at some length in his account of "Spiritual Concerns" the "blessed interior Peace" in which he now lives. But his gratitude for this inner serenity is beset by grievous fears, since he is uncomfortably aware that it may be "the fruit of carnal security" and does not, alas! stem from the "indwelling of God."

IV

THE PARSON IN PARISH AND CHURCH

"I MAY remember," writes the parson early in his ministry, "that Jesus Christ, my divine Master, went about on foot long before me."

This pious and wholesome memory surely stood him in good stead, for his parish, even within the boundaries of Bluehill, was a farflung one. When he called upon the Hinckleys, Ebenezer, Isaiah, and Nehemiah, as he often did, "to converse with them" and their large families "upon religious subjects," he must needs climb four miles of hills to "the upper part of the town"; when he visited the Osgoods, Daniel, Phineas, Nathan, and Christopher, more steep hills awaited him; and when he journeyed to the Tide Mills to discover the spiritual state of Parkers, Holts, Woods, Candages, and Carletons, his round trip meant some seven miles of rough road, "honey-combed" with mud in spring, buried in snow in winter. A walk to Sedgwick, often undertaken for conference with the pastor there, or for meetings of the Hancock Ministers' Association, founded in 1797, added eighteen miles to his carefully kept account of "distances travelled"; one to Penobscot, fourteen; and one "through the forest" to Union River, twenty-eight. When an expedition to Long Island became a seeming necessity in order to minister to the many Carters and Chattos settled there, a trip by boat was added to the seven miles by road. And once he had summoned sufficient zeal and courage to essay the arduous journey by compass through the woods to Morgan's Bay, eight miles distant, to look after the souls of various Morgans and of their scattered neighbors, he started at dawn and returned at midnight.

Occasionally he borrowed a horse among the ten which he lists

as the number in the village at the time of his settlement, or
later among the "near one hundred" owned in 1806, for it was
not until 1824, when he was fifty-six years old, that he dared
afford one for himself. He seems, however, to have sat a horse
badly, for he is constantly falling off or being thrown; and, although "Divine Providence" usually intervenes to prevent serious injury, he records many lame backs and thighs and more
than one "sadly torn surtout." When Mrs. Fisher accompanied
him as she sometimes did in his attendance upon funerals and
weddings, Mr. Asa Clough or Col. Nathan Parker generously
lent "a chaise" or a sleigh. Both occasions, most frequent in the
pages of the Diaries, entailed more journeyings; for although
the funerals were at times held in the meeting-house, the weddings were apparently always solemnized at home.

The schools of Bluehill became at once of deep interest and
concern to Parson Fisher, who was for most of his life a valued
member of the Board which governed them; and the countless
miles which he walked for the purpose of examining the "good
learning" dispensed within them and for the even more exalted
purpose of "catechizing" their children added literally thousands
to his earthly pilgrimages. By the year 1800, when, according to
his careful tabulation of figures, there were 442 inhabitants of
Bluehill, the town had divided itself into six school districts,
each some two miles distant from the next; by 1807, when the
number of persons had increased to 597, among which were 95
families, the number of schools remained the same. It is impossible to ascertain from the town records for how many weeks
each school was in session during a given year, nor does Mr.
Fisher, usually so lavish with all manner of statistics, anywhere
so inform us. But, since he writes of catechizing in various districts in autumn, winter, spring, and summer, it is safe to assume
that terms of school were held each season. These were probably
of rather brief duration, since the money appropriated by the
town from 1800 to 1812 for teaching never exceeded $200 yearly
to cover all six districts, and since, therefore, each could spend

only some $35 in any year on the education of its young. The
teachers of these common schools, from the several names which
are accorded "certificates" in the Diaries, were generally women,
who received, the parson says, from one to two dollars a week for
their services, plus room and board. Evidently, then, each district
school was in session some sixteen to twenty-four weeks during
the year, depending upon what it was necessary to pay the
teacher. Provision, however, was wisely made as early as 1798
that the opening of "School No. I" at the Tide Mills should be
"on Sept. 20th" and that each of the other schools "should open
a week later" than its immediate predecessor. Since there was
no restriction as to which school a child should attend, it was
possible for him, by means of long walks or by boarding with
friendly families, to continue his education in another vicinity
if his parents or he himself were sufficiently avid for more knowledge. The age named for "scholars" was also expansive, since
they might begin school at four years old and continue until
twenty-one.

Tradition is still rife in Bluehill concerning the parson's catechizing of his schools. I myself can recall tales of it told by men
and women, old while I was still young, but not so old as to have
forgotten its terrors. Like Elijah, who always appeared suddenly
before the frightened sinners of Israel, he, too, appeared without
warning, stepping briskly to the door of some schoolhouse and
rapping sharply upon it with his stout, self-made walking-stick,
his white neckcloth severely folded, his leather bag bulging with
tracts. My grandmother, who encountered him around the year
1835, when he was no longer young and she a mite of a girl, was
given to telling us how, when he entered the schoolhouse of her
own isolated district, the scholars sprang to their feet, the boys
with bows from the waist, the girls with curtseys, and the agi-
tated teacher "picking at her handkerchief and fluttering like a
poplar leaf"; and a certain old man, whom I knew in my childhood and who lived to a vast old age, never tired of relating to
groups of fascinated children the most humiliating of experi-

ences. He, it seems, had been making his way to the out-house one cold winter afternoon when he spied to his horror the familiar figure ascending the snowy hill and then and there concluded to remain in frigid concealment. But he was not allowed even that sorry place of refuge! For Father Fisher, who knew every child in his parish, regenerate or unregenerate, came in person to haul him bodily from his hiding-place by the scruff of his neck and back within the catechumenical circle. This ancient swore also to us as one, he said, not far from death and, therefore, careful of his speech, that the parson commanded him to read aloud before the palpitating audience a verse from the 139th Psalm: *Whither shall I go from Thy spirit? And whither shall I flee from Thy presence?* These words, he told us at ninety, had given him "creeps" all his life long! What the parson as catechist may have been like in the days of his more youthful vigor, whether less ominous or more, is, unfortunately, long since buried with those who perhaps knew too well its answer.

There were many journeys on foot for the purpose of baptizing the numerous babies of the large families of those days. Father Fisher was a stout adherent of infant baptism, believing it to be the new covenant stemming from the Abrahamic rite of circumcision and finding it, if not explicitly commanded by the New Testament, surely implicit within the Savior's injunction that young children should be brought to Him that He might lay His hands upon them. There were still other journeys to the sick and the dying, to the latter for spiritual comfort and to the former not infrequently for physical ministrations as well, for the parson seems to have possessed no small store of curative knowledge. His many notebooks are lavishly interpolated by remedies of all sorts, for cuts and bruises, sprains and fractures, toothache, diarrhoea, "severe sore throat," and "stubborn winter coughs." In his Diary for November 1, 1800, he writes of himself bleeding Robert Wood's son, Haskell, wounded by a fall; on another occasion two years later he is called to attend a man suffering from "a strange nervous disorder"; and in July, 1799, he carries itch ointment, concocted by himself and used generously on his own family, to the house of Mr. Daniel Osgood. Since it was not until 1814 that Bluehill voted "to invite a Physician who can be well recommended to settle in this town," the village for many years seems to have been dependent upon Dr. Nathan Tenney of Sedgwick, nine miles away; and, therefore, for minor ailments the parson's knowledge and skill were evidently often employed.

Mr. Fisher was gifted with no small store of legal sense and language as his carefully recorded cases of church discipline bear clear witness. There are at least a dozen entries in his Diaries which mention long walks for the purpose of drawing up wills for the old or for the dying in his parish. "Went to Esq. Peters for the drawing of his will." "To Asa Clough, very sick, to make a will for him." There are even more entries which tell of repeated trips from one end of the town to another for the solemn bearing of stern admonitions or eloquent confessions to those under the censure of their fellow Christians.

And in his make-up there was surely not a little of the instinct and the practice of the itinerant peddler. For fully thirty years he is busily engaged not only in extorting subscriptions for various missionary magazines, *The Panoplist, Panoplist and Missionary Magazine, Missionary Herald,* and for *The Christian Mirror,* which from 1805 followed one another in publication, but also in carrying the issues of these each month to their willing, or unwilling, subscribers. Nor is he above selling, upon every opportunity which presented itself, his own ballads, essays, and books; indeed, he travels miles in the hope of adding a few dollars to his meager income. He seems to have been a genius also at raising subscriptions for divers and sundry missionary enterprises, both for those at home and in foreign lands; and the money which he patiently collected and to which he added far more than he could afford, meant eager sallyings-forth for a holy cause. Nor did his pockets and bags contain only spiritual provender. His itch ointment accompanied him on many an excursion as did the buttons, which he made by thousands, and the hats, which he fabricated by hundreds from delicately shaved poplar shoots.

Small wonder that the Diaries hold numberless entries of the repairing of pastoral shoes, sometimes by the hands of Oliver Sargent, at other times by Deacon Seth Hewins or by Jeremiah Faulkner, all of them apparently cobblers by profession or avocation. Mr. Fisher's sense of democracy and of fair and generous business dealings, always strong within him, obviously caused him to distribute his frequent favors among all three.

2

Like other towns in the Penobscot Bay area settled around the year 1762, when the termination of the French and Indian Wars promised a less precarious and more permanent existence than most earlier settlements in the Province of Maine had known, Bluehill was first contained within the county of Lincoln, formed in 1760. The wide boundaries of this new county included all lands from the Androscoggin River to Nova Scotia on the east and to the farthest northern limits of the Province of Maine. In 1789, the date of the incorporation of Bluehill as a town, the counties of Hancock and of Washington were established. Hancock, within whose vast area Bluehill was now located, included at that time practically all the Penobscot river basin and extended eastward to Gouldsboro Bay and northward to the Laurentian Highlands, where it gave place to the county of Washington. Within this faraway region, this huge area of heavily forested country and rocky seacoast, the settlements in relatively close proximity to Bluehill formed a sort of oasis in an untraversed wilderness so far as their religious activity was concerned. By the year 1797 seven Congregational churches had been formed: at Bluehill in 1772; at Deer Isle in 1773; at Southwest Harbor on Mt. Desert in 1792; at Brooksville and Sedgwick in 1793; at Penobscot in 1795; and at Belfast in 1796. To this frontier nucleus of faith and piety the nearest Congregational church eastward was at Machias seventy-five miles away, a church founded in 1782.[1]

The Bluehill church and that of Deer Isle had been the result of missionary labor on the part of two ardent itinerants, the Rev. Daniel Little, pastor of the Second Congregational Church of Wells, Maine, and the Rev. Oliver Noble, a friend of Parson Fisher and one of the most untiring of missionaries "to the eastward." Daniel Little, who was known as "the Apostle of the East" and who for his good works had been granted by Harvard College the honorary degree of Master of Arts in 1766, had served the Bluehill settlement, then known as Newport, Plantation No. 5, for one or more summers prior to 1772. On October 7th of that year, according to the *Sketches of the Church of Bluehill*, written by Jonathan Fisher, the early parts of which, he says, are copied or compiled from "original documents," Mr. Little "embodied a Congregational church" in the ten-year-old settlement which was bound together by a "Covenant" subscribed by the following names: Ezekiel Osgood, Nicholas Holt, Jonathan Day, John Roundy, Thomas Coggin, Peter Parker, Jr., Joseph Wood, and Nathan Parker. On August 20, 1774, the Rev. Mr. Little met again with his new church "for prayer and Christian conference" and for the election of two deacons, Ezekiel Osgood and Nicholas Holt, they being the senior members of the group of founders. Surely by this time there was a meeting-house of some sort, probably in the Tide Mills district, since town records as early as 1769 speak of "voting to repare the old Meeting-house," but the place and nature of such a building are no longer known.

The Covenant which bound together this little band of men and women in the wilderness is touching in its straightforward simplicity and suggests that Mr. Little's was no mean hand at effective composition:

[1] A most valuable and interesting work on the religious history of Maine is the Rev. Calvin Clark's *History of the Congregational Churches in Maine* in two volumes, published in 1935, by the Congregational Christian Conference of Maine. I am indebted to Mr. Clark for much of the material given in this paragraph and in the one following.

We whose names are underwritten, being by the Providence of God at a very great distance from the Christian Societies to which we formerly belonged and more than 100 miles from any church, think it our duty to form into a new Church State.

We do, therefore, seriously and solemnly, and with one heart and hand, own and adore the one only living and true God, the Lord Jehovah, the Father, Son, and Holy Ghost, to be our God.

We believe the Sacred Scriptures to be the Word of God, and the only perfect rule of our faith and practice.

We own and confess ourselves sinners, and unworthy of God's mercy; and we would penitently ask forgiveness of God, who alone can forgive sin.

We believe in Jesus Christ as the only Mediator between God and man, by whom alone we can obtain pardon and salvation, even eternal life.

We engage together as a particular Church, or covenanted body of Christians, to promote as far as we are able the ministry of the Word and the Ordinance of Christ's kingdom among us.

And we promise, by the Grace of God, to practice all the duties, public and private, that belong to our Christian profession.

We also receive the discipline as used by the Congregational Churches in New England, as to the substance of it, agreeable to the rules of the Gospel, as the discipline of this Church.

And, as a Church of Christ, we covenant together in faith and love, and promise in love to watch over one another, and by all means in our power to promote the honor of Christ, and the peace and happiness of the whole Church.

Now may the glorious and gracious Covenant God forgive us all our offences, assist and bless us in this our Covenant, and accept us now and forever in Jesus Christ, our Lord.

	Ezekiel Osgood
Bluehill Bay	Nicholas Holt
No. 5, Oct 7, 1772.	Jonathan Day

3

Before the ordination and settlement of Jonathan Fisher the Bluehill Church had been administered under the rules of the so-called Half-Way Covenant. This device, established as early as 1662 in Massachusetts and a bone of bitter contention between Richard Mather and his son Increase, allowed the baptism of children whose parents, one or both, had been baptized, to be sure, but who, nevertheless, had not clearly experienced regeneration, were, therefore, not in full communion with the church, and were known as "Half-Way Members." Mr. Fisher, to whom half-way measures of any sort were never attractive, refused from the beginning to countenance the Half-Way Covenant in his congregation. He admits that his stand "has been attended with some difficulty arising from the infant state of church discipline in this Eastern country," but he trusts that "a merciful God, through Christ, will pardon some undesigned errors."

In October, 1795, shortly after his call to Bluehill was given him and before his acceptance of it, he says in his Diary that he has "spent a morning in drawing up a Confession of Faith and a Covenant" for the Bluehill church. These were put into final form shortly after his arrival in December, 1796, and adopted formally on July 13, 1797. The Confession of Faith consists of sixteen Articles, explicitly expressed, each explaining and substantiating itself by many Biblical references. They affirm the existence of one God, "infinite, eternal, and unchangeable," the infallibility of the Scriptures, Old and New, the total depravity of the human creature, "which descends naturally to all his posterity," the immutable truth of Divine Election, the free offering of salvation, determined always by the absolute necessity of a change of heart and a re-birth in Christ, the Divine Ordaining of the Sacraments of Baptism and of the Lord's Supper, infant baptism, provided one parent or both are in full communion of the visible Church, the resurrection of both Just and unjust, and the Day of Judgment "when the wicked shall go away into everlasting punishment and the righteous into Life Eternal." The Covenant is a far more brief document, which translates the Confession of Faith into terms of human practice and which has for its chief Article an explanation of that church discipline commonly in use at this time not only among the orthodox Protestant churches of New England and the Atlantic seaboard, but also among those of the new frontier.[1] The Article reads as follows:

In matters of discipline we promise to conform to the instruction of Christ given in the 18th chapter of Matthew, verses 15, 16, 17:

If thy brother shall trespass against thee, go and tell him his fault between thee and him alone; if he shall hear thee, thou hast gained thy brother.

But if he will not hear thee, then take with thee one or two more, that in the mouth of two or three witnesses, every word may be established.

And if he shall neglect to hear them, tell it unto the church; but if he neglect to hear the church, let him be unto thee as a heathen man and a publican.

Thanks to the parson's zeal and care in composing, copying, and preserving the records of his church, we know a great deal concerning those shortcomings and sins common to "depraved human nature" in Bluehill during the first quarter of the last century and doubtless as common to all other like communities in Maine and elsewhere. We know also of those upheavals which rent family life, those divided loyalties discussed in country stores, blacksmiths' shops, and homes, those scandals which, ruthlessly revealed, kept many listeners willingly from sleep, those humiliations, ironies, and bitter furies, the legacy of all life everywhere, but not often so carefully, even minutely, described and by such a facile pen as that of Jonathan Fisher.

The men who called Mr. Fisher to settle among them could not have been ignorant of his uncompromising position on matters of discipline, for even in the summer of 1795, while he was sojourning for his second summer in Bluehill, the first of his "cases" arose, that of Mr. Joseph Osgood, guilty not only of

[1] For cases of church discipline on the frontier see William Warren Sweet, *Religion on the American Frontier*. New York and Chicago, 1931-1939.

The Fisher Parsonage, 1814

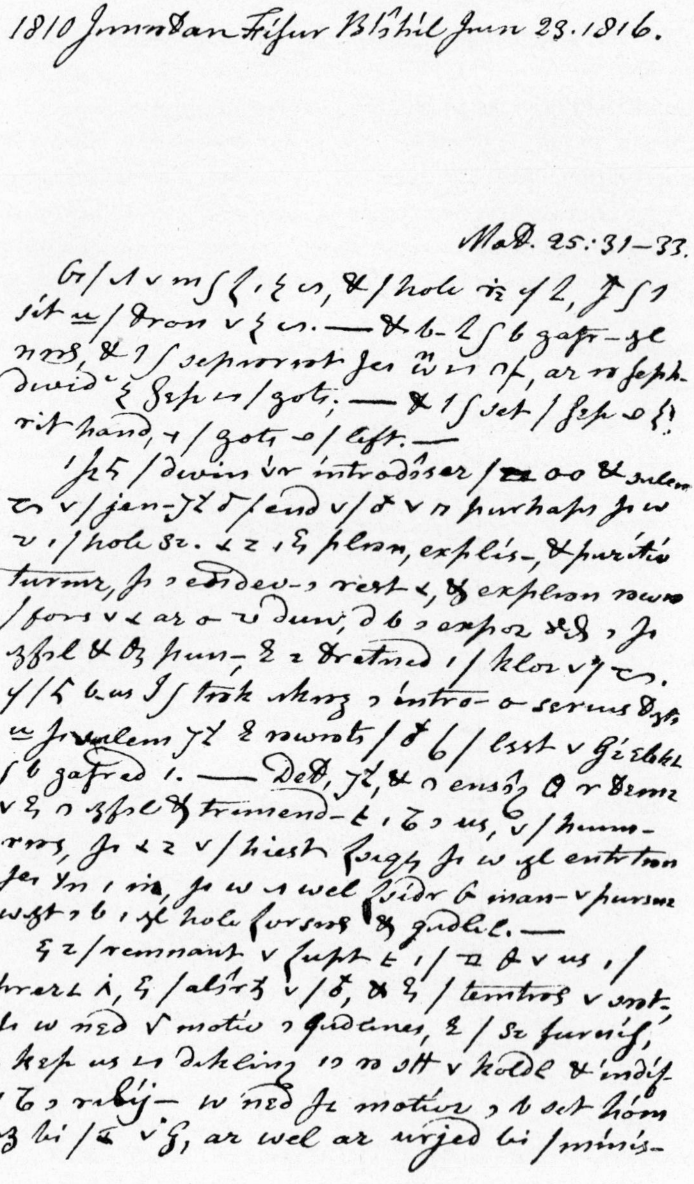
1810 Jonnathan Fisher Bl'hil Jun 23. 1816.

Mat. 25:31-33.

A Sample Page of Jonathan Fisher's Shorthand Code

unbecoming and angry passion, but of indecent behavior. On October 27, 1795, Mr. Osgood, by a unanimous vote of the church, had been suspended from its communion until he should make a public confession of his sins before the church and congregation. This he, pleading innocence, had steadfastly refused to do; and on September 11, 1796, his pastor, now settled in Bluehill, wrote him a robust letter threatening not only formal excommunication from the "body of Christ," but both his temporal and eternal ruin. Mr. Osgood being two years later still unpersuaded, although twice admonished in the interim, his iniquities were again brought to light on August 16, 1798, before a full meeting of the church.

This case of Joseph Osgood occupies some five lively pages in the church records and is most thoroughly delineated with the testimonies of the three witnesses duly recorded and signed. Apparently, since it was the first instance of excommunication under his pastorate, the Rev. Mr. Fisher determined to spare no detail in using it to serve as a test case for the spiritual justification of such disciplinary practice in his church. The sorry affair, which in three years had assumed such gigantic proportions, arose from a dispute, which took place "about the middle of August, 1795," between Mr. Joseph Osgood and Mr. Joshua Horton over the placing of a ridgepole upon Mr. Daniel White's barn. The ridgepole, however, was at last amicably placed to the satisfaction of both, and the quarrel seemingly settled.

On their way home at nightfall, accompanied by Mr. Benjamin Clough and a certain Widow Edwards who unfortunately joined them, the disagreement again arose, and, doubtless increased in importance by the presence of witnesses, suddenly grew into a scene only comparable to those described and depicted by Fielding and Hogarth at their best. Mr. Osgood and Mr. Horton were both dubbed "damned liars," each by the other; Mr. Osgood with a large cane threatened mortal injury to Mr. Horton; Mr. Clough unwisely intervened, and Mrs. Edwards, not to be overlooked, sprang upon Mr. Osgood and tore at his hair. She also, according to Benjamin Clough, the chief witness in the case, "spoke obscenely," upon which Mr. Osgood outdid her "in disgraceful and filthy language," in the course of which he twitted Mr. Horton with the lewd behavior of his wife before Mr. Horton's marriage to her. And, as an even more shameful episode of this wayside drama, Mr. Osgood, according to the sworn testimony of both Benjamin Clough and Sarah Edwards, attempted both with his teeth and his hands to injure Mr. Horton "in his secret parts." Upon this crowning indignity, both the Widow Edwards and Mr. Clough seized Mr. Osgood and "hauled him off" Mr. Horton.

These testimonies having been weighed "with great care and justice" by the church (and, needless to say, with not a little excitement), "a sentence of excommunication was solemnly denounced in public on August 19, 1798, against Mr. Joseph Osgood, who saw not fit to be present." This sentence is itself of great length, since its author obviously embraced this early crisis in his church as an opportunity further to set forth the justice of those scriptural injunctions agreed upon in the Covenant. Somewhat deleted, it reads as follows:

Our Lord and Master, Jesus Christ, both in his own instructions and in the instructions of his apostles, has given his Church certain rules of discipline by which it is to govern itself and its members. Every faithful church will desire to conform itself as closely as may be to these instructions. The most clear and definite instructions which Christ gives us are found in the 18th chapter of Matthew, 15, 16, 17 verses. These instructions relate particularly to the private offences of one individual church member against another; in which case private endeavors to obtain satisfaction are first to be used; if these succeed not, the matter is to be made more public; if satisfaction be not then obtained, the matter is to be brought before the whole church; if the offending person still refuses to give satisfaction, he is to be considered a heathen man and a publican, in other words, is to be considered as out of the church.

Joseph Osgood, one of the members of this church, has been long since accused of having been engaged in an unhappy quarrel with two or three of his neighbors, a quarrel originating from a dispute upon a very trifling subject, and a quarrel in which Mr. Osgood was guilty of conduct very shameful in any person and disgraceful in a professor of religion. On the 27th October, 1795, the accusation was brought forward before the church, when the person accused and the accusers confronted each other and the charge appeared so far supported that the church unanimously voted not to restore the said Joseph Osgood to their communion without a public confession. The church has long since waited with much lenity to see the event. In the meantime Mr. Osgood has received private admonition and admonition in the name and behalf of the church.

On the 16th of this month (August, 1798), in order that the matter might be fairly examined and no injustice done Mr. Osgood, the pastor of the church was at the pains to take down in writing the testimony of the several witnesses, they being at a distance from each other, and not being permitted to see or hear each other's declaration, that any partiality might be the more easily detected; the testimony of each witness was signed by the witness, that which the witness was ready to declare on oath. On the 16th of this month, the greater part of the brethren assembled, and Mr. Osgood appeared before them. The testimony was exhibited which represented the conduct of Mr. Osgood in such a light as is much to the reproach of the religion of which he has made profession. Mr. Osgood, it is true, was ready to make a partial confession, but not a satisfactory one; a part of the charge he still denied, and he did not discover that humility and sincere penitence which was to be expected from a real disciple of Christ. Of course, the church voted, and voted unanimously, to confirm the sentence of excommunication on condition of the want of a satisfactory confession.

Accordingly the Church of Christ in this place do now by their Pastor, agreeably to their vote, excommunicate Joseph Osgood from among them. He is now cast out and rejected from church membership so that he is now no longer one of our brethren; no longer under our peculiar watch and care; no longer entitled to our special friendship as a member of the same body with us, the head of which is Christ. He is now to be considered as an unbeliever, as an heathen man and publican; he is now, in the sense of the Apostle, delivered over to Satan, that is, he is now to be considered as visibly without the limit of Christ's kingdom and within the limits of the kingdom of Satan. I say this is visibly his sad case; but if he have been falsely accused, he is really and truly a subject of this invisible kingdom and redeemed from the kingdom of Satan. And though he be now from circumstances necessitated to suffer this as an affliction, if he suffer it patiently, he will be crowned hereafter with superabundant glory. But, which we fear is the sad case, if he be really guilty of what he has so solemnly, in the presence of God, angels, and men denied, we have reason to tremble for him lest he be one of those whom it is impossible to renew to repentance. The Lord have mercy upon him and give him repentance if it may be. The Lord bless this solemn transaction for his most humble repentance and final salvation. By this we are to witness this day to this assembly that it is our desire to remove the scandal thrown upon religion by the conduct of its professors.

Through regard for modesty and from tenderness to Mr. Osgood, I do not exhibit in public the testimony advanced against him, and I hope that such a step will not be necessary; but the testimony may be open to such as desire further satisfaction to remove any prejudice that may rest upon their minds. In the meantime I would urge, *seriously* urge everyone present to take a solemn warning from this event to avoid cautiously every opening to sin lest the time come when they may be brought into a similar condition.

God grant that we may all hear, and fear, and shun the rocks upon which others have made shipwreck. Let everyone who thinketh he standeth take heed lest he fall, and let us all remember that by Grace we are saved. God grant that we may be, for Christ's sake. Amen.

August 19, 1798.   Jonathan Fisher.

There is among the church records no evidence that any confession was ever deduced, or even wrung, from Mr. Joseph Osgood; in fact, his name does not appear upon the list of those "restored" to fellowship, a list carefully kept by the parson from the time of his settlement. He apparently lived his long life, for he died in 1854 in his ninety-fourth year, without the ministrations of church or pastor, whether in spiritual calm or anxiety, who can now tell? From several entries in the Diaries it is clear that Mr. and Mrs. Fisher, singly and together, called upon him

from time to time, and once it is explicitly stated that Joseph
Osgood worked at brick-laying at the parsonage. At all events,
he lived to see the stern prophet of his destinies borne to the
grave seven years before his own departure thither!

That Jonathan Fisher was not himself unmoved on August 19,
1798, over Osgood's sin and humiliation is clear from his entry
for that day. He writes: "Declared sentence of excommunication
against Mr. Joseph Osgood. What do I deserve better? My heart
is full of evil, if it do not break forth. May God have mercy on
me, for Christ's sake forgive and humble me."

4

In the records of the church at Bluehill, kept by its pastor
from the date of his settlement until March 25, 1832, there are in
all thirty-two cases of discipline for various offences. These cases
are fully described with testimonies of all witnesses and with
careful copies of accompanying admonitory letters, of confessions,
and of excommunications. They are written in Mr. Fisher's clear
and beautiful handwriting and bound in a notebook obviously
made by him. A subsequent notebook, which may have recorded
more cases and which is known to have been in existence, is now
missing. It is safe to assume, however, that such cases did not
continue in any number from 1832 to Mr. Fisher's resignation in
1837. The list of excommunications and restorations, already
referred to in the case of Joseph Osgood and covering the period
from 1832 to 1837, names not one case of excommunication during these years. Moreover, in his Diary for 1829 Mr. Fisher admits
with evident distress that many among his flock have become
reluctant to accept "those disciplinary measures enjoined by
Christ upon the Church"; and in the same year he writes his
son that he is concerned and depressed over this reluctance, even
among some of the most staunch of the Brethren, and fears lest
the "prostration" of church discipline be at hand. The last two
cases occur in 1829; in the Diaries from 1829 to their close in
1835 no reference is made to further discipline; and in the

many letters written by the parson between 1829 and the year of his death, 1847, the matter is not mentioned.[1]

Actually few of the thirty-two cases in the Bluehill church resulted in excommunication, since the greater number of the culprits submitted to public confession of their sins and were thereupon granted re-instatement to church fellowship and communion. These confessions, all but one of them obviously composed by the pen of Mr. Fisher, were in the early years of his ministry not only read before the church in the presence of the one censured, but also "exhibited in public," which phrase would seem to mean that they were not concealed from the ears of non-members, who might well decide to be present upon so exciting an occasion, and that they were likewise posted within the precincts of the meeting-house for anyone entering to read. As early as the year 1804 such objection was raised by various members against too great publicity of misdemeanors, which publicity in their opinion brought scandal against the church in the minds of those unconnected with it, that the pastor was forced to accede to a majority vote of his anxious children in Christ and henceforth consent to the hearing of confessions only within the circle of those in communion with the church. Although he states in his recording of this vote that he, "together with some of the brethren, disapproved," his stout adherence to the democratic principle in church government demanded his submission to the declared wishes of the majority.

The thirty-two offences which in the opinion of the church demanded its discipline include most of those human frailties to which flesh is heir: sinful anger, extreme intemperance, false-hood, abuse of wives by husbands and of husbands by wives, flagrant neglect of family worship, betting on horse-racing, dis-

[1] In a most interesting book, *History of American Congregationalism*, by G. G. Atkins and F. L. Fagley (Boston and Chicago, 1942) church discipline is said to have continued "well into the nineteenth century." William Warren Sweet in his volume, *The Congregationalists*, in *Religion on the American Frontier*, lists such discipline in Illinois as late as 1838. Doubtless the location, size, and character of church communities determined its continuance. As is well known, certain sects, such as the Mennonites, continue it to the present time.

honest business dealings, desecration of the Sabbath, profanity, adultery, propagation of scandal, lewd behavior, contention with a mother-in-law, and fornication. The last-named sin, indeed, was apparently so common in Bluehill and elsewhere (for the parson on many pages of his Diary deplores its prevalence both at home and abroad) that on July 17, 1799, the following confession is offered before the church "according to the form heretofore exhibited":

We, the subscribers, trusting that by the Grace of God we have been brought to see the evil of sin in general and especially of the sins we have committed, do now humbly, we hope, and penitently confess the sin of fornication of which we have been guilty; and this we do from a conviction that it is reasonable to bear public and marked testimony against scandalous offenses whereby we may have been instrumental in weakening the bonds of society and injuring the cause of religion. We ask the forgiveness of all Christians and also that God for Christ's sake would forgive us and keep us from offending in future.

Signed:

> Lois Mirich
> Isaiah Hinckley
> Nabby Ingalls
> Joshua Parker
> Elisabeth Parker

The case of Miss Molly Clay, guilty of the same sin in large measure, for she had boasted to Mrs. Bethany Oakes that she had four times "received clandestine addresses," proved far too detailed and disgraceful to be covered by a form confession. She, upon refusing to make public acknowledgment, was excommunicated on June 3, 1804. Mr. Andrew Wood, whose various misdemeanors over a period of twelve adventuresome years occupy much space in the records of his church, began his series of downfalls by fornication also, and for his impenitency was excommunicated on July 18, 1805. Brother Wood, however, upon a delayed confession on March 8, 1807, was restored to fellowship and communion. A few years later he is charged with neglect of family prayer and not long afterward with "yoking his oxen on the Sabbath and loading hay between three o'clock and sunset." By this time he seems inured to the act of confession and quickly escapes excommunication by his alacrity to make amends.

Mr. Benjamin Clough, who will be remembered as the chief witness against Mr. Joseph Osgood and the somewhat belligerent restorer of peace in that unseemly fracas, himself fell from grace on December 5, 1799, through a number of inadvertent, even profane, remarks over a horse-trade with Mr. Jonathan Clay. Although three days later he was quick to make a public confession of his guilt, he again diverged widely from the straight and narrow way in the year 1800. In that year he was accused, first, of breaking the Sabbath both by "singing a dancing tune" and by buying sugar and tea on that day; second, of a breach of truth; and, third, of "speaking reproachfully of church members." At a meeting on March 13th, to which Brother Clough was summoned to answer these charges, so many witnesses flung back at him his reputed remarks over a period of two years that one is tempted not only to condone his fury but even to admire his skilful and apt employment of language in his defense. In answering his accusers he affirmed that he could "glorify God in a dancing tune as well as by any other," that he had "suffered all for the sake of religion" and meant to endure this anguish no longer, that the church was not only "hardening him in sin" but was, indeed, "as the blind leading the blind," and that, in short, it was "in the same ditch" from which it was vainly trying to haul *him*. Upon this torrent of language the Brethren voted unanimously for excommunication.

Like Mr. Joseph Osgood, Mr. Clough for the rest of his many days lived "outside the church." An entry thirty years later in the parson's Diary states this fact and describes him as dwelling in poverty with sons who have married unregenerate women. Mr. Fisher in this entry, with a sympathy not always characteristic of him, forbears to attribute "old Mr. Clough's sorry state" to its quite evident cause!

Miss Mercy Lowell on May 1, 1818, is charged by the "Brethren of the Church" with propagating a scandalous report against Stephen Holt and Edith Parker, who, she has steadfastly asserted, "were seen on Long Island in an indecent act." Mercy is, however, induced by her pastor to eat her ill-advised words in public on September 20th and is thereupon restored to fellowship.

On a certain Sabbath morning, "about the middle of July, 1818," Mr. David Osgood so far forgot himself and that humaneness which all Christian professors should show toward dumb beasts as to abuse a flock of geese, belonging to his neighbor, Mrs. Joshua Oakes, by beating three of them to death with a stick and by throwing others of them over a fence. Mr. Osgood added to his cruel behavior the sin of falsehood, for, upon being questioned by the church concerning the size of the stick used in this maltreatment, he reported the diameter of the little end of the stick instead of the considerable size of the stick itself. But upon receiving a stern admonishment from his pastor both for his inhumanity and his "degree of deception concerning the stick," together with the command to pay Mrs. Oakes "one dollar as soon as he should be able," he promised amendment and escaped further punishment.

Deacon Peter Parker confesses to driving horses "on the Lord's Day without necessity"; Mrs. James Candage and Mrs. Patty Clay are sincerely sorry that they have spoken harshly to their respective mothers-in-law; a dispute between Mr. Daniel Faulkner and Mr. Joseph Treworgy over five dollars rises to such a state of altercation that it is settled by the church and pastor assembled in solemn conference; Mr. James Savage, who is accused by Nicholas Gray of adultery with an Indian squaw, proves to the entire satisfaction of his "fellow professors of religion" that he was in his own door-yard at 4 P.M., the hour named by Mr. Gray as that when the untoward incident occurred; and

Peter Parker, Jr., who is accused not only of kicking his wife but of boasting of this act before his neighbors, confesses his two-fold crime and is restored to fellowship. A year later, however, Peter sees fit to withdraw to the newly-organized Baptists!

The problem of intemperance during the first quarter of the nineteenth century obviously was productive of many searchings of heart. In a day when, according to William Warren Sweet in his *Religion on the American Frontier,* "whiskey was considered with meat and bread as one of the necessities of life" and when in Illinois and Ohio country stores a whiskey-pail with cups attached invited all visitors to help themselves, it was difficult to draw the line between generous and genial hospitality and sin. Maine towns and villages may not have equaled those on the Western frontier in the use of ardent spirits; and yet from the parson's Diaries it is quite clear not only that Mr. Andrew Witham, the leading store-keeper in Bluehill, did a thriving business in the sale of such beverages, but that Mr. Fisher himself more than occasionally purchased them of Mr. Witham. Whiskey and rum serve as the basis, indeed, for many of the parson's medicinal remedies; and in one of his notebooks he writes that if pickles "are placed in 1 qt. of molasses, 6 qts. of water, and 1½ qts. of good New England rum, there will need be no worry whatever about their excellence for any amount of time." Wine and spirits were certainly hospitably served in all homes, even in the parsonage, during at least the early years of Mr. Fisher's pastorate; and in 1814, when the new part of his house was raised, the gallon of gin provided by the host at $1.50 was, one imagines, as efficacious as the "bountiful supper" in promoting that great good cheer of which he writes in his Diary.

It is significant that of the thirty-two cases of discipline recorded in the annals of the church between 1797 and 1832, only two, those of Brothers Thomas Coggin and Freeman Hardin, have to do with intemperance, one in 1797, the other in 1818; and that each is accused, not with the use of spiritous liquors, but with "too free a use" of them, which indulgence has been the cause of family neglect and of other unseemly behavior. The temperance movement, which, with Neal Dow as its principal advocate, was in later years to bring Maine into national prominence, was but a feeble spark in the first quarter of the century; and, although Mr. Fisher often records graphically in his Diary the sad effects of intoxication in Bluehill and elsewhere, he himself was not an entire convert to the movement until 1829, when he finally, perhaps even a bit reluctantly, gave his support to an organization in Bluehill for the suppression of intemperance. Once having given his support, however, he espoused this new cause with his usual relentless fervor.

Two other cases of discipline within the church merit special attention, one because of the culprit's later tragic connection with the Fisher family, the other because, like that of Mr. Joseph Osgood, it throws such light upon church administration and upon the manner in which it became inextricably involved in village society.

The first was the case of Mr. Joshua Wood, who, alone of all those under censure, clearly composed his own confession, a document sadly characteristic of the young man himself and as sadly prophetic of later events. Joshua Wood is often referred to in the parson's Diary and at first with the greatest respect. He was a young candidate for the Christian ministry, who lived at intervals with the Fisher family for several years, recited in Greek and Latin to the parson, and occasionally attended a term at the Bluehill Academy. He seems to have been a most valued member of the family group, and the accusation against him on July 13, 1820, while he was still under the Fisher roof, must have caused many hours of embarrassment and distress to his host and tutor. His accuser in the church records is a certain Miss Phebe Horton, a "Baptist professor," who testifies in the following words against Mr. Wood, "both being at the Meeting-House in the presence of the Brethren of the church."

About the time of the Baptist association Mr. Joshua Wood

came down for me to go and watch at his brother's. Just before we got to the door, he attempted to pull up my clothes. I laid out what strength I had and prevented it. Not long after, I told one of the sisters of this church of it, for I have felt hard towards him; and I have reported it again, though I think I have not done right in doing it.

Then follow questions and answers:

Question by Mr. Joshua Wood:
Did the whole transaction take up more than the ¼ part of a minute?
Answer by Phebe Horton:
I don't know that it did.
Question by Mr. Fisher:
Did Mr. Wood use any violence?
Answer by Phebe Horton:
No, he did not.
Voted, That Mr. Wood read a confession which he had prepared. He read it.
Question to Phebe Horton:
Is this confession satisfactory to you? Is it sufficiently full?
Answer:
Yes.
Voted, That the church is satisfied with the confession, that it be offered in public by Mr. Wood next Lord's Day, and that there is liberty for others of the Baptist Church to attend.

Mr. Wood's confession was duly offered, without doubt to a large audience, and seemingly read by himself. In the light of his future behavior and of the few years of life remaining to him, its illuminating protestations are worth careful scrutiny:

My Christian Brethren:

Our blessed Savior commands us to confess our faults one to another. I confess to you and to the world that I have done wickedly and have sinned, O Lord, against heaven and in thy sight. I confess that one evening in the fore part of September, 1817, now almost three years ago, walking from the house of Mr. John Horton to my brother's house in company with Miss Phebe Horton, I, in an unguarded moment, conducted unbecomingly and wickedly in that I offered to put my hands beneath her clothes. My God beheld, I instantly sighed, and exclaimed, I am a wicked wretch! Soon after upon my knees with my heart full of anguish, with tears flowing down, I confessed my crime to my God and Savior and pleaded earnestly for pardon, and for the sanctifying influence of the Holy Spirit to keep me from sin; but conscious guilt has stood opposed to my asking for forgiveness almost to this day. But I have asked her forgiveness and obtained it. Now, my Brethren, I ask your forgiveness, I ask your prayers, I entreat you to be faithful to me in your reproofs and admonitions. I have wounded the cause of the blessed Redeemer. I lament it, and when I take a retrospective view of my life and have some discovery of the wickedness of my heart, I tremble. Again, my Brethren, I ask your forgiveness, the forgiveness of all, and especially of God. O pray for my thorough conviction of sin, for my sanctification, and that I may never more bring a reproach upon the cause of Christ. O pray that I may not be a stumbling-block over which sinners may fall into hell! Pray that sinners may not consider such conduct to be the fruit of the benign religion of the prince of Peace, but the fruit of a depraved, wicked heart and of the prince of the powers of darkness. Once more I ask your forgiveness; for I have such a view of my own wickedness, and of the justice, holiness, and purity of God, that if he, with barbed arrows, dipped in the dregs of the cup of his indignation, should pierce my guilty soul and drink up my spirits, and with the mighty weight of both his hands should crush me down to the bottomless pit, where the smoke of my torment must ascend up forever and ever, I must exclaim, Just and righteous are thy judgments, O God!

Signed: Joshua Wood

Attest: Jonathan Fisher, Pastor.

The second case, which was to trail in its stormy wake controversies as yet unforeseen and virtually result in the end of church discipline in Bluehill, was that of Mrs. Roxana Ray. Roxana was the wife of Matthew Ray, the village smith, to whom the parson in his Diaries is constantly going for repairs of tools or for the purchase of metal objects of all sorts. This conflict, which opened on June 8, 1817, and soon involved both husband and wife, continued until October, 1829, when it was at last pronounced "settled" so far as a rent and unhappy church was concerned. It rocked, if not wrecked, the peace of village society, caused bitter criticism against the church and its pastor, as his Diaries attest, and finally made necessary the calling of a Council of delegates outside Bluehill, an act which injured Mr. Fisher's staunch belief in the independence of each local church only slightly less than it hurt his pride.

Mrs. Ray's sins are many. "A repeated indulgence of sinful anger" first engages the attention of the church, but to this the accused easily confesses. Five years later, however, a mere misdemeanor such as anger is forgotten in the accusation against her by her neighbors of enough crimes to illustrate in full the Seven Deadly Sins. She is guilty, they assert, of falsehood, "dirty, foul-mouthed language," unbecoming arrogance and pride, slander, and even of adultery. Her daughter, Loisa, admits to Miss Tempe Floyd, that while she, Loisa, "was lying on the transum of Capt. Thomas Nichols' ship on a passage to the westward" in July, 1820, she heard her mother, then in a berth together with Capt. Nichols, say that she "would not have her behavior known even for the ownership of all Bluehill." Faced with such charges as these, coupled with the total lack of humility and deference on the part of Mrs. Ray, the church, after several sessions of prayerful and serious consideration, excommunicates her on April 22, 1822.

On March 5, 1823, Brother Matthew Ray angrily springs to the defense of his still impenitent wife. He accuses the church of neglect of duty in not giving friendly warning and instruction to Roxana "as promised in its covenant." He further makes accusation of the church's dependence upon "mere hearsay" for evidence against her "modesty," and he finally upbraids the Brethren and their pastor for not permitting him to vote with them upon the matter of his wife's excommunication. These accusations the church denies, except that it admits its conclusion that Mr. Ray's presence would be "unbecoming" upon the occasion of his wife's sentence. On March 20, 1823, Mr. Fisher writes, with some evident circumspection and care, a confession for Brother Ray, which states that he himself has broken covenant with the church and exhibited towards it an "un-Christian-like spirit." This Mr. Ray steadfastly refuses to sign, and in the following May is likewise excluded from its communion.

This unsavory and sorry strife continues for several more years, interspersed by frequent "waitings upon" the still recalcitrant Mr. Ray by various brethren of the church. By 1826 a new element injects itself into the affair. Matthew Ray by this time has become a Major in the State Militia; by 1828 his title has been advanced to that of Colonel. It is quite evident that such recognition has advanced also the social position of the Ray family and that certain accusers of the past years have now become friends and adherents of both Roxana and her colonel. Like Jonathan Edwards, who found church discipline most hazardous in Northampton because "the best people" were involved, Mr. Fisher and his church discover their problem increasing both in magnitude and in intricacy. Finally after appealing to the Sedgwick church in 1828 for unofficial advice and hearing its unwelcome judgment that "Col. Ray censures the Bluehill church abroad and has influence," a Council was called of the pastors and delegates from at least four Hancock County churches in July, 1829.

This Council was, in fact, precipitated by Col. Ray himself, whose action in so doing suggests revengeful shrewdness rather than spiritual concern for the outcast souls of him and his wife. Sometime in March, 1828, Col. Ray applied to the Rev. Mr. Mighill Blood, pastor of the Congregational Church at Bucksport, for membership for him and Mrs. Ray in that church. Upon such application Mr. Blood, a devoted friend of Mr. Fisher and a man of fine intelligence and character, had no other recourse than to inquire into the religious status of his new candidates, a subject upon which he, together with practically everyone else in the region, must have been already well-versed. He thereupon advised the convening of a Council in order to determine the truth of a controversy which was obviously getting out of hand and threatening the cause of religion.

This calling of a Council to settle an affair within his own church and parish was a bitter blow to Jonathan Fisher, and that he never entirely recovered from it is clear both from his Diaries and his letters, even although their statements are brief and often only suggestive. In common with Congregational ministers and churches everywhere, and especially in New England, he held unswervingly to the principles of democracy and self-government within the individual church; and to be forced to yield to the counsel and criticism of others, was a shock to his sense of justice, mitigated only by the knowledge within him that Divine Providence, for some inscrutable reason, must have so ordained it for the good of his immortal soul. Moreover, his own undeviating honesty must have been outraged almost beyond endurance by the trap so skilfully laid for him by Matthew and Roxana Ray.

His Diary for July 14, 15, and 16, 1829, records tersely and with no personal comments the sitting of the Council in the Bluehill meeting-house. Opening "after dinner" on July 14th, the Council deliberated "until sunset," reconvened the next day at 7:30 A.M., sat again until sunset, and finally closed on the third day at the same hour. The result of the deliberation was even more humiliating and distressing than the necessity which occasioned it. It was voted by the Council that the Bluehill church should "annul as improper all its past votes expressing any suspicions of Mrs. Ray's modesty" and "that the pastor of the church should communicate the doings of the Council to Col. Ray."

Whether Col. and Mrs. Ray were ever received into the bosom of the Bucksport church, we are not told. If they were, the Rev. Mighill Blood must have been beset by uncomfortable doubts as to their spiritual contributions to his own flock. And although the name of Brother Ray in later years appears in the parson's Diary as a "collector for foreign missions," there is no evidence, direct or indirect, that he and Roxana were ever restored to the Bluehill communion of saints.

In a letter to his son-in-law, dated June 21, 1828, the distracted parson writes that there is "an Achan in the camp of the church" and, he fears, "more than one." And writing to his children on November 13, 1829, he says: "We have had some serious trials this Summer and Autumn in the Church. . . . The prevailing indifference about religious privileges is a grief to my mind, and sometimes in a measure discourages me. O that the Spirit from on high might be poured out upon us! Then the wilderness would become as a fruitful field, and the desert blossom as the rose. Pray for us, that God may revive his work among us, and for me, that I may be faithful, and may not faint in the day of adversity."

On October 20th of that difficult and fateful year, 1829, he makes a statement in his Diary which would seem inconsequential enough, were it not the only entry in forty years to chronicle for him a complete holiday:

"A brisk northwest wind. I went all day after partridges to relax myself with a ramble in the forests. Saw but two partridges. I killed one of them."

5

Early in his ministry in Bluehill Mr. Fisher found occasion to put on the whole armor of God in his wrestling against what was to him spiritual wickedness in various forms. But although he kept his loins girt about with truth, as he saw it, and wore uncompromisingly the shield of faith, the helmet of salvation, and the sword of the spirit, he seldom forgot that gospel of peace with which the Apostle Paul would have Christian feet well shod. His Diary is filled with the suppers, beds, and breakfasts hospitably given to itinerant Methodist and Baptist missionaries seeking converts among the settlements of Hancock County. Nor did they hesitate, as he was well aware, to seek these converts within his own sheepfold!

As early as 1799 he records in his Diary several calls made upon him by traveling Methodist preachers; in August, 1805, Mr. Upfold, a Baptist evangelist, visits him; in September of the same year Mr. Carpending of the same unfortunate persuasion tarries for the night; and in October Mr. Baker, a Methodist preacher "with Universalist leanings," is given supper and a lodging. These were, needless to say, hardly so welcome as Father Jotham Sewall, that intrepid man of God, who, like Elisha, seemed to have "passed by continually" and who shared the theology of his host. They were doubtless stoutly assailed on many points of doctrine as they tarried by the parson's study fire; but there is ample evidence that they were hospitably received and set on their way well-fed and assured of friendliness and good cheer upon any future visits.

Two itinerant Methodists (in name at least) in January, 1803, gave the parson perhaps his first opportunity to gird on his armor and go forth to battle. On the 18th of that month a certain Mr. Metcalf reached Bluehill and began a series of "lectures" there at the home of Col. Nathan Parker, who, probably through frontier hospitality alone, allowed his house for that purpose. Apparently a persuasive speaker, Mr. Metcalf drew a large audience for his first and succeeding discourses. His initial text for the series, *He that is an hireling seeth the wolf coming and fleeth because he is an hireling,* was perhaps unwisely chosen, for it so impressed Parson Fisher that he determined to guard his flock and never to fail to be present at any of Mr. Metcalf's lectures. Nor did he fail, once Mr. Metcalf had concluded his evening sermon, to "put to the preacher some irrefutable questions and objections" which the slower mind of the visiting lecturer found difficult to answer. Mr. Metcalf's Methodism was dangerously undermined by "Arminian heresies," for he summarily declared that "the heathen who do as well as they have known will meet with us in glory," that "no person is totally depraved," and that "Divine Election is a mistaken and un-Scriptural doctrine." These pernicious tenets laid him open to Mr. Fisher's powers of argument; and the meetings at Col. Parker's must have been stormy sessions, indeed. In March, 1803, Mr. Metcalf, still tarrying in Bluehill, but evidently fearing himself in danger of complete defeat, called in the help of a Methodist brother, Mr. Goodhue by name, himself tainted by heresy, who "dared to state in the presence of a large company that with God there is no distinction between saints and sinners"! Whereupon such a battle of wits ensued, accompanied by such "insolence" on the part of Messrs. Metcalf and Goodhue toward Mr. Fisher, that "almost all the audience" left in disgust, and Arminianism was "for the time routed."

The year 1803, indeed, was destined to be a fatal one in its ominous prophecies for the future peace and spiritual prosperity of Jonathan Fisher and his congregation. In that year three persons who were examined for admission to the church, Susannah Floyd, Lydia Parker, and William Johnson, "expressed scruples respecting Infant Baptism." They were, however, "not withstanding these doubts," received as members. By 1805 the scruples of the three had developed into convictions. They now declared themselves dissatisfied with their own baptisms, thoroughly converted to the doctrine of immersion as the only door of admission to the Church of Christ, and, therefore, conscientious subjects for immediate withdrawal. In the same disastrous year similar convictions had assailed and conquered some twenty-five others of Mr. Fisher's flock, who by the close of that year had also withdrawn from his church.

A persuasive Baptist missionary, Elder Isaac Case, had been preaching in the Bluehill region from time to time since 1796; and the spread of Baptist influence can doubtless be largely attributed to his eloquent faith. In 1805 his untiring zeal had reaped a rich reward in the town of Sedgwick, where since 1793 the Rev. Daniel Merrill had been the intelligent and indefatigable pastor of the Congregational Church. This Daniel Merrill had already written his name large in the District of Maine by his energetic labors in the cause of God. His church numbered in 1805 nearly 150 members, the largest at that time in Hancock County; revivals under him had been both plenteous and plentiful; indeed, more than once in his Diary his friend, colleague, and neighbor, Mr. Fisher, had yearned volubly for similar manifestations of Divine Grace in his own far smaller church. Along with his other zealous projects for the increase of the kingdom of Heaven upon earth, Mr. Merrill had taken upon himself the training of able young men in his parish for the Congregational ministry. Within this group of candidates were several who, in the year 1803, found themselves beset by grave doubts as to the Scriptural validity of their own baptisms. In attempting to allay these doubts their teacher was himself so attacked by similar misgivings that on May 13, 1805, he, his wife, and 66 of his church were, in a single spectacular hour, immersed in the cold salt waters of the Benjamin River.

This was an event which the Rev. David Benedict, in an old, but interesting book called *A General History of the Baptist Denomination* and published in 1848, describes as "exacting no small attention throughout the United States." "The Congregational church," he says, "continued to repair to the water until 120 of them were baptized." Mr. Merrill's church thereupon became the Baptist church of Sedgwick; and the small handful which remained firm to the earlier faith thenceforth became a part of the Congregational society of Brooksville.[1] It was with Mr. Merrill's new church in Sedgwick that the first Baptists in Bluehill united, until a year later on February 13, 1806, eighteen of them organized themselves into a Baptist church in Bluehill "under Elder Case and Elder Merrill with their delegates."

This first serious defection in his church, which from 1796 to 1803 he reports as "living in general peace and pleasantness except for some trying cases of discipline," was a sad and heavy blow to Jonathan Fisher. To lose from a congregation, number-

---

[1] Other accounts of this spiritual and ecclesiastical triumph for the Baptists are found in the Rev. Joshua Millet's *History of the Baptists in Maine* (Portland, 1845) and in a much later book, under the identical title, by Henry S. Burrage (Portland, 1904).

ing in January, 1806, but 98 communicants, almost one third of its members meant not only grievous disappointment but genuine forebodings of a practical nature. It also meant to a mind like the parson's much careful searching of heart as to his own theological position. All these resultant emotions and anxieties he describes in his Diary for February 9, 1806:

During the twelve months past I have had a season of trial. The Rev. D. Merrill of Sedgwick, having been led with a number of his church to renounce the mode of Baptism by any other way than immersion as a nullity, and having withdrawn from the fellowship of the churches and received Baptism and ordination anew, and a number of his church also having withdrawn from the fellowship of the rest, and about 30 of the church under my care having followed their example, it has been a time of serious inquiry with me whether immersion be essential to the ordinance of Baptism.

During these inquiries, my feelings have been variously exercised. Sometimes for a little while I have indulged hardness towards those who have withdrawn; at other times I have felt indifference towards them, and this through stupidity of heart; at other times I trust I have been divested of prejudice and hard feeling and have felt a little tenderness towards my dissenting brethren as children of God, and grieved for their departure.

Such a number have withdrawn that I have serious apprehension that my settlement will be broken up. Were the evidence equal, I think the temptation would rather be to embrace the Anabaptist sentiment. In such a situation I think I have the advantage of contemplating the subject with a good degree of freedom from the secret influence of self-interest. I have labored to contemplate it and to inquire concerning it.

With regard to the mode of Baptism, after serious inquiry and meditation upon the subject, and after carrying the case repeatedly to God, I feel an inward and general satisfaction that sprinkling water on the face is acceptable to God, and so pouring water upon the head, and so rubbing water upon some part of the body with the hand, and so immersion in water, total or partial, each of these modes being in some degree suggested and approved by Scripture intimation and allusion, and in some way signifying the great thing intended, which is the cleansing away of sin by the blood of Christ.

On February 13th his entry is brief:

This day 18 persons, 12 males, 6 females, all but one members of my church, were gathered into a Baptist church by Mr. Case and Mr. Merrill. To me a mournful event. But the Lord reigneth!

And on February 14th he remarks succinctly and with no comment that the Rev. Daniel Merrill, before returning to Sedgwick on the day following the forming of the new church, called very early and took breakfast with him. One would give a great deal to know what was said at that breakfast table by the two close friends of many years! But that Mr. Merrill both felt assured of his welcome and desired to come speaks eloquently and well both for Parson Fisher and for himself.

The subsequent life of the two churches now established in a small and isolated village, which in the year 1807 numbered but 597 souls, seems to have been far more long-suffering, even amicable, than one might with good reason expect. There doubtless were hard words on both sides, long since buried in oblivion with those who uttered them; and yet in the parson's Diaries, in his carefully kept church records, which review in detail the whole story of the "Baptist controversy," and in the *Sketches* of his life, there is little resentment and less bitterness. Moreover, in a neatly tied bundle of letters, preserved among his papers and written between 1803 and 1825 by him and some leading Baptists in the town concerning controversial matters, the tone of the writers on either side is one of mutual, if at times distant, respect. There may, of course, have been other correspondence of a far less pleasant nature; but when one takes into account the parson's honesty and candor, together with his life-long reluctance to destroy a scrap of paper unrecorded or uncopied, it seems reasonable to assume that at least those in positions of authority in the two societies walked in ways of comparative friendliness one with another. And it is pleasing to note in passing that the language and composition of all the letters thus exchanged speak admirably for the cultural and intellectual tone of so small a community.

Mr. Fisher, it is true, does upon one occasion "feel prejudice against the ungrammatical utterances" of a certain Baptist preacher, but he chides himself immediately for so doing; he describes two Baptist Elders, John Roundy and Amos Allen, former members of his church, as "men of good character but of small education"; he regrets that preaching is "licensed," even encouraged, among the Baptist denomination without the necessity of ordination; he occasionally looks askance at the tendency toward Republican or Jeffersonian sentiments on the part of several Baptist brethren, at variance with his own staunch Federalist position; and he wishes that in general the rival denomination set greater store "upon a learned clergy." He is, it is true, cruelly hurt when, in February, 1809, the Rev. Mr. Merrill is invited to preach the funeral sermon of one of his own oldest parishioners, a recent convert to the Baptist ranks; and he occasionally writes of "hard things," never explained, said against him by members of the new congregation. But, for the most part, he has little to record of rancor, and he frequently writes of "pleasant religious conversations" which he enjoys with "Baptist professors" in Bluehill and elsewhere.

In February, 1806, he is careful to see that by a vote of his church those withdrawn from his congregation "for conscientious reasons" are immediately excused the payment of the .12½ "Communion Table Tax" levied upon each communicant. He is less amenable toward the "Ministerial Tax," which, still demanded of the Baptists for the payment of his salary as minister of "the Established Church," caused trouble as early as 1806 and, still unremitted in 1813, resulted in the legal incorporation of the Baptist church; but he insists that such a matter is one of official taxation and lies wholly and only within the province of town government. He is glad to receive back into his fold from time to time, between 1806 and 1820, five who have changed their minds about their earlier discontent and now desire re-instatement; but he does so without undue rejoicing. Not until July, 1822, is he asked to preach in the new Baptist meeting-house, erected in 1817, and then only upon the occasion of a funeral; but in August, 1817, he writes of uniting with the Baptists at the village schoolhouse in the monthly "concert prayer-meeting," apparently the first union service held by the two churches.

Perhaps no happening during these difficult years throws more kindly a light on the relations between Congregationalists and Baptists than does the case of a certain Mrs. Eliza Day, a member of the Baptist church, who was employed for some months in 1812 as a servant in the Fisher family. On July 12th of that summer the ninth child of Jonathan and Dolly Fisher was born, only to die two weeks later. Mrs. Day, whose imagination must have been more rampant than accurate, circulated about the town a report that the baby's father had hastily baptized it but a few hours before its death. This tale, evidently current for several years, did not reach the ears of any member of the Fisher family until 1819. Naturally distressed over a report so false and so "damaging to his standing as a minister of the gospel," Mr. Fisher asked for an investigation of the matter by the Baptist church. Such investigation was held unnecessary by the Baptists, who, in a letter dated September 11, 1819, express themselves as convinced that "Mrs. Day was mistaken" upon the basis alone of "Mr. Fisher's truth and piety." They further determine that "she be reproved and admonished by the church to which she belongs." This action proves unsatisfactory both to Mr. Fisher's thorough-going mind and to his church, who straightway reply that no decision concerning his innocence should rest alone upon his "truth and piety," but rather upon the whole revealed evidence of the case in question. The Baptist brethren, convinced of the justice of Mr. Fisher's position and that of his church, thereupon on September 25th hold such an inquiry, at which both Mr. and Mrs. Fisher are present and at the close of which Mr. Fisher is fully exonerated and Eliza Day informed of the necessity for public acknowledgment and confession. That such a report was for seven years not carried to the parson by some trouble-maker in either camp and that during so long a time no use whatever was made of it in fomenting dissension and strife, provide at least negative evidence of the regard and confidence in which he was held by his dissenting brethren.

Mr. Fisher lived to see the Baptist church steadily amass far more members than his own; but he lived also to see a far greater degree of friendliness between the two congregations. By 1826 he is attending at Mr. Andrew Witham's home Elder Pinkham's "lecture," which he pronounces "very good" and before which he is requested by the Baptist Elder "to open the meeting with prayer." In the same year he sees the two churches "unite in a season of prayer and fasting for the outpouring of the spirit among us all." In 1827 his church is joining with the Baptist "to form a common Sabbath School Society"; in 1829 he is working for the cause of temperance with the Rev. James Gilpatrick, the newly-ordained Baptist minister. Before his retirement in 1837 he has more than once spoken in the pulpit of the Baptist meeting-house and more than once conducted a Baptist brother up the stairs to his own.

And always, through his long pastorate, he could solace his doubts and anxieties by his irrefutable knowledge that the least circumstance or happening in Bluehill, or elsewhere, had been ordained from the beginning of time by that God whose mysterious, inscrutable ways were past finding out by man's feeble and flickering intelligence. This comfort the Rev. Jotham Sewall extends to him in a letter of sympathy written in April, 1806, from one of his missionary outposts far eastward:

To have your children torn from you and so far alienated in their affections from you as to disown you, while you feel all the tender concern for their welfare which can fill the heart of a Spiritual Father, is grievous, indeed. To have such things prevail and God in the strange course of his Providence ordaining such peculiar measures may well cause to stumble such as adhere to the uniting spirit of the Gospel. God's ways are often in the sea, and his footsteps hidden in the great deep, and they are not to be scanned by mortals. But, dear brother in Christ, still believe in him who rides upon the whirlwind and the storm and whose mysterious ways with the children of men will some day be revealed as goodness and as wisdom.

6

The founding and the nurture of Bluehill Academy belong rightly in any portrayal of Jonathan Fisher in relation to his church and parish, for this "infant seminary" was fostered by the church and in a very real sense fathered by its pastor. To the Congregational clergy of New England the advancement of all good learning had been held for nearly two centuries a sacred charge, second only to their concern for souls; and the Rev. Mr. Fisher was not one in this high respect to dim the glory of God. Moreover, his memory of "Tully" and Virgil and Horace lay warm within him as he tunneled his way through many a snowdrift on his winter visits to his people; and his Diary often records that he snatched "a pleasant hour" with one or another of the "ancients" in his study.

Shortly after his settlement in Bluehill, then a village of 350 people, distributed among 63 families, according to his census, he began to agitate the community with the desire for higher learning than the common schools could provide; and he was ably seconded and aided by "several other Gentlemen residing chiefly in Bluehill," first among whom was John Peters, Esq. That the Rev. Jonathan Powers of Penobscot and the Rev. William Mason of Castine were among the "several Gentlemen" proves the interest of the neighboring clergy in the adventurous undertaking. By the year 1801 the parson's shrewd and methodical mind, together with those of his associates, had worked out the ways and the means to attain their end. The cost was to be borne by one hundred shareholders (a number which speaks well for so small a village) who pledged themselves to maintain the school for ten years. On March 8, 1803, Bluehill Academy was incorporated under the laws of Massachusetts, twelve trustees were appointed, and a building was erected on the same long hill with the meeting-house, a quarter of a mile below it. It was formally dedicated on April 5, 1803.

One wishes that the records of this old school, which, with Gorham and Hampden Academies, was one of the earliest among the rural academies of Maine, had been as carefully kept and preserved as those of the church; but from what remain, together with many entries in the parson's Diaries and numerous letters written by him, it is possible to gather not a little information concerning its aims, its conduct, and its course of study. The following announcement, which was evidently an advertisement in dignified form, appeared on October 30, 1806, in *The Gazette of Maine,* published at Bucksport, then Buckstown:

Bluehill Academy

After a short recess of instruction in Bluehill Academy, as agreed by the Trustees, it will again be opened on the first Monday of November next, under the direction of the former Preceptor, Mr. Elias Upton, who has hitherto given universal satisfaction. The Trustees return their cordial thanks to those persons who have from time to time encouraged this infant seminary and again solicit their assistance and that of the public in general; they flatter themselves that in so doing they will find their reward in beholding their tender offspring possessing that degree of literature as will, by Divine Assistance, make them a peculiar comfort to themselves and a blessing to the rising generation.

Bluehill,   Reuben Dodge, Sec. to
October 24, 1806.   the Board of Trustees

N.B. Tuition at said Academy is 20 cts. a week and one dollar (of new students) for admittance.

The preceptors, who from the parson's Diaries and from various letters on the subject were obviously chosen and secured

by him, were young men of established Christian character and
"of sound theology." Many, if not most, of them were candidates
for the Congregationalist ministry, students either from the
Andover Theological Seminary, or, as the years went on, from
the younger seminary at Bangor. They are "to open all school
sessions with prayer and Scripture," "introduce their students
to new readings, give especial attention to health, and urge the
habits of industry." It is their duty also "to delineate the beauty
and amiability of virtue and the deformity and odiousness of
vice." They are to demand punctuality from their scholars, to
inflict "corporeal punishment when necessary for profane and
indecent language," to encourage attendance at church, and "to
inculcate good manners at all times, especially upon the entrance
of trustees or other notable visitors when every scholar is to
stand at respectful attention." For all these duties, together with
practically single-handed instruction in all manner of subjects,
they are to receive their "passage to Bluehill," from $9 to $10
weekly and board themselves, or from $8 to $9, together with
board. Most of them, as a matter of fact, boarded with the
Fisher family, and to vast mutual advantage as will be seen in
later pages of this book. In addition to their strictly scholastic
as well as to their inspirational services, they were expected to
occupy the meeting-house pulpit when the pastor was away or
whenever he was stricken with the sick-headaches and conse-
quent temporary blindness which were his thorn in the flesh
throughout his life.

The boys and girls were taught separately, the latter being
under the tutelage and equally strict supervision of a preceptress.
This hard-working woman, who is always carefully termed "a
female assistant," received for her services as late as 1830, "a
passage to Bluehill, her board, and $3 a week." There is no
mention of other teachers except for one imported in 1805 and
for several years thereafter to instruct the scholars "in the art of
sacred music." Money for this was appropriated by the town
since the town participated in the "singing schools." Painting

was apparently also taught, since in a letter to Dr. Leonard
Woods of the Andover Seminary in 1825 Mr. Fisher is eager to
obtain the services of a preceptor trained in that art, in which
teaching the parson himself assisted from time to time. This
subject was obviously dear to his heart and continued to be
taught after his death, since in a catalogue for 1852 the cost of
painting is ".75 for 12 lessons" and that of "crayoning $1.00,
material not included." In this same catalogue "24 music lessons"
cost $6 with $1.50 added "for the use of a Piano."

Beyond the elementary subjects of spelling, geography, grammar, and arithmetic, instruction was given from the start in
Latin, Greek, and French, algebra, geometry, "philosophy,"
chemistry, navigation, and surveying. In a notebook, now preserved in the Bluehill library and kept in 1810 by John, the
son of Andrew Witham, at the age of sixteen, there are, in addition to arithmetic problems, several pages given to problems
in "navigation and currents." One page contains "A Method of
Keeping a Journal at Sea," which sadly gave little help to John,
since he died at Port au Prince two years later. Mr. Fisher without doubt assisted also in the teaching of surveying, for in his
Diary he mentions "surveying land, roads, and the surface of
ponds with boys." He quite likely helped in the teaching of
navigation as well, for although, according to his own admission, he was "ever a poor hand at boat management," he had
been well-grounded in navigation under Mr. Webber at
Harvard.

The terms of the Academy were evidently of varying lengths,
dependent upon the money available to pay for instruction;
but there were certainly four each year and generally from
eight to ten weeks in length. In a letter dated March 30, 1830,
Mr. Fisher states definitely that at that time the autumn,
winter, and spring terms were ten weeks each and the summer
term six. The days were long, from 9 to 5 in the spring and
summer, and from 9 to 4 in the fall and winter. Only Saturday
afternoon, "Election Day," and July 4th were allowed as holi-

days. No notice was made of Christmas, if the fall term extended that late or the winter term began that early; indeed, it is not until well into the 1830's that the parson finds occasion to deplore certain "riotous and wicked celebrations" on that day, which he has observed fortunately *without* the confines of Blue-hill. The tuition remained for over fifty years at .20 a week, although in 1852 the charge for "Languages and Navigation" is listed at .25, "all other Branches at .20."

There seems to have been no definite age specified for admission, nor was a scholar required to complete a year or even a full term. In February, 1808, Jonathan Fisher, Jr., "commences going to the Academy" just before his tenth birthday, and other Fisher children come and go at various ages and times, dependent without doubt upon the condition of their father's purse. Sometimes they are at the Academy for four, six, or ten weeks; again, "seven of my children attend this winter the common school at Beech Hill." The boys and girls who board with the Fisher family from time to time are likewise educated under this extremely flexible arrangement. The result of such an unsystematic system must have been confusion indescribable for the preceptor and preceptress.

The Academy was always a place of consuming interest and concern to the parson, who for many years was President of its Board of Trustees. His visits to it are innumerable, for inspection, for prayer with the students, for godly counsel, especially concerning "profane and careless language." In April, 1817, upon one of his frequent inspections "with the other trustees" he notes that "the scholars appeared very well except in reading and speaking too low." The other trustees also seem to have taken most seriously their responsibilities in regard to their school. According to Mr. Fisher's Diary entries, they met each month for consultation, for examining and choosing text-books, and for conferring "concerning the general state of our institution of learning." In 1834 they were able to erect on the same site a new and beautiful brick building which still stands, a monument to their enterprise as well as to their good taste.

A touching comment upon the affection and concern of these sponsors for their Academy is found in a letter written by the President on February 9, 1830, to Mr. Reuben Dodge, who for many years had been a leader in all things true and of good report in Bluehill and who was then nearing the end of his life:

Dear Sir:

We feel it a painful affliction that, in the course of Providence, we are called at length to accept your resignation as Secretary of the Board of Trustees of our Academy. The institution sustains a loss which we fear will not soon be repaired. The ways of God are to us mysterious. He often takes away the most useful, and leaves those who are a burden upon the community. Yet, we may have this to console us in part: his friends are taken away from the evil to come, his enemies are left, sometimes that they may have longer space for repentance and sometimes that their perverseness may be a living witness to the truth of human depravity.

We thank you for the careful, correct, and even elegant manner in which the duties of the office have been discharged. We doubt not but that in connexion with other services, this office has been a source of much labor and solicitude. Whenever the time of your departure shall come, we hope it will be an endless removal from all painful solicitude, labor, and care, and an introduction to most pious, spiritual, soul-satisfying, and ever-enduring felicity.

Yours, with undissembled affection,

Jonathan Fisher
By order of the Trustees of
Bluehill Academy.

To Reuben Dodge, Esq.

7

The Rev. Mr. Fisher was both scrupulous and generous in his statistical records of the size and the progress of his church in Bluehill. At the close of each year of his ministry he drew up a neat list of his assets and liabilities in terms of the souls in his keeping. Nor was he content merely with a tabulation in the church records and in his Diaries. Besides these, he made, sewed, and bound in heavy paper tiny notebooks with the same figures tidily set down. As though these were not enough, he amassed his spiritual riches or deplored his dearth in meticulous reckonings in letters to his mother, to his brothers Samuel and William, to his classmates and friends, John S. Popkin and Abiel Abbot. And, finally, again and again in those hundreds of small books in which he bound his sermons, the identical numbers appear either on the back covers or on blank pages at the close. He is like a child who adds his few coins or counts his few treasures over and over in the wistful hope that, through some magic, they may perhaps have increased since the last careful summing-up.

When he arrived in Bluehill in 1796, his actual communicants numbered 23, "males 9, females 12, under censure 2." This number does not, of course, suggest the size of his congregations, those who were regular attendants at church. The majority of the forty pew-owners were obviously not "professed" church members; but many, if not most, of them doubtless were present at his Sunday services since he often writes of a "large auditory" and of "a full meeting-house." His first considerable gain in numbers occurred in the spring of 1799. "About the last of February, 1799," he writes, "there were pretty evident indications of a commencing revival. Light beamed upon many minds, and they attained to a joyful hope of salvation. It was like the shaking of dry bones in Ezekiel. By June, 1799, the healing streams of Divine Mercy and Grace were in full flood." In all, through this "glorious and blessed awakening," 57 persons were received into fellowship, "the greatest harvest for the Lord," he says years later, "that I have ever been permitted to gather in."

Never again throughout the forty years of his ministry did the parson find his fields so ready for harvest, his presses so bursting with new wine. "Mercy drops," to be sure, did fall from time to time, but such abundant "showers of blessing" were denied him, fervently as he pled for them at the throne of Grace. "Why

God withholds his blessed rain from us," he writes, "when refreshing waters flow in Castine, Bucksport, and Machias and
yield rich increase, I know not. It is a sore trial, but hidden, like
all else, within his mysterious and all-embracing Providence."
He reports slight seasons of refreshment in 1816, in 1822, in
1826, and in 1834, through which more souls were added to his
flock, besides those few who in most years "attained to a blessed
hope." The inevitable inroads of death and of removal elsewhere
depleted his numbers; "discipline," which in several cases did
not result in its desired end, took others from him; and always,
after 1806, there was the Baptist fold to which discontented and
ill-fed sheep might wander—and *did!* The Baptist preachers,
Elders Roundy, Allen, Pilsbury, Pinkham, and the ordained ministers, who, after the year 1818, shepherded that church, surely
lacked his learning, but they just as surely possessed greater
powers of persuasion. Whether or not he recognized this fact,
he never divulges; and in a theology which attributed all to the
providential dispensation of God, it probably did not greatly
distress him. Throughout his ministry his communicants rarely
numbered above 60 or 70 in any given year and often fell far
below that modest mark.

His preaching schedule was a rigorous one and always, except
in illness, rigorously discharged. On Sundays there were two
services, one at 10:30 and one at 2 o'clock, those of his congregation who lived at a distance bringing their luncheons with
them. Save for portable foot-warmers and soapstones, the meeting-house and its occupants were unheated until 1817, when
he purchased in Boston a stove for $24. In 1820 he writes that
its warmth yields "sensible benefit." There was the weekly
"lecture" on Thursday afternoon, sometimes held at the meeting-
house, but more often in schoolhouses or in homes. There was
also the "monthly concert prayer-meeting," held on the first
Monday evening of each month and again usually at schools or
homes though sometimes at the church. There was the yearly
March or April Fast, a day set apart for fasting and prayer; and

there was as well an occasional day or half-day, when circumstances of any sort became crucial, devoted to the same purpose, sometimes for much-needed rain in time of drought, sometimes for less tangible "dew from Heaven." In the winter of 1823, being "seriously depressed over the indifference of the young toward their immortal souls," Mr. Fisher writes of giving at various homes a series of twenty-two lectures for children and young people. From his Diary for that year one is convinced that the attendance at these lectures was large, 50 on one night, 45 on another, rarely fewer than 30. He carefully states the topics of his addresses: human depravity, the fear of God, the importance of the Holy Scriptures, *This night thy soul shall be required of thee.* It is difficult to believe that so many young people came eagerly, or even willingly, to hear of these matters. Perhaps the parson employed a follow-up system which held far more terrors than did the attendance upon his solemn words!

The several societies and organizations within his church, which seem to have held at least monthly meetings, must have demanded much of his time since he reports himself as present at most of their sessions. These flourished mightily not only in Bluehill, but throughout New England during the early years of the nineteenth century.[1] There were in Mr. Fisher's parish the Tract Society and the Female Tract Society, the Gentlemen's Society for Foreign Missions and the Female Missionary Society, the Female Mite Society and the Female Cent Society, the latter of which demanded of all "ladies" .01 weekly for foreign missions.

A volume, and perhaps not of too dull a nature, might be written of Jonathan Fisher as a preacher. The three thousand sermons which he left behind him (and more, if one counts the résumés which he gives of many uncatalogued discourses) provide ample material. Needless to say, his biographers, for reasons of time, strength, and courage, have not delved deeply into this

[1] The Rev. Calvin Clark in Vol. I of his *History of the Congregational Churches in Maine,* Chapter X, gives an interesting account of these many organizations, especially of those run by women.

unexploited mine of stern and unrelenting Calvinism. We have, however, deciphered some one hundred of the three thousand (for all, without exception, were written in code), assisted in our choice by the parson's meticulous tabulation of texts from year to year and from Sabbath to Sabbath. He always read his sermons, being unable, he often states, "to speak well extempore" except when "visited by Divine Providence with a measure of freedom." Friday and Saturday were given each week to the preparation of his Sabbath discourses; and he rarely used "an old sermon" except when he had returned late from a journey or when illness had exhausted his energies. He is particular to state in each sermon booklet the exact dates of its delivery in Bluehill and wherever else it has been preached. The text is often, though not always, rewritten in the original Hebrew or Greek; frequently a Latin and a French translation are also given. These languages were even sometimes imposed upon the puzzled ears of his congregation "in order that they may have their ears attuned to tongues other than their own."

No amount of admiration for the parson must obscure the undeniable fact that he was without doubt neither persuasive nor eloquent as a preacher. The Rev. Swan Pomroy, who with an essay of his own complements the interesting biographical sketch of Jonathan Fisher in William Sprague's *Annals of the American Pulpit,*[1] says that his voice "had great compass," but that, "being destitute of an ear for music, his emphasis was sometimes misplaced and his intonations inappropriate." In language and thought he was usually logical rather than impulsive, rational rather than imaginative, controversial rather than sympathetic. He did not know how to pour oil on troubled waters, nor, had he known, would his conscience have allowed him to employ so conciliatory a method. Believing that his adversary, Satan, was ever at his right hand contending for the place of God, *he* was ever ready with refutation and defiance.

---

[1] This sketch is found in Vol. II of the *Annals* in seven volumes. Boston, 1853.

Early in his ministry he writes that two sermons on Divine Election, which, next to human depravity, seems to have been his favorite theme, "caused much excitement, no small opposition, and even distress bordering on despair"; and yet he feels that he must persist "in enlarging upon and illuminating this irrefutable Doctrine." His way was always to meet a situation or to tackle a subject head on; he spurned any circuitous approach. The wrath of God sounded more often in the ears of his listeners than did His mercy, and the utter depravity of the human creature left little room for its possible decency. He obviously knew nothing of diplomacy except to scorn it as artful cunning; and, intent upon saving the human soul from an agony of future torment, he was far too little aware of the intricacies of the human mind. People to him were, first of all, immortal souls rather than mortal men and women. And, although his sermons are filled with addresses to his congregation, "my dear children in God," "my dear Christian friends," and, most frequently, "my dear impenitent hearers," a study of them must, I think, result in the inevitable conclusion that his love for his erring children, real and even warm though it actually was, could not easily, or often, be discerned among the fearsome accents of his many discourses to them. Surely a survey of hundreds of his texts results in the discovery that the dialectics of the Apostle Paul, the *Dies Irae* of Zephaniah, and the exhortations of Ezekiel appealed far more to him as subjects meet for elucidation and for solemn warning than either the story of the alabaster box or of the woman taken in adultery. Compassion to him was the reward of necessary repentance and salvation rather than the free and gracious means to a desired end.

His scientific mind loved method and organization, and his sermons, so far as their form is concerned, are models of clarity. This clarity did not, unfortunately, extend always to his language, which, especially in doctrinal sermons, is usually ponderous, involved, and dull. When, however, he now and then forsakes matters of doctrine for those of more practical and personal nature, his style and diction are noticeably simplified. In this he is like his favorite apostle, who, at once involved and abstruse in his letter to the Romans, becomes simple and even tender in expression when he writes to his "dearly beloved and longed for" children at Philippi.

Mr. Fisher's procedure in all his sermons, involved or simple, remains the same. He is given to stating his text, commenting upon its source and the occasion of its utterance, defining it, if necessary, and explaining precisely how he proposes "to enlarge upon it"; he thereupon preaches his sermon, "proceeding," as he is fond of saying, "by regular steps," makes his applications, and draws his always solemn conclusions. He is rarely pictorial, except when he describes the sufferings of the damned or the ecstasies of the redeemed. If his Sunday afternoon discourse complements or completes that of the morning, as it often does, he is careful to review the propositions of the earlier sermon before proceeding to the later. He always assumes an amazing store of theological, Scriptural, and even ecclesiastical knowledge on the part of his hearers; he assumes also an equally amazing agility at extricating themselves from the frequent intricacies of his language. It is interesting to surmise what may have been the effects of these assumptions on the farmers, tradesmen, shipbuilders, mill-owners, and shop-keepers of Bluehill even in an age when theological disputation was not relegated to the theologians, when the Bible was read and studied in most homes, and when the well-being of the soul was of paramount and fearful importance to its owner.

At the risk of boring the readers of this book so that they forsake the parson before they learn of the lighter aspects of his nature, I quote, as briefly as possible and omitting many paragraphs of explanation and argument, from a typical sermon, apparently a favorite of Mr. Fisher's, since he preaches it between 1816 and 1819 in four different places, one of these being the Old South Church in Boston. Its subject is "The Sin of Unbelief," its text from John 3:18: *He that believeth not is condemned already, because he hath not believed in the name of the only begotten son of God.*

In discoursing from these words, my dear hearers, I have it in view to speak seriously of the greatness of the sin of neglecting to believe on the Lord Jesus Christ. The neglect of believing on the Lord Jesus Christ may be shown to the serious, reasonable, and contemplative mind to be a very great evil, a sin of the highest magnitude and one especially deserving a severe punishment in the future state. Also when the conscience of a sinner is truly enlightened and is properly awake, the sin of unbelief must be felt as a sin of dreadful and overbearing weight.

I pray you now, my dear hearers, to attend seriously to the circumstances which render the sin of unbelief a very great sin.

1. The sin of unbelief is great because it is in opposition to the plain, explicit command of God. This is the work of God, says the blessed Savior, which God requires you to perform, that ye believe on him whom he hath sent.

2. The greatness of the sacrifice made on the part of a benefactor to accommodate a sufferer is a circumstance which aggravates the ingratitude of the sufferer in refusing to accept or acknowledge the favor. The sacrifice which God has made to accommodate or benefit sinners of the human race is the greatest sacrifice that even an infinite God could make: it is the sacrifice of his only begotten son.

3. The dignity and authority of the person who makes a sacrifice for the benefit of another magnifies the sin of refusing to embrace the favor. In this regard, the sin of rejecting the Lord Jesus Christ is infinitely aggravated because God who gave him up to die for sinners is of infinite dignity and authority.

4. The ill-desert of those for whom a sacrifice is made magnifies the sacrifice and aggravates the sin of those who refuse to accept the benefit of the sacrifice when it is offered. In this regard, the sin of unbelief is greatly aggravated, for man is an exceedingly ill-deserving creature, being a rebel against an infinitely holy God before the offer of a Savior is made to him.

5. The degree of suffering to be sustained to procure a benefit for another aggravates the ingratitude of refusing and neglecting the favor. Man, in refusing to believe on the Lord Jesus, throws contempt upon this infinitely valuable and unspeakably great suffering, so that the guilt of his sin becomes exceedingly great.

6. The evil, to redeem for which the sacrifice was made, magnifies, in proportion to its greatness, the value of the sacrifice and aggravates the ignominy of refusing it. If it were a small evil from which man is to be redeemed, a comparatively small sacrifice might suffice to redeem him. But the evil from which man is to be redeemed by believing on the Lord Jesus Christ is exceedingly great. How unspeakably great then must be the sin of refusing the precious Savior!

7. The greatness of the favor in regard to the happiness to be procured by the sacrifice is another circumstance which aggravates the ingratitude of refusing the offer of a benefactor. The favor in regard to happiness to be procured for man by the sacrifice of the Son of God is a state of endless glory and happiness in the Kingdom of God. The benefit to believers from this sacrifice is, if I may so speak, *doubly infinite salvation,* from infinite evil to infinite good.

8. The difficulties to be encountered in providing favors for those in an evil case are, indeed, possible with God; but some things considered in regard to themselves are far more difficult than others. How great was the difficulty of man's redemption? (1) It must be accomplished in such a way as not to impair the divine authority. (2) It must be accomplished in such a way that sin may be seen to be a loathsome and abominable thing. (3) It must be accomplished in such a way that the complete and dreadful obstinacy of the human nature must be subdued and brought from a state of perfect opposition to God into a state of obedience and submission. (4) Finally, the work of redemption must be accomplished so that the rational creature could never have the least reasonable ground to charge the blessed God with injustice or partiality. All these difficulties have been surmounted in the work of redemption. How awfully great then must be the sin of refusing to believe!

9. The freeness of a favor magnifies the benevolence of it, and aggravates the sin of ingratitude in the refusal of it. In this regard the sin of man is exceedingly great in rejecting the divine Savior. God was not under the least obligation of justice to bestow any such favor. Man's redemption on the part of God is a matter of self-moved Goodness. How great then is the offer of salvation, and how vastly it must aggravate man's future condemnation to neglect, to slight, to refuse the great salvation!

I have thus endeavored to show in a number of particulars

the greatness of sin of refusing to believe on the Lord Jesus Christ. In this great guilt each of you, my dear impenitent hearers, who is yet in unbelief, is involved! Why do not unbelievers see the sword of divine justice drawn for them, and made bright, and ready to be bathed in their blood? Why do they not see the arrows of the Almighty dipped in poison and fitted on the string, ready to fly and fix an eternal wound? Do, my dear hearers, who are yet rejecting the Savior, look at the greatness of your guilt and danger in the light of the subject this day before you.

A study of dozens of Mr. Fisher's sermons pronounces the one just quoted, in small part, as characteristic both in matter and manner of many of his discourses. A series of nine, preached on the subject of baptism and delivered in 1804 when the Baptist influence was beginning to make itself felt, differ little in approach, development, and language. Nor do several on the Scriptural authority for church discipline, given at various seasons when that matter was causing disaffection among the brethren. The parson, wisely or unwisely, always seized upon the temper of the moment to strike while the iron was hot; nor did he hesitate to use his pulpit as a means of disseminating his opinions on the current happenings in state or in nation. In 1812 he delivers such a discourse on the evil and iniquity of the war with England that two of his congregation, who, he states in his Diary, differ from him in political sentiments, march from the church in the midst of his pronouncements. He preaches against the carrying of mails on the Sabbath, against slavery, intemperance, and the treatment meted out to "the poor Indians," against the proposed separation of Maine from Massachusetts, against the inroads of sin in high places of governmental authority. But, in general, his concern is with the souls of men; and, in general, too, he is more given to elucidating orthodox theology and commending its unquestionable truth to his hearers than he is to healing their wounds or to aiding their faltering steps along the rough roads of human existence.

Occasionally his sense of drama, his love of the spectacular, the astounding, and even of the horrible, lends wings to his imagination, speed and power to his pen. At such times categories and dialectic give place to vivid pictures. Involved constructions are abandoned, and the force of the question is employed to excellent and exciting advantage. With all his honest concern over the destiny of the souls of his children, one can hardly imagine that he did not take some pleasure, even pride, in the following paragraphs from a sermon delivered on October 16, 1825. The title is taken from Hebrews 12:29: *For our God is a consuming fire.*

In Isaiah 27:4 God challenges: *Who would set the briars and thorns against me in battle? I would go through them, I would burn them together.* Those who revolt against God he here compares to a fire which must consume them as the dry, withered briars and thorns are consumed by the burning flame.

We, my dear hearers, are all involved as transgressors of the Divine Law. How shall we escape the consuming justice of the Most High? God will not trifle with us, nor will he let the course of his justice suffer. He may forbear the execution of his vengeance for a season, as he does in the case of the fallen angels, who, as we may gather from the Scriptures, are not yet receiving their full measure of torment. It is further said that they are reserved in chains, under darkness, until the judgment of the great day.

My dear impenitent hearers, do you try to escape the truth that bye and bye the delay of your punishment will be at an end and that you will have judgment without mercy? When God makes inquiry for blood, will he not remember you? When he calls a fallen world in question, what will then be your plea? Will you say that you have not sinned? But your consciences will testify against you, and you will know that you cannot deceive the Divine Omniscience. Will you plead that your sins are but small? But you know that they have been directed against infinite order, infinite power and majesty, infinite holiness, and that they cannot be small. Will you plead that they are but few? But you will know that they are as the sands of the seashore for multitude. Will you dare to plead ignorance of the Divine Law, you who live under the blaze of the Gospel sun? Should you attempt such pleas in that great day, your speech will falter on your lips.

Our God is a consuming fire. My dear hearers, there is no way to escape Divine Justice at the great day. I will briefly describe its course according to the light of the Scriptures: Bye and bye God will send you a summons. It will call you to his bar. Death, natural death, will be the messenger. When your souls have departed the body, they appear before the throne of God. They will be subjected to a measure of inquiry. Being found the transgressors of the Divine Law, your never dying spirits will be sent into the world of spirits, into that place where the rich man, mentioned in the Scriptures, lifted up his eyes being in torment. Your souls will then feel a relation in every part of this body they now inhabit, an exquisite torment as it were in every member. You will be the subject of inward horror and burning anguish. *You cannot avoid this. There is no escaping.* You will be forced away into this place of eternal fire, prepared for the Devil and his angels. Material fire like salt will constantly penetrate and torment, but *never* decompose or annihilate your bodies. In all this you will find what it means that God is a consuming fire. In the language of Dr. Watts:

> Almighty vengeance, how it burns!
> How bright his furnace glows!
> What magazines of plagues and storms
> Lie treasured for his foes!

Can you endure the thought of falling, world without end, under this dreadful vengeance? Here in the present state you shrink from the scorching heat of the touch of fire; yea, the disease of one member, an aching tooth, a pounded finger, discompose your spirits, drive you almost to distraction. How will you endure to be destroyed both soul and body in Hell?

I desire you to understand your danger, the dreadfulness of the distress you risk, and the way of escape through a Divine Mediator. I desire you to ponder upon this; therefore it is that I bring before you the same interesting subject so frequently. May God this day give you grace to serve him with veneration and godly fear. *For our God is a consuming fire!*

Mr. Fisher was frequently drawn to exhort the young of his church and parish and even to give them explicit precepts concerning their conduct. For these discourses he often chose texts from the Epistles to Timothy and Titus. In an early, and long, sermon, preached in the summer of 1795 before his permanent settlement in Bluehill, he is especially concrete in his suggestions for behavior upon social occasions. He takes his text from Titus: *Young men likewise exhort to be soberminded.* After many paragraphs on the importance of the period of life between fifteen and twenty-five years, "a time of strong temptation because of the ripening passions of youth," on the necessity for at least one half-hour daily, spent in meditation and prayer, for "immediately expelling all profane and impure thoughts" at all moments, for "grave and serious behavior on the Sabbath," and for "constant diligence" in whatever occupation they may have entered upon, he gives several concrete suggestions for the profitable spending of their leisure hours.

I cannot recommend large companies to young people. To meet together once in a while in small parties of three or four may be useful. When the company is larger, it is not easy to maintain that sobriety recommended in our text. Cards on these occasions should be wholly abandoned; and you should avoid entirely gaming for money, or for any reward whatever. It may be well to store your minds with pleasant and useful historical anecdotes, or with stories which have a good moral and may be applied in the cause of virtue. These may keep alive your conversation and preserve you from blasting the character of your neighbors and from polluting your own hearts. If anyone in the company should be so void of sense as to introduce anything indecent, you who detest such a thing should endeavor to divert it by starting some other subject which need not be ashamed of the light of day.

When three or four young men meet together for the purpose of amusement in an evening, I would recommend something in arithmetic to try their quickness in reckoning, or the solving of some ingenious problem in science as an agreeable and useful amusement. Young women should always have some sort of work in their hands and the pleasure of conversation besides; and instead of scandal, which is too apt to be *their* failing, they may entertain themselves on the subject of family government in the home, or on the management and education of

children, until that time when Providence shall please to communicate to them the mysteries of a family. When young people of both sexes are together, and their voices admit of it, I
can recommend singing as a source of useful entertainment. The
mutual study and examination of maps may serve as instructive
amusement, whether maps of our own country as a means of
instilling knowledge and patriotism, or one of Palestine where
the Blessed Savior walked.

But your social meetings should not always be devoted to
amusement. Two or three of you should sometimes meet together to converse upon religion. Such as meet for this purpose
should be intimate friends; and by free and serious intercourse
they may improve their minds and quicken one another in spiritual things. In such meetings, you will be soberminded, not
through restraint, but with delight.

Dwell upon these things, my dear young friends, in proportion to their importance. Surely they will banish levity from your
hearts, they will keep you steady on every occasion, and cause
your demeanor to be that of men and of Christians.

And, happily, there were rare and pleasant Sabbaths when the
parson's earthly loves intruded themselves into his pulpit, ousting
for a brief season the pangs of Hell and even the Apostle Paul
on justification by faith. His passion for mathematics was
vindicated even there, since it could satisfy itself with celestial
computations. In July, 1813, he preaches upon the many mansions in his Father's house. He assumes their incredibly vast
number by a consideration of the redeemed in the blessed period
of the Millenium, the dawning of which he expects to see in the
year 2000.

I doubt not, he says, that the greater part of the inhabitants of
the earth during the Millenium will be pious. I am satisfied also
that the earth will be abundantly inhabited during this Blessed
Period. As there are now about 900 million in one generation
upon the earth, we may suppose with probability that upon an
average during the Millenium there will be more than twice this
number, or about 2000 million in a generation. Supposing 3
such generations in every 100 years during the Millenium, 30
generations at 2000 million in a generation would amount to

60,000 million souls. Admit ⅔ of these to be the happy subjects of redeeming grace, the number would be 40,000 million. Then for the 6000 years previous to the Millenium, allow 180,000 generations of 500 million on an average, and it gives 90,000 million. Admit but 1 in 100 of these to be a subject of grace, the number yet would be 900 million, which, added to 40,000 million gives 40,900 millions of Redeemed Ones, or at least more than 10,000 million more than Methuselah could have counted one by one at the rate of 60 a minute during his whole life, night and day, for 969 years. Now, allowing 1 square rod for each of these to move about in, they would cover a plain containing 399,414 square miles.

I have made these calculations, my dear hearers, not presuming that any mortal can assign the certain number of the redeemed, but to show that it will be as great as I here have supposed and to impress our minds strongly with the idea that in our Heavenly Father's house there must be many mansions to contain so great an assembly.

Again, in 1832, at the time when he was preparing his book, *Scripture Animals,* or *The Natural History of the Bible,* for the press, he preaches a sensitive and even touching sermon on God's goodness to His creatures, of which the Hebrew poet sings in Psalm 104. The beasts of the fields, he says, yea, even the ant and the swallow, the two sparrows sold for a farthing, the young ravens which cry—all these and their happiness are dear in the sight of God, who has formed them all "for the delight of man and probably for even that of the holy angels." For these evidences of the abounding goodness of God, He should be loved and praised.

This proof of his generous benevolence calls loudly upon man to feel an interest in the happiness of all living creatures. For if the happiness of the animals is not beneath the notice and care of God, surely man ought not to be too proud or too indifferent to notice and to care for them. It is a mark also of the goodness of God that he has provided abundant means by which man's mind may be fed with knowledge. He has raised up from time to time men of understanding, who have written upon interesting subjects, such as insects, birds, and beasts, so that the minds of children and men may be stored with that information and so that their hearts may be interested and enlightened and their happiness refined and greatly exalted.

For these gifts, my dear hearers, man has surely reason to love and to praise God.

V

THE PARSON AT HOME

T|HAT of all "earthly and, hence, transitory possessions" his home and his family were most loved and valued by Parson Fisher is surely evident from many entries in his Diaries. Indeed, his affection for both results in a warmth and even tenderness of expression not elsewhere to be found in those thousands of pages which chronicle in laconic, terse, and objective language the daily happenings of his life. Nor is he usually fulsome even about those things which lie nearest to his heart. He seems, in fact, to have allowed such expression to have its way with him only upon his return from a journey and upon his wedding anniversary or his birthday. But, since he is frequently on the road for one purpose or another and since two occasions yearly condone, if they do not demand, thanksgiving, we are happily not denied these closer glimpses of himself:

"I returned home at nightfall, very wet and weary, to find all well, blessed be God! When I consider what joys always await me in the welcome of my dear consort and my pleasant children, and in the warmth and cheer of my home fires, I am transported in thought of what welcome God has to give to those worthy of a heavenly home. O may I and mine be found worthy of that bliss prepared for the faithful servants of the Savior!"

"The 15th anniversary of our marriage. Blessed be God in respect to my connection with Mrs. Fisher! They have been 15 comfortable and happy years, and, without boasting, I can say to the praise of Providential Grace, they have been to a good measure free of altercation and strife. Eight pleasant children have been the fruit of our marriage and their lives yet kindly spared. What shall I return unto God for all his benefits?"

"This day is my birthday. Bless the Lord, O my soul, for sparing mercy! He has upheld me in life and indulged me with such a variety of comforts, with so many and great favors, that I am a living monument, however unworthy, to his mercy. My consort is in health, my children live to our mutual joy, life still holds endearing moments of tenderest affection. My land brings forth its increase, my food is sweet to my mouth, my sleep, for the most part, is refreshing and wholesome. Though accounted but poor in the goods of this fleeting world, we have the joys of contentment, free from strife. It is God who gives all. May his be eternally the glory!"

Sometimes fear assails him lest these earthly affections are stealing from him the love which he owes to God:

"I have sound reason to fear that the cares and even the pleasures of this life, my consort, my family, my plans for transitory comforts, occupy too much space in my mind. Of late, for a number of months past, I have been in what I may consider a cold, unfeeling state with respect to divine things. For a day or two I have been stirred up to a measure of engaged concern for my soul, for the souls of my consort and my children, and sometimes for the souls of my people. But presently the curses of the world have drawn me away. Plans for the cultivation of my land, fencing it, building my new woodhouse, providing necessities for my family—these have occupied my thoughts and made me barren in my prayers, barren in my sermons, and barren in my conversation about heavenly things. I receive many gifts from the hand of God for which I have cause to be thankful. Sometimes I think I do feel some small emotion of gratitude, but oh, how infinitely it is surpassed by the blessed favors I daily enjoy."

Although he often writes of the solemn necessity of fighting against what he terms "I-interest" and of cultivating with equal zeal "I-abasement," Mr. Fisher was given to the lavish use of the first personal pronoun in its possessive sense. His land is always *my* land, his home, *my* house, his children, *my* children. "My sons and I went after blueberries today to the ledges. Together we picked 12 quarts, and clean." "This afternoon my sons and I fished for trouts in the Peters brook. Jonathan caught 4, Josiah, 3, I, 20." "I fashioned this morning a little wheelbarrow for my son Jonathan." "Today I ground 4 little knives for my children and fitted handles to them." "I walked with my daughters in the fields on the edge of the evening." "My rabbit, which I found hurt in the woods, died today of his wounds. Poor, poor Bunny! I had made a little cage for him." And Dolly Battle Fisher is never once referred to in forty years by her Christian name, either in his Diaries or in his countless letters written to relatives and friends. When she is not "my consort," as she often is, she is merely "Mrs. Fisher."

2

Mrs. Fisher was undoubtedly a good wife, although she is never accorded even that companionable name. What she was really like as a human being, we do not know, since her husband was not given to character delineation of any member of his family and only directly of himself when he is urged thereto by his everpresent sense of sin. She is seen in the Diaries only in terms of prodigious activity and incredible industry. She most certainly emulated, if she did not surpass, that virtuous woman in Proverbs in seeking wool and flax, laying her hand to the spindle and distaff, rising while it was yet night to give meat to her household, and eating never the bread of idleness. She may, indeed, have often opened her mouth with wisdom even although that gift is nowhere stated of her. She comes and goes in the Diaries and in her husband's letters only as an active shadow, constantly referred to, but never described.

The arrivals of her nine children, who were born between 1798 and 1812, are always carefully recorded by their father in similar words and almost identical tone. Little time and space are allotted to each, and, since no suggestion is ever given that a new child is expected in the family circle, the brief announcement comes as somewhat of a surprise:

"Mar. 12, 1798. Mrs. Fisher sent for help about 10 o'clock A.M. At 7 hrs. 30 min. P.M. she was, through kind Providence, delivered of a fine son, after severe labor. God be praised!"

"Oct. 22, 1799. A.M. Turned an augur handle. P.M. Bored upon a log. Mrs. Fisher sent for help this P.M. At 40 min. past 8 o'clock she was delivered of a fine daughter. Oh, may the Lord make us thankful!"

"Jan. 7, 1801. In the morning went for help for Mrs. Fisher. At 15 min. past 12 P.M. she had a fine daughter born. The Lord give us grace to be thankful."

Since no mention is made of the attendance of a doctor, Mrs. Fisher doubtless, like the other women in Bluehill, survived her ordeals with the help of some experienced neighbor. She seems to have recovered slowly from the births of her younger children, for in the case of three of them the parson writes of a stubborn fever and the calling in of Dr. Nathan Tenney of Sedgwick after some days or weeks of illness.

Like their mother the children are constantly mentioned in their father's Diaries, but almost never described or delineated in any way. Jonathan, the eldest, who died at seventeen, seems to have been a serious boy, too old for his years, whose soul is a bit too closely on his father's mind. Sally, the eldest daughter, was diffident and shy, although this fact is known only when she is twenty and also only by means of a letter written by the parson to a young preceptor in Bluehill Academy, whose "unwelcome advances to my oldest daughter have caused sad distress to her shy and diffident nature." Sally, however, escaped oblivion by characterizing herself on her death-bed at twenty-four. Betsy, Nancy, Polly, and Dolly would remain as shadowy as their mother did not their own letters, written after they had left home to teach school and after their marriages, reveal them as lively and charming girls, devoted to their parents. Josiah, the second son, born in 1802 and known as "Josie" in the family, was apparently the problem child, as a note of exasperation not infrequently creeps into his father's comments concerning both his physical and spiritual mishaps: "Josie cut his ankle badly with an axe today through carelessness." "Josiah jumped from a load of hay this afternoon and sprained his knee. He will be kept from work for some days in consequence." "My son Josiah borrowed a boat without leave a week ago. This has cost me $1.00 and considerable embarrassment." "Much concerned over Josiah's soul. I fear that the hope he has been indulging is but feeble." Willard, the third son, born in 1806 and named after President Willard of Harvard, under whose administration, and friendly interest, the parson had received his education, is not characterized at all save by being negligent, or perhaps stupid, in his studies and very late in his ultimate salvation. His conversion was, in fact, to his father's reiterated distress, delayed until after his marriage when, at last, the parson can record thankfully that he is at peace "about the souls of Willard and of Mary, his wife." The other children "indulged a hope" relatively early, much to their father's relief and joy.

The Fisher children must have taken delight in the various works of their father's hands, for the Diaries are filled with the things which he fashioned for their pleasure. "I made a little wagon for Jonathan today. I also made a hat for him." "This morning I made a squirrel cage for my children's pet squirrels." "This afternoon I fitted the handles to small axes for my sons." "I spent the morning in making little chairs for my various children." "Made a little sleigh, placed it on runners and painted it red, for my seven children to take to school with them." "Today I made a wooden sword for my son Josiah." "Ground paints and made a little set of water-colors for each of my children." "I made and painted a little book-case this morning for my children's library."

It is hardly necessary to say that the Fisher sons and daughters were early trained in habits of industry and frugality. Jonathan at ten years old is clearly responsible for carrying, by a borrowed horse and wagon, the family grain to be ground at the Tide Mills. At thirteen he is working out by the day for various neighbors. Sally at eleven in the year 1810 has herself woven "23¾ yds. of woolen cloth.' In 1813 the parson writes: "Mrs. Fisher and my daughters have woven in 6 months 56 yards of cloth." The boys had each his own plot of ground upon which they raised vegetables which they sold to their father. "My sons and I dug our potatoes today. My bushels 126, Jonathan's 50, Josiah's 19½, Willard's 12." The children were obviously paid for their farm and household chores, for their father is meticulous in setting down his accounts with them as well as theirs with one another. "Sept. 1, 1813. I paid my children in full for chores: Jonathan .25, Betsy .05, Josie .02, Willard, Nancy, and Polly .01 each." Willard at the age of seven has earned $1.35. In June, 1813, the parson records that Josiah has lent Jonathan $1.75, Willard $1.45, and Dolly .25; in September, 1814, that Jonathan owes his father for ploughing .50. The boys evidently also owned shares in the livestock on the farm. "Mr. Joseph Johnson sheared 19 sheep for me today, for Jonathan, 1 sheep. In all 56 lbs. of wool, of which the shearer's share is 2½ lbs."

3

The parsonage was, indeed, a hive of industry compared to which our busiest days seem relatively free from labor. The head of the family rose by five o'clock, sometimes earlier, made the fires, laid the table for breakfast, and then repaired to his study for an hour of Hebrew before breakfast, which was held at six o'clock, followed by prayers at six-thirty. From then on, except on schooldays, every member of the household was busy at an incredible number and variety of activities, necessary not only for the smooth running of the house and farm, but also for the increase of a salary never larger than $280 yearly. The parson, who carefully sets down every penny spent, keeps no account of the yearly amount accruing from his many enterprises; but, all told, it must have been almost equal to his salary when one reckons the money earned from the sale of numerous Fisher commodities. The wool spun and woven yearly by Mrs. Fisher and the girls was sold at from $1.00 to $1.50 a yard in Bucksport or exchanged for the same price at Mr. Andrew Witham's store for foodstuffs. In August, 1810, these are listed carefully: eggs .10 a doz., beef .05 a lb., rum .33 a qt., butter .17 a lb., potatoes .25 a bu., vinegar .32 a gal., turnips .40 a bu., cheese .11 a lb., halibut .02 a lb., shad .05 each. In no year does the produce of the farm seem entirely sufficient either for the family or for the animals, for supplementary meat and vegetables were purchased for home consumption and extra hay and grain always had to be bought for the five or six cows kept and the twenty or more sheep. The several pigs seem to have been sustained largely from Fisher left-overs, although a Fisher left-over seems a complete contradiction in terms!

Literally nothing which could be turned to monetary gain was wasted or overlooked. The bones of slaughtered farm animals were kept and made into thousands of buttons, filed and pierced by the entire family, sometimes dyed in various colors, and sold at .25 a dozen. Since this button industry is mentioned in the Diary entries of practically every year, it must have occupied many hours. It was surpassed, however, by the incredible number of hats made by hundreds and sold at $1.00 or $1.50 each, or exchanged for necessities. In 1811, "a bonnet, value $1.00, exchanged for a pound of tea"; in 1818, "a bonnet for a pair of shoes for Nancy." This "chip braiding" is first mentioned in 1804 as "evening work for the entire family" and is continuing fifteen years later, for in 1819 the parson is still "getting out bonnet stuff." In September, 1805, he writes that he has "gotten from the woods 2600 ft. of poplar shoots for bonnet strands." He does not tell us how these strands were prepared for braiding, although he does once mention dyeing them in colors. The hats or bonnets fashioned from them were evidently made for men, women, and children, for their purchasers, frequently listed, are of each sex and every age. A bundle of strands was even taken on vacation trips to Dedham in order that profitable work might not cease, for the parson writes of "braiding hats" in the cabins or on the decks of schooners sailing "to the westward." And there is also mention of the sale of such hats in Dedham.

One suspects that this pastime was sometimes thrust into the hands and laps of evening callers, of which there were many at the parsonage. Concerning such callers Mr. Fisher writes in 1799: "I consider most visits from friends and neighbors unprofitable and fruitless." Perhaps this comment suggests an uneasy conscience, since during the same year he deplores his want of courage in guiding conversations of visitors into religious channels and condemns himself for such unworthy cowardice. If he saw that their fingers were at least busy during their calls, his anxiety may have been at least partially alleviated, since a pair of idle hands was anathema to him throughout his life.

Many hours were given also to the making of baskets from reeds, twigs, and grasses, and of brooms as well. Nor was the rose conserve, concocted for profit during the parson's college days, forgotten as a means of income. In July, 1813, the children gather "185 white roses and 35 damask," which are ground and made into conserve, "2 lbs. in all, sold to Andrew Witham at .15 a lb." Innumerable butter molds are whittled from wood, planed smoothly, and engraved by the parson's tools with various designs. Rolling-pins are also made and sold for .25 each. A cure for sore throat is brewed "from sweetened pine booze"; itch ointment is frequently in preparation; and the tooth powder for family use and for sale as well is made from "pulverized hardwood coal, rendered savory by a few drops of oil of lavendar." The seeds of the caraway, which whitened the Fisher fields in July, are always carefully harvested. "My children gathered 6 qts. of caraway seeds for me to sell in Dedham."

The parson's own business enterprises, unaided by his family, are many and diverse. He apparently worked often on the meeting-house, painting and numbering pews, repairing the roof, setting new window sashes and panes of glass. The town paid him at the rate of $1.00 a day for such labor and the same price for his work at surveying and helping to lay out new roads. It paid him also $1.50 each for "guide-boards with signs." Individuals hired him for all manner of surveying projects for which they paid in cash, in labor, or in provisions. One of the many sources of added income lay in the making of pieces of furniture, chests of drawers, bureaus, tables, bedsteads, kitchen chairs, trunks, and literally hundreds of picture frames. In 1800 he makes "a chest for Ruth Horton at $1.50"; in 1804, "2 light stands for Mr. Andrew Witham to help discharge bills"; in the same year, "a chest for D. Clough and several kitchen chairs"; in 1805, "3 tables, a cradle, and a chest for Joseph Johnson." His picture frames at $1.00 each must have hung on most Bluehill walls just as scores of "piggins," pails, and butter firkins at .50 stood in their kitchens. His Diaries are filled with jobs at painting, a bureau painted at .58, chairs at .50 each, chests at the same price. In 1800 he makes "a pump for the Rev. Daniel Merrill"; in 1801, "a pump for Mr. Hewins"; and in 1806 he makes and "installs 2 pumps for the Widow Wood and the Widow Parker." A lucrative job was painting sleighs, which began in 1798 with the painting of Col. Nathan Parker's sleigh, "decorated with the picture of a horse." This work of art apparently so impressed the men of Bluehill that he receives in following years like commissions, at $2.50 each, from Daniel Spofford, Jonah Holt, Daniel Emerton, Ezra Dodge, James Peters, and Deacon Theodore Stevens. Mr. Dutton of Union River in 1800 even pays him $4.00 for a similar accomplishment. Another less profitable but frequent enterprise was painting the names of vessels built and launched in Bluehill. This task was, he says, "in certain ways unpleasant," for it must needs be done by standing in a small boat beneath the stern of the ship or schooner to be marked and at times "caused a loss of balance or even seasickness." Since it brought in $1.00, however, it was gratefully executed, for Capt. Jonah Holt, who graciously named his schooner the *Sally and Betsy,* and for at least thirty others over a period of as many years. He mends numberless looms and spinning-wheels, rebottoms chairs, repairs clocks, fits new handles for rakes and hoes,

makes latches for doors, designs, makes, and fits kitchen cup-
boards, constructs a horse-trough for the village, turns cabin-
posts for schooners, paints names on the knapsacks and canteens
of the local militia, makes drumsticks at .25 a pair, frames
dozens of "hair-combs from wood," binds volume after volume
of books for himself and others, and makes a sign for Bluehill
Academy at the lavish price of $10!

No source of food or of income on the farm and in the
neighboring countryside was ever neglected. "My boys and I
tapped all my maple trees today." "My children and I gathered
in and stored my apples, in all 40 bushels." "My daughters and I
gathered strawberries today, very plentiful. In the evening we
prepared them for preserving." "Jonathan and I went to Norris
Pond to fetch chalk. The earth there resembles, when wet, a
bluish-white paste. This, rolled into balls and dried, or burnt
in the fire, becomes excellent chalk, especially for carpenters'
use. It is valuable also for scouring silver, black tin, and the like."
The sea and shore yielded up their sustenance. Entries recording
the digging of a bushel of clams are frequent; and when mackerel
were "running," the boys took to borrowed boats and caught
hundreds for "salting down." In the early spring the smelts and
alewives, which filled the brooks on night tides, could be scooped
up in great quantities for many a costless meal and pickled for
winter use as well. In 1819 and 1820 the parson writes of the
"vast flocks of passenger pigeons" which pass over his fields.
Sadly enough, since they meant food for the family, father and
sons aided in the work of their extermination, for they killed
the birds by hundreds. "We killed many pigeons today. Josiah
brought down 23 at one shot." When one or another of the
family cows (whose names are carefully set down and apparently
repeated as one cow gave place to another, Naka, Lil, Pink,
Blackberry, Broadhorns) was slaughtered, its bones and horns
were as carefully preserved as its beef or veal. And even the
evident hosts of family cats were not allowed to pass into prudent
extinction undivested of their skins, which served for gloves and

for the binding of books; in fact, perhaps the only distasteful
entries in the Diaries concern these creatures. "I killed and
skinned 6 of our cats today."

With all these manifold activities there was as well the work
on the farm and the daily inescapable chores of milking, feeding,
pasturing in spring and summer, cleaning out and bedding down.
These latter with the parson's standards of order and cleanliness
could not have in themselves been light, for he writes as often
of "cleaning and setting my barn in order" as of "dusting and
tidying up my study." According to the town records of 1798, the
parsonage land consisted of 140 acres. Much of this was in
woodland, which he is often clearing and cutting over, and a
considerable extent in pasture. He does not say how much land
was under cultivation though he speaks of three hay-fields, the
further, the middle, and the near. In 1823 he reports that the
ground grain from his crop amounts to "21½ bu. rye, 5 bu.
wheat, and 20 bu. Indian corn"; in 1824 his potato crop is 157½
bushels. He writes in several years that Mr. Joseph Johnson
slaughtered his hogs for him and helped him cut up and salt
down his pork. In 1811 he got from one hog 270 lbs. of ham,
pork, and bacon. Occasionally he speaks of men with oxen
working at clearing out rocks, making stone walls, and building
fences; but apparently most of the labor on the farm was done
by himself and his family. He himself is often ploughing, with a
hired, or borrowed, horse, or with oxen, planting, hoeing, pruning and "liming" fruit trees, and fighting against "grubs and
insects." The boys seem constantly at work "on the woodpile
next the door"; and together he and his sons "get out our winter
wood over the deep snow."

4

In addition to the positive and even grateful pleasure which
Parson Fisher undoubtedly experienced in labor, in the sense
of its orderly accomplishment, in the knowledge that he could
perform it quickly and well, and in the pride which he justly

felt in the multifarious, useful, and even beautiful works of his hands, there were other enjoyments which he savored to the full, for the abundance of his nature allowed no halfway measures. There were, first of all, his studies, to be considered later; and there was, perhaps next in importance, the paying of his bills. This payment of bills was almost a rite with him; and the feeling of tidy relief with which he ascended the long, steep hill homeward on the days set apart for this ceremony must not be overlooked in any description of his several delights.

About once in every month in the Diaries there is an account of this important occasion, which usually took place either at the beginning of the month or at its close. Early in the morning Mr. Fisher set aside all other duties and obligations and prepared to go "to the head of the bay." Not infrequently he loaded a wheelbarrow with those creations of Fisher hands which could serve either for sale or for barter, woolen cloth, hats, buttons, rolling-pins, rose conserve, remedies of sorts, and, in later years, copies of his own literary works. Having descended the hill with a fine view of the harbor before him and the Mt. Desert range beyond, he went first to the home of the town treasurer, Mr. Reuben Dodge or Mr. Nathan Ellis, to draw a portion of his salary. This amount varied from $10 in one month to $50 in another, dependent either upon his needs of the moment or upon the condition of the treasury. He thereupon repaired to Mr. Andrew Witham's to discharge his account in part or in full, in cash or commodities, to receive the statement, and carefully to "paste the receipt" upon it. Having done this, he purchased, on a new account, supplies for the next month: "1 gal. molasses, 5 lbs. sugar, 2 lbs. rice, 1 lb. tea, 5 lbs. red ochre, 2 lbs. red lead, 3 pencils, 1 qt. N.E. rum, 1 lb. assorted nails, 2 lbs. flax seed, 1 quire paper," and, on a rare day, "a new pen-knife." He always lingered at Mr. Witham's "to read the newspapers," which were evidently kept there for the interested thumbing of the village, although what newspapers they were we are not told. "Thence to Mr. Ellis to pay him $5, thence to Mr. Hartford's, $2.34, thence to Lydia Day, in full, $2, thence to Mr. D. Osgood's, $6.54 for shingles, thence to Mr. Sargent's, .54 for shoe repair, thence to Jonathan Darling's, to pay my bill to him by 2 bonnets, thence to the Widow Clough's, 1 doz. buttons in return for 2 lbs. cheese, thence to George Stevens to pay him in full $9.57. These duties honestly discharged and as fully as circumstances would permit, I returned home in time for dinner with thanks to God for his loving bounty."

It is the frequency of such entries as this which makes especially touching—and exciting—the unusually long paragraph written in the Diary for March 22, 1820, when Jonathan Fisher was fifty-two years old:

"This night for the first time in 25 years, through the great goodness and favor of that God who is the father of the fatherless, I am free from debt to earthly creditors, not knowing that I owe any person anything but to love and to do good. In the meantime I have a comfortable house and outhouses, a comfortable supply of food and decent raiment, and a small sum of money on hand. I pray that I may be grateful for these temporary concerns and especially for the great favor of a knowledge of the way of salvation by Jesus Christ. Thanks be to God for his unspeakable goodness."

There were other and more careless joys which he permitted himself now and again to savor. Chief among these was troutfishing. Perhaps, indeed, he excused his frequent indulgences in this pleasant pastime by the indisputable fact that fish, which cost only his time and patience, could be eaten. He seems to have been an expert fisherman. He always carefully records his catch, usually in the plural: "20 trouts today"; "only 16 trouts, but 4 of excellent size and all of fine flavor"; and, on one banner afternoon, "52 trouts from Second Pond brook." Sometimes his sons accompanied him, but more often he set forth alone; and the miles he traversed from brook to brook in one afternoon seem incredible to one familiar with the topography of Bluehill. "Today I fished first in the Norris Pond brook with small success.

I then tried the Little Peters brook. Caught 10 there. I then followed the village stream, by road, to the Horton Meadow brook where they took the worms well. The afternoon in all yielded 38. In the Norris Pond brook there are some small, but sublime waterfalls, very cool and pleasant."

He obviously dearly loved also to pick berries and in July and August is constantly going "to the ledges" or "to the pastures" with his children. Wild strawberries are more abundant in the fields in late June, 1811, than he has ever known them; raspberries also are always plentiful in August in tangled thickets, and there are "some wild gooseberries good for sauce." In most years "the ledges afford plenty of blueberries and huckleberries." On August 12, 1805, he reports "a town picnic in Capt. Jonah Holt's schooner to Long Island," seven miles distant, to gather blueberries. The cost of this voyage was .25 a person, and the parson, "although exercised with a severe headache, enjoyed a fine time."

Although he made conscientiously and by the thousands his pastoral visits and received hundreds of visitors in the parsonage on both afternoons and evenings, it is quite clear that he did not take real delight in social occasions. He writes frequently and with obvious irritation that "visitors kept him from his reading and study." He did not enjoy weddings, although the $1.25, which, according to the church records, seems to have been the fee expected from each, must have somewhat compensated him for his aversion. Even the marriage of his daughter Polly, held at the parsonage on November 11, 1829, was a gloomy occasion for him as he acknowledges in a letter to his other children:

"Your sister went off with good spirits, but before her marriage she had some very pensive hours. I hope she will find a pleasant home in her new situation, and, with the blessing of God, I doubt not but she will. In this world, however, we are not to expect an uninterrupted course of happiness; the 3rd chapter of Genesis may well assure us of this. We had rather a large company at the wedding, and we could not well avoid it, as circumstances were. The number, including our own family, was 42. We had no wine nor strong drink; but there was quite high life enough, too much for me, for it made me gloomy as the grave. Whether I am so sensible to my own faults as I ought to be, may be a question; but for some years past, if I am in large parties where a measure of levity or vanity shows out, I retire from them with a dark cloud over my mind, and even in the midst of them my heart is heavy."

The Diaries, in fact, record very few purely social gatherings in which he took part. He mentions attendance upon but two of the many ship launchings, which during his years in Bluehill from 1796 to 1847 numbered some seventy-five and which were apparently gay town affairs. "Mrs. Fisher and the children" go to several of these, but he remains at home. Sometimes he goes to "house raisings," but usually, one surmises, for the purpose chiefly of assisting his neighbors and parishioners who from time to time establish their own new roof-trees. On October 11, 1819, he joins in a "town bear hunt in which the principal part of the inhabitants went a-bear hunting. No bear was killed, none was, in fact, seen, and I returned home quite weary." He loved the sight of wild animals, as his many careful and beautiful paintings of them prove; and there is a pathetic note in his renunciation, on July 14, 1825, of an opportunity to look at "a caravan" of them on exhibit in Bluehill. "My family and boarders went to see the caravan of wild animals. I denied myself this sight to be more able to assist in the missionary cause."

He vastly enjoyed singing, although certainly he had small ear for music and evidently did not sing well. Perhaps the recognition of this deficiency, which must have hampered him in his church services where hymns were regularly sung, caused his great eagerness both in 1799 and again in 1805 for the establishment of a singing-school in Bluehill. He writes in January, 1805, that he went in one afternoon, "when the going was tedious in slush," to all the other Trustees of the Academy to obtain their permission to hold the singing-school in the Academy. During February and March it was in session there, at least three or four evenings each week, under the instruction of a certain Mr. Samuel Wood, who received $17 from the town for his services in full; and Mr. Fisher's Diary both for that year and for 1799 would suggest that he was a regular attendant upon both schools.

It is abundantly clear that the parson's love of the dramatic, even of the harrowing, neither diminished with the years nor ceased to give him intense, if melancholy, pleasure; and, although his many accounts both in his Diaries and letters of the tragic happenings in Bluehill and its environs are usually well-buttressed with pious reflections, the very fact that he chronicled so many of them and that he rarely failed to reach the scene, if possible, suggests that a quite human excitement triumphed often over spiritual concern. The two fullest descriptions in all his Diaries portray hangings, in 1811 and 1824, to both of which he was an eye-witness and no detail of which is omitted. A brutal murder in Ellsworth in 1815 keeps him from sleep, especially since it was committed by a doctor of the town, who slew his wife, and since he must needs "prayerfully meditate upon such awful wickedness." In 1798 a certain Reuben Dyer sees a figure in white approach his bedside, which pronounces in awful syllables the certain guilt of Mr. Joseph Osgood, already excommunicated that very year, and then descends to dictate in less terrible accents a text upon which God desires Mr. Fisher to preach. Although the parson's rational mind is inclined to discredit Mr. Dyer's vision "as the result of a derangement," he evidently enjoys describing "this unparalleled occurrence." There is no record, however, that he preached the sermon commanded! Early one morning in 1802 he discovers "in a horse-stable near the meeting-house a stranger deranged and in a dying condition." To his distress this man proves to be one, Eben Lyon, once a student at Harvard, who has taken arsenic! In 1813 a girl dies from the bite of a mad house-cat in Belfast; in the same year two young boys, disobedient to their mother, drown off Long Island, entangled in fish-nets, and "so far as anyone knows, completely without a hope of the Savior." In 1820 Delia and Horatio Floyd, brother and sister, dead of consumption, "are laid in one grave on the same day." A dwarf "with child by fornication cannot bring forth after three days' agony and dies, clearly in sin"; a baby falls backward into a kettle of scalding water and is, "alas, parboiled as any vegetable"; two men are found in the woods, "frozen in the snow as stiff as iron rods," having fallen from intoxication; a feeble-minded boy "with no gleam of sense whatever has such amazing dexterity that he can balance two staffs on the tips of his forefingers simultaneously"; a yoke of oxen and nineteen sheep are killed instantly in Sedgwick "by one clap of lightning." He lists in June, 1827, the "solemn acts of Divine Providence" in one generous week in Bluehill: "Within one week Phoebe Faulkner was thrown from her horse and had an arm broken; Mr. John Horton's second son by the fall of a cart-body had a thigh broken; Mr. Floyd Hinckley by the oversetting of a wagon had an arm broken; Mr. Eben Guptill fell through the Carleton Locks, through intoxication, and was dangerously wounded. We know not what a day will bring forth!" Mr. Fisher's letters to his mother, whose ears were always eagerly open for these manifestations of a watchful Providence, never fail to announce all these catastrophes. In 1822, after listing for her the names of all those who have been taken from Bluehill in 1821, "through the mournful strides of Death among us," together with the fatal disease of each, he tells her of a discovery he has made "by means of simple mathematics": From the date of his settlement in 1796 to January 1, 1822, he has computed the average span of life in Bluehill to be but 27½ years. This startling figure, he says, "should excite a serious religious concern in the minds of youth." For this reason he is taking pains "to reveal it whenever possible."

The parson has little to say about food in his Diaries other than to list his farm produce, his purchases of provender, and an occasional welcome gift, "a keg of good molasses, thanks be to

God," "a Penobscot river salmon," "a fine piece of beef." The intemperance in eating which troubled him during his boyhood and his days at Harvard does not seem to have been a spiritual stumbling-block in his more mature years. He does mention frequent attacks of "colic" and "summer complaint" with attendant discomforts, but nowhere does he suggest over-eating as the cause. Nor does he anywhere express a delight in any particular form of sustenance except in the case of his melons. But on the subject of melons he becomes as nearly lyrical as he was ever able to be about merely physical and sensual pleasures.

He began his cultivation of these luscious fruits, for he raised both musk and watermelons, as early as 1800, since in September of that year he writes of inviting "Col. Nathan Parker and wife, Mr. and Mrs. Stetson, and Mr. Seth Hewins and wife to eat watermelons with us." He states, moreover, that together they "spent a most pleasant evening" in this innocent gratification. Perhaps, indeed, he was a pioneer in this form of agriculture, for melons, except as an interesting experiment, have never been looked upon as a steady, or stock, product of the short summer seasons on the Maine coast. Even today on Bluehill farms, if raised at all, they are largely a venture for interest or pleasure rather than a sure and certain source of food for home tables or for the market. Some warm slopes in the parson's fields, however, set him to growing them; and his pride in his yearly crop was exceeded only by his positive delight in their consumption. Almost every year from 1800 on, either in his Diary or in his letters, he writes of his extreme satisfaction in seeing his melons swell and ripen in the sun, and in several years he carefully counts his treasures. The watermelons do not seem to have flourished so well as the musk, for references to the former early give place to those of the latter. In 1826 his bumper crop occurs. In that year he begins counting on the 26th of August, when the first melon is ripe and ready for eating. On every day thereafter he names the exact number which have ripened, until on September 30th he has reached 60 in all. He even underlines his exciting tabulations for greater emphasis. "One melon," he writes, "is in length 12 in., in girth 23 in., and in weight 8 lbs. I am unconscionably fond of melons, and I have enjoyed eating them, with, I trust, thanks to God for his great bounty. We gathered and ate the last of this large crop on the 30th day of September with some friends invited in for the occasion." There is something very pleasing in this picture of Parson Fisher, his tape-measure in his hand, stooping over his melon patch in the sun and anticipating not only the succulence of his evening repast, but also the pride of exhibiting his blue ribbon winners to his friends and neighbors, for once perhaps more welcome than usual.

And always there is his undiminished joy "in the manifold works of God" in field and countryside at all seasons and in the winter skies. The weather always interested him. Most of the Diary entries are prefaced with a careful notation of the wind: "Brisk S.W. Scattering clouds, warm and misty"; "high N.W. Fair and quite cold"; "brisk E. Several thunder showers during the night with an almost continual blaze of lightning and roar of thunder"; "low E. Pleasant showers." He obviously loved the excitement of great snowstorms, regardless of their attendant problems. Again and again he writes of the depth of the snow: "Snow 4 to 6 ft. deep in the fields, 8 ft. in my swamp. Drifted into hills throughout the neighborhood." Once he says that the problem of getting out wood has become crucial. "My neighbors came with 7 yoke of oxen to get wood for us. We all labored together through the gigantic drifts." On one occasion, walking home from Bucksport on a cold and very snowy night, he is struck by "the blessedness of the white expanse" which, without the help of moon or of stars, by its own whiteness "guides the steps of the traveller." On another night he is entranced by a clear and very bright rainbow in full color, which, after a shower, is cast by the moon, breaking through the clouds in the eastern sky. During the autumn and winter months northern lights are a constant pleasure to him; and in March, 1821, he describes a "blazing comet in the western heavens." Falling stars, tracing their sharp, bright paths through the darkness, always delight him. After an ice-storm the drooping trees are "like rich chandeliers in some great room. I call this encrusted ice the bloom of winter." On April 2, 1827, he remarks with evident pleasure that "the frogs now begin to sing on the edge of the evening." Fireflies in July are "an astonishing revelation of God's generous plan for the delight of his children upon his earth." He catches one and watches it glow in his hand. He spies a gray squirrel in the woods, "the first I have ever seen in these parts." He knew a great deal about birds as his sketches of Bluehill prove, for he not only lists them by name, but describes their familiar habits; and he loves to watch the barn-swallows with their blue backs and beautiful flights swooping over his fields. In June, 1818, he writes: "This year for the first time in more than twenty years in this place the crowfoot, or yellow buttercup blossoms, are seen as an apron, whither away through the fields as far as the eye can extend."

5

The illnesses which Mr. Fisher carefully enters in his Diaries, a season of widespread influenza throughout the town in several winters, the frequent occurrence during the summer months of an epidemic of cholera morbus, or "summer complaint," "a bilious, putrid fever prevailing among us from July to December in the year 1806," did not, of course, spare his own family, nor did the usual diseases of childhood, mumps, measles, and whooping-cough. In January, 1807, he writes that all his children are "very ill with the fever"; and, in 1813, that "for 11 weeks from September through November all my 8 children continue ill, some so seriously that I fear the outcome." In this latter crisis Dr. Tenney's visits from Sedgwick are forty-seven in number, and the cost, together with his medicine, amounts to $94, which staggering sum worries the parson as does "the bustle of sickness

in the house, making study very difficult." He "watches" conscientiously through many nights with his sick children, although,
according to the Diary, various neighbors in turn are there also;
in fact, he particularly cites the "great kindness of many friends"
when the long siege is safely over.

The remedies and treatments listed by the parson in both
Diaries and notebooks are many and various. Dr. Tenney is
given to "bleeding" generously, especially for fevers, and Mr.
Fisher himself not infrequently performs this operation within
and without his family. "Pueking" is second on the list of treatments. "Dr. Tenney came and gave Nancy a puek." "I gave
Polly a puke, which relieved her headache and stomach pain."
Ipecac or tartar given in molasses seem to have been the agents
most generally employed for this unpleasant exercise. Castor oil
is administered in huge quantities and calomel as well. "Spirits
in hot water" is given for chills and hard colds, until 1829, when
his alliance with the temperance movement caused the parson to
use "hot peppermint water" instead, which he pronounces
equally efficacious. In 1815, as a cure for a pain in his chest, he
drinks "a pint of hot pennyroyal tea," and his consumption of
"hot mullein posset" is almost unbelievable. On one of many
occasions he drinks "1½ qts. to excellent effect." Hardly a month
goes by that some Fisher is not stricken with "painful diarrhoea,"
for which the standard cure seems to be "1½ tablespoons of castor
oil." Camphor and snake-root are given for headaches; "blisters
of mustard" are placed on congested lungs; horehound tea is
used to cure a cough; an onion poultice is bound about a stiff
neck; and "a hemlock plaster made by boiling hemlock boughs
to a gum" proves very helpful in 1829 on Mr. Fisher's lame thigh.
The Fisher ointment for itch seems in frequent use at home and
elsewhere, since all the children are more than once "anointed at
bedtime" and since the parson often carries a jar of it on his
various journeys. In 1826, beset by a stubborn earache, he tries,
first, "a stuffing of hot camphor on wool"; then, the pain con-

tinuing, "hot tobacco smoke blown in" (he does not say by whom!). Finally relief is gained "by plentiful droppings in the cavity of very hot West India rum."

On the whole, however, the health of a large family in a severe climate seems to have been reasonably good; and Mr. Fisher is constantly thanking God for His merciful Providence in sparing him and his from year to year. The first severe blow fell in 1812 when his infant son, Samuel, died less than two weeks from birth; and, in 1815, a far more cruel one in the death of his oldest child, Jonathan, who succumbed to "a lung fever" on the 10th of March at the age of seventeen after several weeks of failing health.

To one reading today in the Diary those brief entries which chronicle this boy's illness and death, there is much about them which seems distressing and pitiable, even harsh and shocking. At first they are mere statements of a steady decline, sandwiched in among details of household work and parish duties. "Jonathan's cough continues." "Jonathan still going down." "My son very feeble." "Distressed over my son's spiritual state." As the boy's "mounting fever and painful cough" make their inevitable inroads upon his father's consciousness, and the recognition of his approaching death grows clearer, his father's grief seems actually little in comparison to his fear concerning the state of his son's soul. Jonathan has made no public profession of a hope and a desire for salvation. What, therefore, may be his awful fate? On the day of his death, however, his father's fears diminish:

"I conversed with my son with much satisfaction upon the solemn subject of death and eternity. Blessed be God, he expressed a calmness in the expectation of near approaching death, expressed his astonishment at the richness of redeeming love, and exhibited a calm confidence in the Savior. In the afternoon he took a solemn leave of the family and of a number of young people who called. In the evening, several singers being present, he requested us to sing:

Lord I am thine, but thou wilt prove
My faith, my patience, and my love.

About 10 mins. before midnight he expired, after a hard conflict
with death. We have reason to hope that he has gone to rest
in the bosom of Jesus. Amen, glory to redeeming love."

There are but two further references to his son in all the many
Diaries which follow, although brief descriptions of his death
and of his father's hope for his soul occur in letters written at
the immediate time. Two days after his funeral the parson writes
that he has found among his son's possessions a letter, written a
month before his death to his sisters, Sally and Betsy, then sixteen and fourteen years old, and that he is transcribing it.
"Occasionally," he adds, "my bowels yearn and my bosom bleeds
on account of the loss of my dear son." And on March 17th, a
week after Jonathan's death, he records simply: "Went to the
head of the bay and paid Mr. Savage for the coffin of my son,
$2.10."

The letter of Jonathan Fisher, Jr., to his sisters may well be
given here, not only because it somewhat ironically sets aside
as unnecessary his father's concern for his son's immortal soul,
but also because it serves as the one remaining legacy to characterize a life so sadly brief, so grave beyond its years:

Dear Sisters,
God has now raised you up from sickness, and what is it for?
Is it that you might pursue a carnal course of pleasure, and
gratify your senses with earthly scenes? No, my dear Sisters, that
is not the end for which you were made. God is now giving you
an opportunity to make your peace with him, and to do him
service, and will you improve this opportunity? Will you continue to waste the time, which he has graciously given you? God
can easily take away this opportunity, if you do not rightly improve it.
Suppose a king had procured a ransom for a poor, miserable
criminal, who had been doomed to perpetual servitude, and had
conferred money and other privileges upon him, and promised
to make him great in the world, provided he would well im-

prove the benefits, which were conferred upon him. Now if this man convert the money, which had been given him, to other purposes than that which the king had assigned, and should spend his time in luxury, & disregard the king, and treat him with contempt, would he not be considered as very ungrateful, and would not the king have just reason to be angry with him, and take away his privileges? How much greater reason has God, then, to take away our opportunities, if we thus misimprove them?

Fly to Christ now, while there is time, and then you are safe. How would it gladden the hearts of your parents to see two daughters in the prime of life, walking in the ways of piety? On the contrary, if you refuse to embrace Christ, all the learning and all the instruction you have received, and all the sufferings of Christ will be lost to you, and not only lost, but they will increase your future misery. Can you think of it without emotion? Can you endure the thought that at death you must be separated from Christ, & from all your future happiness? Can you think of it without emotion? Can you endure the thought that at death you must be separated from Christ, & from all your godly friends? If you cannot bear the thought of this, fly now to an arm of safety, now quickly, while you have an opportunity allotted you; then you are safe; and though tempests roar around you, and sickness invade the land, you need not fear.

A few remarks that follow, though imperfectly written, yet if rightly improved, may be of use to you.

1. Consider that your time belongs to God, and whatever you do, do it to the glory of God; whatever you take in hand, ask yourselves, Will this serve in any way to promote God's glory?

2. Keep always upon the watch against Satan; guard every side, leave no place unguarded. If you do, Satan will be sure to enter; he is constantly upon the watch, ready to seize upon the weak side.

3. Do to others, as you would have others do to you; whatever you say about others, or whatever you do, which may in any way injure them, ask yourselves this question, Should we be willing that they, under the same circumstances, should do the same to us?

4. Live in peace with all men; avoid everything, that is of a tendency to raise a difficulty. Study to keep peace in the family;

when there is a blaze of discord kindled, let every one remove a brand from this blaze, and it will soon be extinguished; but, on the contrary, let everyone administer a handful of fuel, and it will soon kindle into a large flame. If there arise any dispute, let not your voice be heard in it, unless it be necessary—except it be to reconcile the parties.

5. Preserve due reverence towards all that are worthy of it. If the ways of aged people be not always so pleasing to you as you would wish, overlook it in them, & speak not disrespectfully of them when you are behind their backs.

6. Be diligent in your studies, at your work, and in whatever you take in hand; strive to improve your persons, and to preserve a decent carriage towards all.

These, and various other things must be attended to, if you would be exemplary in the world; and if you regard the feelings of your parents, conform, as far as in your power, to these things.

From your loving Brother,
Jonathan Fisher, Jun.

6

At no time during their fifty years of married life did Jonathan and Dolly Fisher live one short week, even one brief day, by themselves beneath a roof-tree unshared by others. When they first came to Bluehill in December, 1796, they brought with them Dolly Battle Newell, a seven-year-old niece of Mrs. Fisher, who lived with them until her marriage to Nathan Ellis in Bluehill in the year 1818. What manner of child she was, we have no idea as she is barely mentioned in the Diaries; but she was a *child,* needing, like all children, care and attention, eating Fisher food, and occupying parsonage room.

Three years after their arrival in Bluehill the Fishers received also into their home Seth Hewins of Dedham, who had married in September, 1799, Katharine Fisher, a younger sister of Jonathan. The Hewins remained a year at the parsonage while their own house was being built a short distance above the ministerial lot. Seth discharged the cost of their board and keep by helping the parson on his farm during those odd hours while he was not employed in erecting his own house. Always referred to as "Brother Hewins" by Jonathan, he seems to have been a congenial companion, perhaps because, according to his obituary in 1844, "his hope of acceptance with Christ," like that of the parson, "was checkered with doubts and expressed with caution." For many years he was a deacon in the church and evidently a man highly respected in the parish and town. Certain veiled references to Katharine Fisher Hewins would suggest that she was a difficult woman, who may not have added much grace to the Fisher household during her sojourn therein.

With a son and a daughter settled in the same place, the visits of Katharine Avery Fisher to Bluehill quite naturally held for her great interest and purpose; and in the early years of her son's pastorate she comes frequently to stay for a considerable season. In 1800 she is there from early spring until late fall; in July, 1805, she comes and remains through much of the winter; in the summer of 1807 she is again a visitor; and in 1812 she is present for the birth and the death of her grandson, Samuel. In the light of the parson's respect for his mother and of his long and congenial letters to her throughout her life, it seems odd that so little mention is made in the Diaries of her presence in Bluehill. Except for the brief notations of her arrivals and departures, literally no comments are made concerning her or her stays with her children and grandchildren. But, again, she was there, and room must needs have been made for her.

The parsonage, indeed, seemed capable of magical expansion; but to one who knows the present house, built in 1814 when the Fisher family in itself numbered eleven souls, the questions of where all slept, all washed themselves daily, and all presumably bathed once a week, are of engrossing complexity. Of the original house, erected by the parson and his willing parishioners in the summer of 1796, we know relatively little except that it was "1½ stories high with 7 windows." In 1814, when the new and far more commodious house was built, the older served as an ell until it was torn down by a Fisher descendant in 1896, a sad

recognition of its centenary, since, with the parson's passion for
design and for divers and sundry work on wood, it must have
been an interesting building, within and without. Since Mr.
Fisher early writes of constant projects in carpentry, "outhouses,"
"a woodhouse with a chamber," "a shed," the additions to the
original house must have been substantial. Perhaps, indeed, at a
time when no heat was expected in sleeping quarters, some of
the perennial Fisher overflow slept in the out-buildings.

The 1814 house contained downstairs a large and beautiful
paneled living-room with a fireplace and a correspondingly large
chamber above, also with fire-place. Opposite, beyond the hall,
which held the staircase and a brick oven, was the parson's study
facing west, a small, two-windowed room about 14 by 9 ft.,
sheathed in pine and paneled to window height. His fire-place
must have "drawn" well, for he speaks often of studying his
early morning Hebrew in the winter "by the sole light of my
study fire." The study bed-room above was similar in size. Although the large attic was unfinished, it had a back dormer
window and could easily have accommodated some half-dozen
hardy youths. One suspects that the various boys who boarded at
the parsonage from 1817 on may have been bedded down there
together with Josiah and Willard Fisher. The 1796 house must
have served after 1814 as a kitchen with also extra living and
sleeping space.

All the five Fisher daughters at fourteen or fifteen went to
school, for at least two years each, in Castine or in Bucksport.
Perhaps their father wanted wider experience for them; or perhaps, since they apparently worked for their board in the homes
of the Castine and Bucksport ministers, he wisely figured that
their room in the parsonage was more valuable than their company, since the $1.00 to $1.50 paid weekly by the several boarders
added substantially to the family income. The preceptor of Bluehill Academy from the founding of that institution usually made
his home at the parsonage. Board for him in 1806 is worth $1.00
a week; five years later it has risen to $1.50; and in 1824 a certain

Mr. Clapp pays $1.83. The boys, who from 1817 to 1824 live with
the parson, either to read their Greek and Latin with him
personally in preparation for the Academy at Andover or for a
theological seminary, or to attend the Bluehill Academy, number from three to six in various years. In 1822, in addition to the
preceptor, he names Mighill Blood, Jr. and George Moulton of
Bucksport, Danforth and George Pond and Hosea Kittredge of
Mt. Desert, each of whom pays $1.50 weekly for sustenance and
for the privilege of pastoral care.

7

The three years between 1822 and the close of 1824 marked
in their generous months both the zenith and the nadir of
Fisher fortunes. They were crowded with events, both grave and
gay; and the parson, acutely aware of the bountiful design of a
wise, if not always welcome, Providence, is unusually fulsome in
his description of them. He himself in 1822 at the age of fifty-
four seems at the height of his powers; and, although he occasionally says in both Diary and letters that he feels "the in-
firmities of old age creeping stealthily upon him," there is surely
no sign of their inroads in the daily patterns of his life. He is
painting pictures, transcribing "15,000 lines of verse composed
since 1787," making plans for various other literary ventures,
and excitedly beginning the study of Malay from a New Testament in that language given to him by the Rev. Mighill Blood
of Bucksport. He builds himself a sleigh, which he paints gaily
in "broad yellow stripes on black," and in 1824 buys himself a
five-months old colt, which he hopes "to make tractable in two
years." The purchase of this colt was evidently hastened by an
unprecedented windfall in the Fisher family. Mrs. Fisher has
received in 1823 a legacy of $50, which, "according to her own ex-
pressed wish," they invest in a "second-hand chaise." By 1824
the Fishers find themselves well and eagerly prepared, once the
new colt is broken to saddle and to harness, for equestrian adventures of every sort.

The parson apparently enjoys his large family in 1822, perhaps because it is affording him unusual financial security. Sally and Nancy are teaching in neighboring villages; Polly at fourteen is at school in Bucksport; Betsy, who is preparing for marriage, Dolly, Josiah, and Willard remain at home. The five boarders help with the wood-pile and the chores. The preceptor of the Academy, now Mr. Joshua Wood, is a valued member of the family. He preaches now and again for the parson; and his fairly recent humiliation at the hands of his fellow Christians seems forgotten, or at least overlooked. Mr. Fisher describes at some length and with evident satisfaction the family life in the winter of 1822:

"I arise at 5 A.M. and prepare the table for breakfast. I then repair to my study where by the light of my fire I pursue my work on Hebrew while my family of 12 or 13 is rising to prepare for the day. I now read the historical parts of the Bible easily in Hebrew. The prophets are more difficult for me. At 6 o'clock the family descends. Between 6 and 7 we breakfast and have family worship. I sometimes read the Scriptures in French, in Hebrew, in Latin, or in Greek in order that our ears may become familiar with the sound of other tongues."

He chronicles also at some length his great joy over the "engaged concern" not only of his son Josiah, but of his boarders over the state of their souls. Young George Moulton is "under a deep impression with some faint gleams of comfort"; in general, however, he "seems in deep mourning over his wretchedness." Hosea Kittredge also "indulges a hope." Dolly, at twelve years old, apparently is affected by the general seriousness at large in the family circle and begins "to entertain some measure of concern." This her father encourages by leaving about the house notes for her in French. He even fastens one "upon her pincushion." He feels, he says, that the French language, which he is most anxious for her to learn, may make her less shy about her spiritual state and at the same time increase her linguistic knowledge. He is deeply affected when, in the spring of 1823, four of the young beneath his roof, including Nancy and Josiah, make a public profession of their faith. "We rejoiced together," he writes, "in our common joy."

In September, 1822, Betsy Fisher was married to Capt Jeremiah Stevens, formerly of Mt. Desert, now of Portland, a widower with three young children. The parson is immensely gratified by this union and records with obvious satisfaction that Capt. Stevens is not only a professor of religion, but that on his ship, which plies from Portland to the West Indies, "he holds daily prayers and always commands decent language from his crew." He reports Betsy's wedding "a very pleasant Day," and then carefully lists the presents which he has given her. These amount in all, he says, "to the considerable sum of $71." They include a chest of drawers, a trunk, three paintings by her father, one volume of sermons, one volume of the *New York Missionary Magazine,* one book on Garden Life, and Mrs. Hannah More on Education. Mr. Fisher reckons meticulously that these articles amount to $20, which, with a cash present of $51, add up to the $71 proudly set down in the Diary.

The three years were marked by other events of a nature not so pleasing. For our knowledge of the first of these we are indebted to a small packet of poetry found among the parson's countless papers and suggesting a village tragedy to which Mr. Fisher himself gives little space. And yet, because it reveals such suffering in the hearts of a group of young people more than a century ago, it deserves, I think, a few paragraphs in passing, if only to rescue it from that complete oblivion which is perhaps the most bitter and touching certainty of human life and love.

Catharine, the daughter of Seth and Katharine Fisher Hewins, died on February 16, 1823, at the age of twenty-two of "a consumption" after a wasting illness of several months. In such a community and at a time when the death of the young was in no way unusual, such an occurrence in itself might perhaps merit little attention. But within the packet of poems written to Catharine Hewins there are included certain writings of her own which show her to have been a girl of great promise and charm. At fourteen, while attending Bluehill Academy, she writes in a beautiful hand a poem on Friendship which she inscribes as composed "for Miss Sally Fisher"; in the same year, within intricate and exquisitely designed scrolls, she writes some verses on Fame and four lines which she entitles *The Wish:*

> I sigh not for beauty nor languish for wealth,
> But grant me, Kind Providence, virtue and health.
> Then, richer than kings and more happy than they,
> My days shall pass sweetly and swiftly away.

Parson Fisher himself has little to say about his niece except for some brief entries during her illness in 1822 in which he deplores not so much her "continual decline in health" as her "lack of any change in heart." At her funeral, which was held at the meeting-house on February 18th during a "severe snowstorm," he reports "a great collection of people present."

The question of Catharine's ultimate repentance and salvation, however, does not seem to have been uppermost in the minds of young Hosea Kittredge, Josiah Fisher, and George Moulton, all of whom quite clearly loved her. Perhaps, unlike the parson, they could not conceive of Divine vengeance against one so cherished. During the night following her death the three of them sat with her body in the Hewins' house, and each composed a poem to her:

"Lines occasioned by the death of Catharine Hewins on Feb. 16, 1823." By Hosea Kittredge.

> There, there she lies, a lifeless form of clay.
> And was she ever more? Ah, yes, most sure!
> Those limbs, which now are still and deadly cold,
> Were once with vigor strung, and blooming youth
> Flushed roses on those cheeks which now are pale.
> Those eyes fired beauty and that bosom glowed
> With hopes high-fixed, with laughter, and with grace.
> And was this all? Was she but this to me?
> Ah, no! Something that's worth the world and more to me
> That lovely form possessed.

"Lines composed while sitting up to watch the remains of Catharine Hewins the night after her death." By Josiah Fisher.

> As thus I sit to watch her dear remains,
> I hear the steady clock repeat its hours,
> A solemn sound! With silent tread the hearse
> Shall bear her slow away. One, and the last
> Fond look, I now must take. Her friend, her lover, too,
> I bend once more o'er faded loveliness,
> Then bid a long farewell.

The lines composed by young George Moulton on this memorable night in the Hewins sitting-room, when they are compared to those of his now harmless rivals in love, are turgid and pious enough, an appeal to youth to repent while there is yet time. From them alone we might, indeed, quite reasonably assume that George's soul to him was of far greater importance than any condition of his heart at that moment. But fortunately among the poems is one which was written by him four days after Catharine had been laid in the graveyard (where, the parson writes, the snow lay three feet deep). These verses clearly reveal not only his love for her, but also the real impetus compelling his conversion some weeks later. The Rev. Mr. Fisher had been quite evidently misled concerning the reason for George's "deep mourning" in December!

"Lines occasioned by the death of Miss Catharine Hewins, who died February 16, 1823." Written by George F. Moulton on Feb. 22, 1823.

> Alas! My Catharine is dead!
> The soul from that dear form is fled.
> That voice, which once so charmed my ear,
> Alas! I nevermore shall hear.
> That cheek, which once so sweetly blushed,
> Shall be no more with crimson flushed.
> All that remains, a lifeless clod,
> Lies buried now beneath the sod.

I loved her! And 'twas my delight
To walk with her by Moon's fair light.
Close to my side her arm I pressed,
Affection glowing in my breast.
Onward we moved with lingering feet,
Our converse then was chaste and sweet,
O'er future scenes my mind would rove
Of much enjoyment with my love
When Hymen should our hands unite,
Nor dreamed that Death our hopes would blight.

But ah! how vain all earthly bliss!
To me no stroke was e'er like this!
In the cold grave they laid my Fair,
And all those hopes lie buried there.

Let me, ah! let me now reflect!
Shall I the love of God reject?
Oh no! the better part I choose,
The Savior's call I can't refuse.
And when my mortal race is run
And every earthly duty done,
Then shall my happy spirit rise
On wings of love above the skies.
There shall I meet that happy one
Whom I once loved beneath the sun,
There look with pleasure on the past,
And while Eternity shall last,
Unite with her in grateful lays
To celebrate Jehovah's praise.

The parson does not anywhere suggest that he was aware of broken hearts in his household in the winter and spring of 1823. In various letters as well as in his Diary he writes of his deep joy over the conversion of "a number of young men" under his roof and especially of his relief over the change of heart of his son Josiah. One hopes that this decision on the part of Josiah helped somewhat to assuage the painful effects of another which a few months later dealt great distress to his father. Shortly after his conversion Josiah determined to study for the ministry, again much to the parson's joy. Plans were thereupon made in March, 1824, for his entrance into "the infant theological seminary" at Bangor, an institution which, from its precarious beginnings but a few years earlier, had won Mr. Fisher's intense zeal and devotion and his untiring activities in its cause. Josiah, however, always seemingly a law unto himself and evidently contrary by nature, was harboring plans of his own which he announced to his father in April. He had decided to enter Bowdoin College and at the close of his four years there to attend the Andover Theological Seminary rather than that of Bangor.

An understanding of Parson Fisher's intimate and cherished connection with "the school of the prophets" at Bangor, which will be described in the next chapter of this book, makes more clear the "great shock" which he sustained upon learning that his penniless son at twenty-two was not only bent upon a college education before beginning his theological studies, but was repudiating the Maine seminary in favor of that at Andover. Few entries in the parson's Diaries show more grieved concern than that which he pens in April, 1824:

"I can hardly bear up under this. For my own son to go to another institution would seem to speak a language unfavorable to the Seminary in Bangor, and in this I find my heart is much bound up."

He records, however, no conversations with Josiah on the subject, and, on August 27, 1824, writes a letter to President William Allen of Bowdoin commending his "oldest surviving son" to his care. He himself, he says, can provide nothing for him save a few books and necessary clothing. He trusts that the American Education Society may be persuaded to assist somewhat and that Josiah himself, "who is accustomed to use his hands, may be able to turn them to useful labor."

Only Josiah's term bills at Bowdoin, three each year in number, dutifully sent his father "for record," and a few letters of the parson to his son begging for news of him, since the family

is in "great suspense" over his condition and even his where-
abouts and his mother "extremely solicitous," reveal his life at
college. The cost of his education was some $18 each term,
which sum included tuition and "chamber rent." He seems to
have foraged for himself as to food. In a letter written by his
father to a relative he says that Josiah has been living for some
weeks entirely on bread and milk at a cost of .75 a week; and,
in one of Josiah's few letters home during his four years at
Bowdoin, he describes with some humor the state of his clothing
just before his Commencement: "My outward person shows some
rather unequivocal marks of decay, my hat bent in, coat thread-
bare, shirts worn out and torn, trousers evidently in consumption, and my heels every now and then look through windows
which they have made in their enclosures as if on purpose to
stare people in the face." His college bills include reports of
his "moral deportment" and his "attention to study." The first
is always "good"; the second progresses from "improving" to
"satisfactory" to "good." From Andover, to which he went in
1829, he writes in a rare letter of his determination to go "to
the Western Territories for missionary work"; but these dreams
do not materialize, for in March, 1832, he is ordained as Congregational minister in the village of Stillwater, a part of Orono,
Maine. Dismissed from there three years later, he goes to Clyde,
New York, where his father, in a letter to a niece, "assumes him
to be established." References to him in the later Diaries are as
infrequent as were, presumably, his letters home, and except for
his marriage to his cousin, Elisabeth Fisher, a daughter of his
uncle Samuel, and for two brief visits in Bluehill, we have little
information concerning him until a few years before his father's
death in 1847. It seems, however, quite fair to conclude that
both the pleasure and the comfort which he afforded his parents
were but slight.

On November 20, 1823, Mr. Fisher married at the parsonage
his eldest daughter, Sally, at the age of twenty-four to Joshua
Wood, then acting as preceptor of Bluehill Academy. Mr. Wood,

in both the Diary and some letters written by his father-in-law
to announce the marriage, is described as a "Licentiate" and a
"candidate for the ministry." He was eight years older than
Sally Fisher, having been born in 1791, the son of Col. Robert
Wood, a highly respected member of the parson's church, a deacon for many years, and quite clearly a substantial citizen of
the town. Joshua seems for some unknown reason to have begun
his studying late, for it is not until 1818 when he is twenty-seven
years old that he is reading Greek and Latin with the parson,
apparently for entrance to Phillips Academy at Andover. He
entered there in May, 1818, but is back again at home in October
of that year with no explanation given for his return. Just why
he boarded at the parsonage for several weeks and even months
at a time from 1818 to 1823 is not clear, since his own home
was little more than a mile away; and yet Mr. Fisher clearly
lists him as a "boarder" in several entries. The parson always
refers to him as "Mr. Wood" although the other boarders are
spoken of familiarly by their Christian names. This tone of respect, however, can perhaps be explained on the score of his age.

In fact, the life of this young man in relation to the Fisher
household presents more than one mystery. The first sign of
trouble between him and his father-in-law occurred on July 19,
1824, eight months after his marriage when his wife was expecting her first child. The parson writes: "Mr. Wood last evening
said to me, 'I have made arrangements to board otherwheres next
week.' I replied, 'Well, it is well.' He said no more. This morning, before I was up, he went away. I know not whither." On
July 30th he closed his school and, leaving his wife with her
parents, went "to the westward." On September 3rd he returned
and took Sally to live "in a room at Mr. Obed Johnson's, a
quarter of a mile from the parsonage." A few weeks later he is
seemingly gone for good, "to Georgia for his health."

Sally, remaining alone at Mr. Johnson's, is reported by her
father as "in a state of extreme ill health and spirits" throughout the autumn. On November 17, 1824, she gave birth to a still-

born son and, after ten days of suffering, died on November 27th. Her father describes the last sad and ironic day of her life, taking pains first to transcribe a poem which she wrote on the day of her dead child's birth:

> How soon from the womb to the tomb
> My first-born dear infant is fled!
> The blossom just came to the bloom,
> 'Tis smitten, and withered, and dead.

"Nancy went to stay with her sister, as did Polly, and her mother. I followed with Dr. Tenney, who came to fetch me. She gave us all present her dying farewell. With calmness she gave directions concerning the disposal of the few things she possessed. Her distress of body continued with but little intermission; but her patience, courage, and connectedness of mind were remarkable in view of her great suffering. When I said to her that nothing can help us on a dying bed but the love of God in Christ Jesus, she said: 'I have had occasion to realize that before now.' She is gone. I think I feel it in my heart to say, The will of God be done. I need this stroke. May it wean me from the world! May God sanctify the event to her dear mother, her brothers and sisters, and to her husband, gone to the State of Georgia for his health."

On the day after her burial he writes that he went "to the head of the bay to put a letter in the post-office," that he then walked alone to the graveyard, and that finally he went to the meeting-house "to clear the stove of the ashes from the fire which I kindled there for my daughter's funeral." In January, 1825, he records the death of Joshua Wood on the 6th of that month near Savannah, Georgia.

Some further evidence, though by no means explicit, is thrown upon this tragedy in the Fisher family through a sermon preached by the parson shortly after Joshua Wood's death. The text seems hardly applicable to what we know, or at least assume, concerning Joshua: *Mark the perfect man and behold the up-*

right, for the end of that man is peace; but the "application" to him in some paragraphs at the close was apparently made in a final effort to make the best of a sad and sorry business, perhaps even to quell village indignation and criticism:

I would urge upon you, my dear hearers, when friends or relatives are taken by death, to contemplate their lives and characters attentively, to mark with tenderness wherein they have failed, and to be on your guard that you may not fail in the same respects. We miss from among us one who was lately a member of this church, who, though not without failings, was a person of fair promise. One who was free to acknowledge when he had been led aside from the path of duty and appeared to be watchful that he might not offend again; one of some powers of mind from whose first attempts in dispensing the gospel we found reason to believe might have been very useful; one whom I had rejoiced to receive into my family as a son-in-law and who, I truly believed, would one day hold a respectable rank among the ministers of Christ.

But soon after he had closed his education, a latent disorder began to prey with increasing rapacity upon his vitals. We saw him sink under it; we saw the effect upon his mind as well as upon his body; we saw the strength of his mind failing as his mortal part failed. As a last expedient for restoration of health, he journeyed to a distant clime, but it was too late. We trust that he was so far upright in the sense of our text that his end was peace and that he is already with the spirit of his consort, who took her flight before him. We mourn their early departure.

Wherein these, our late departed friends, did exhibit a good example, and, in some respects, they certainly did, let us, their survivors, cheerfully imitate them. They were industrious, prudent in their expenses, and patient under trials. If they were at times reserved, it was probably constitutional. Their early and, we trust, sincere profession of religion, is worthy of imitation in the youth around us. May every member of this church, diminished by their removal, see that *his own lamp* is trimmed and burning!

Except for a brief statement that he and Col. Robert Wood "divided the furnishings of Mr. and Mrs. Joshua Wood between them," there is no further reference either in Diaries or in letters to Sally Fisher Wood and her fleeting romance. But when the parson recorded her death and that of her husband in the Family Register of Bluehill, in the compiling of which he took great care and pride, he placed beneath their names two black bars, together with the old and haunting Latin words,

Sic transit gloria mundi.

8

Except for the housing of the preceptors of the Academy who continued to make their home at the parsonage, the Rev. Mr. Fisher after 1824 relinquished the care and training of young men in favor of small and recalcitrant boys; in fact, from 1824 to 1829 he seems to have run a miniature, but most active, reform school within his home. His first entrant was a youngster of thirteen named Reuben Daniel, the son of a Boston, or Dedham, relative, who, apparently intractable at home, was turned over to the parson for discipline. Reuben endured the doubtless stern, if just, measures of his guardian and the generous tasks required of him about the farm for three years, at the close of which he left on a visit to his mother and refused to return. In a reproachful letter to Reuben and in other correspondence relating to him, Parson Fisher expresses deep regret and disappointment over such ungrateful behavior "just when he was beginning to be of some help in recompense for many trials."

In 1826, while Reuben is still unwillingly at the parsonage, young Ignatius Stevens, aged twelve, the step-son of Betsy Fisher Stevens, arrives from Portland to add his uneasy presence to the household. Ignatius and Reuben together seem to have made imperative a Watch and Ward Society with the parson as police officer. Sent on errands, they "tarry for nine hours on end"; set to "mowing *ruin*" (Mr. Fisher's term for burdocks, thistles, and alders) they escape to the woods; averse to study, they make both parson and preceptor "to despair."

And yet Ignatius Stevens, in comparison with his younger

brother, Joseph Tyler, who in 1827 takes Reuben's place in the ministerial house of correction, seems docile, indeed. Young Joseph at ten is, according to the parson's definition, "an unmanageable Zebra." In a letter to his father, Capt. Jeremiah Stevens, written in June, 1828, Mr. Fisher forcefully and frankly gives his opinion of Joseph, since "fidelity seems to require" that he should state "a few prominent facts." He plays in the house of God on the Sabbath; he speaks both profanely and falsely; he is irreverent to his superiors; he is immodest in his behavior, for which both at school and at home he has been "severely chastised"; he stays away for hours when sent on errands; he abuses his books, having torn from the binding "his new *Vive Roma*"; he makes no improvement whatever in his writing and "his Latin he seems to hate with utter hatred." Mr. Fisher concludes this mounting list of crimes with the assurance that he has not yet given Joseph up "for lost," but is willing to continue his "difficult experiment" for yet another year in the hope that Joseph's "hardened though not entirely seared conscience through severe chastisement, accompanied by calm and serious admonition, may be touched and softened." We are unfortunately not informed of the result of the second year, nor do we know anything of the "Zebra's" longer future except that at fifteen he is at sea "on a whaler," which would seem an excellent place for him.

In November, 1830, Jonathan and Dolly Battle Fisher joyfully reaped the harvest of their years of hospitality to the various preceptors of Bluehill Academy. On the 18th of that month a double wedding was solemnized in the parsonage sitting-room. Nancy at twenty-six was that evening married to Hosea Kittredge, then preceptor, and Dolly at twenty to Robert Crossett, who had come to Bluehill in 1828 to act both as preceptor and as singing-school master. Both these young men seem to have been admirable additions to the Fisher family. Hosea Kittredge, who had already been a member of the household six and eight years earlier, had graduated from Amherst College in 1828, where he evidently made himself distinctly felt. He remained in Bluehill until 1836, built a commodious and beautiful home there, on the hill below the meeting-house, and, if a comparison can justly be made, seems to have been, at least in terms of human personality, the most interesting and lively of the Fisher sons-in-law. The parson, obviously devoted to him, warns him in occasional later letters to guard his "perhaps too quick and lively temper" and to "curb an innate tendency to carelessness, even extravagance, in monetary affairs." The necessity for both these warnings makes one quite drawn toward Hosea and pleased that Nancy's life with him evidently did not lack excitement. Robert Crossett, who had been trained at the Bangor Theological Seminary, had left Bluehill at the time of his marriage to Dolly to become pastor of the Congregational church in the village of Dennysville in Washington County, Maine. Although apparently less prodigal in nature than Hosea, he seems to have been an able and amiable young man and the marriage a most happy one. Since Polly a year earlier had married Benjamin Stevens, a clothier in Bluehill, the lines of the four surviving Fisher daughters had fallen unto them in pleasant places, as their father more than once remarks in various letters. Willard at twenty-four alone remained at home, neither to be saved nor to be married until four years later.

His zeal for reform of the young now cooled, his daughters well married and two of them settled in Bluehill, his household now numbering but three, his financial affairs in a decent state, the Rev. Mr. Fisher has but one anxiety during 1830 and the years immediately following: he is grieved to the heart over the low state of religion in his church and parish. He writes: "In this town there is but little left of life and of engagedness in religion apparent. My mind is much borne down through the divisions, hard feelings, and dissensions in my church and society, rising partly through opposition to church discipline, partly from opposition to the cause of temperance. Oh when will God send his healing streams to us who thirst after them?"

Still, the Diaries and letters for these years reveal their compensations. The colt, "broken well to harness," affords "pleasant expeditions in our sleigh or chaise"; the first yoke of oxen, purchased in 1829, makes "improvements on the farm easier." He sets out "rock maples and other shade trees" in the spring of 1830; his muskmelons continue to flourish; with Willard's help, although Willard now "works for himself," he does most of the labor on his farm "cheerfully and with pleasant thoughts." In the long evenings he and Dolly still "braid hats." His brother Samuel, whom he has not seen for thirteen years, visits him, "a great pleasure"; they part "after a refreshing fortnight, to meet no more in this world." On a cold February morning in 1832 he finds "a little owl" in his wood-house and paints it as it sits quietly on a beam. A friend sends him "a fine eagle's quill" for a new pen, and he trusts it may serve him as well as the last, which he has just thrown away "after using it 18 months for all my writing." At the age of sixty-two he is walking sixteen miles to Castine and back the same day "for the pleasures of solitude, quiet thought, and observation of the glories and gifts of God."

In October, 1831, after an afternoon of burning brush in his pasture, he writes in his Diary: "While my hands were occupied in needful labor, I was led to exclaim in my heart: *Hands, what a blessing they are when employed aright!*"

9

Jonathan Fisher, beset by anxiety and depression over his seemingly fruitless labor in the Lord's vineyard, made a mighty sacrifice in the summer of 1830. He gave up trout-fishing. He describes this renunciation in an entry dated July 8th:

"This afternoon I went trout fishing for the last time. In the Norris Pond brook and the Lemuel Peters brook I caught 15. The scenery was various and entertaining, but the pleasure hardly compensated for the fatigue. In my present purpose I take a last farewell of most of the wild places I have this day visited. May God enable and dispose me to use still greater art and perseverance to *catch men* than I have this day used to catch the little fishes of the brook."

But, like most of us of lesser clay than he, he happily weakened in his resolve. Did he then fall from Grace or rather attain to it? He does not say. Only, when the "benign and serene days" of June, 1831, come again, he finds himself "clearly in such need of relaxation" that he digs his worms and sets forth once more, this time to Col. Wood's brook and to the Horton Meadow brook. He caught 8 in the one and 12 in the other. "It was a happy afternoon," he says. Let us sincerely trust that it was quite free from the faintest shadow of self-reproach!

VI

FATHER FISHER ABROAD

T HE Rev. Mr. Fisher, like his contemporary, William Hazlitt, liked nothing better than to go on a journey. Like Hazlitt, too, he was not in the least averse to going by himself, being, also, never less alone than when alone and doubtless not a little relieved "to get rid of others" and "to be free of all impediments." The parson's wayfarings afford, like those of Hazlitt, an interesting slant on his versatile and at times paradoxical nature. His vacation trips to Boston afforded him as much excitement doubtless as did Hazlitt's to Calais, "the confused, busy murmur" of the one place as alien and delightful a sound in his ears as was that of the other to its eager visitor. He, too, walked miles through the mud of many a country road to witness the embracing of Truth and Genius under the sanction of Religion, even, indeed, to unite them by his own ardor. Nor did Hazlitt mount the Bath coach on his way to watch the famous fight with greater curiosity and avidity than did Jonathan Fisher set forth upon two occasions for the shire town of Castine, Maine, to see two of his fellowmen meet their deaths upon the gallows. But away with pleasant comparisons, and to the parson's journeyings!

1

The first and foremost of his many travels were made in the cause of his "Divine Master." As early as the year 1801, at the age of thirty-three, he is zealously engaged in missionary labor among the farflung settlements of Hancock and of Washington Counties. Father Fisher, indeed, possessed all those many and diverse traits which together form the ideal missionary character.

He was firmly grounded in his faith, in spite of harassing doubts as to the certainty of his own salvation; and he fervently believed that he was called by God to go out into his world and preach it to others. Like St. Paul he gloried in hardships and welcomed perils by land and sea. Nor was he, either, indifferent toward recounting them, even to boasting about them upon occasion. He loved unfamiliar country and odd places of sojourn. He liked to speculate upon the future of any wilderness wherein he might find himself, to look forward to the years "when, under God, it should blossom as the rose and contain, in place of forests, the habitations of piety and peace." He vastly enjoyed meeting unexpectedly from time to time fellow apostles fired with similar zeal, Father Jotham Sewall, the Revs. Abijah Wines, Jonathan Powers, Daniel Lovejoy, John Sawyer, and Mighill Blood, and to hold celestial conversations with them along the way, "a prayer for Divine Grace upon our labors before we each set forth upon our separate paths." He loved solitude, and, although he was given to finding human nature not only "depraved by necessity," but at times "extremely wearisome," he quite evidently bore with it even more charitably away than at home. He could endure with great good nature, if not with humor, a night made trying by fleas for the sake of what the next morning might conceivably hold in new interest and excitement. And he possessed those undiminished powers of physical endurance and resiliency which, whether he recognized it or not, added immeasurably to his treasury of spiritual gifts.

The place of his settlement could not have been more admirably chosen for his missionary labors; indeed, perhaps no other State in the Union has ever afforded more opportunity for such enterprise than has the State of Maine from its earliest beginnings as a province of Massachusetts even until now. The countless inlets, coves, and bays of its long, indented coastline, its many islands, and in the north its vast, thinly populated forest area resulted early in the isolation of its settlements one from another. Its people, scattered over this extensive tract of land, were, in general, too poor and its colonies of settlers too small to support resident ministers; hence they became wholly, or nearly, dependent upon missionary aid. This fact became of burning importance to the several societies established early in Massachusetts and dedicated to the spread of the gospel not only among the Indians, but among "others in remote portions of North America," which phrase came to mean primarily the settlers in the District of Maine.

Nor, had Jonathan Fisher himself been the arbiter of the date of his birth, could he have selected a time better suited for his destined profession as a laborer in God's vineyard both at home and abroad. For the English-speaking Christian world of his young manhood at the beginning of the nineteenth century was stirred as perhaps never before since the early Middle Ages by the need and the desire to evangelize its fellowmen. Not only in England and Scotland were Dissenters of various names, and Anglicans also, aroused to missionary enthusiasm and to the founding of societies to carry it out; but in New England even more than in Old, this sacred responsibility of a man for the soul and the mind of his brother flourished mightily, largely because there were so many near and distant fields already ripe for harvest and awaiting those who might bring in the sheaves. In a letter written by General Benjamin Lincoln in 1790 on the "Religious State of the Eastern Counties in the District of Maine," the sad spiritual condition of that district is graphically described. "Very few of the children born in that country are baptized, nor has the Lord's Supper ever been administered in most of the towns and plantations below the Penobscot. There is great reason to believe that, unless some care is immediately taken to remedy the evil, by sending regular, ordained ministers into that country, the inhabitants will acquire at least an indifference to those important truths." [1]

Care was immediately taken to remedy the evil. In 1791 the

---

[1] A copy of this letter is in *Collections of the Massachusetts Historical Society*, 1st Series, 4: 153-156, 1795.

Massachusetts Society for the Propagation of the Gospel, incorporated in 1787, began in Maine its missionary labors, which it continued for thirty years, often sending as many as sixteen or eighteen itinerant preachers each year not only as far as the Penobscot, but "through the wilderness" east of that river to Machias, Eastport, and Lubec. Some of these indefatigable servants of God carried on schools as well as occupied pulpits, and all of them distributed thousands upon thousands of Bibles, Testaments, hymn-books, primers, spelling-books, sermons, and tracts. The Massachusetts Missionary Society, established in 1799, also began to send its first missionaries into eastern Maine as early as the year 1801, that great stretch of country from the Penobscot River to the St. Croix being evidently considered the most isolated and destitute of all lands in the Province. Of all its ardent apostles the chief was the Rev. Jotham Sewall, who describes himself as "a voice crying in the wilderness." Born in 1760 in the town of York, Maine, brought up to a bricklayer's trade, and quite without any formal education, not to say theological training, Father Sewall spent more than fifty years of his life as an itinerant preacher, mostly in the District, and later in the State of Maine, but also on Cape Cod, in New York State, in New Jersey, Delaware, Maryland, Virginia, North and South Carolina, the District of Columbia, and New Brunswick. At the age of eighty-five he is still on the road and still experiencing "solemn, interesting seasons of Divine Grace." In his Diary for 1804, a diary which he kept throughout his life regardless of the weariness he must have felt at nightfall, he reports that in that year he has preached 412 sermons, visited 482 families and 23 schools, attended 12 church conferences and 3 ministerial associations, received 35 persons to church fellowship, celebrated the Lord's Supper 9 times, catechized 2 groups of children, seized 3 full days for "private fasting and prayer"; and assisted in the gathering together and founding of 2 churches. Father Sewall numbered his sermons, preached mostly in eastern Maine, as in all 12,593. The miles which he rode or walked were numberless, literally thousands in a single year.[1]

The Maine Missionary Society was founded in 1807. Its immediate forerunner was the Lincoln and Kennebec Religious Tract Society, which with thirty-two members had been organized in 1802 chiefly by the Congregational ministers of those two counties for the purpose of distributing tracts and other religious literature among outlying districts. Such journeyings entailed also, of course, missionary preaching. At the annual meeting of the society, held at Hallowell on June 18, 1807, its members, in order "to extend the circle of their influence and multiply their means of doing good," resolved to form themselves into the Maine Missionary Society. Two years later the society was incorporated under the Acts of the Commonwealth of Massachusetts with the names of both Jotham Sewall and Jonathan Fisher among the original petitioners. The latter was a member also of its first Board of Trustees. The Massachusetts Society, after the formation of the Maine, still continued its labors in the District, and State, until 1826, the two working together in a common purpose and their missionaries, like Father Sewall, serving under first the one and then the other. The Massachusetts Society for the Propagation of the Gospel also continued its activities, and it was under the encouragement of this society, together with the cooperation of the Hancock Ministers' Association, that Father Fisher made his first journey into Washington County in 1801.[2]

Practically all these devoted itinerants were already settled as pastors of churches in Maine, or Massachusetts, or Connecticut,

[1] An account of this almost incredible life is given in *A Memoir of Rev. Jotham Sewall of Chesterville, Maine,* by his son, the Rev. Jotham Sewall. Boston, 1853. The book is made up largely of quotations from Father Sewall's Diary, the original of which is in the Maine Historical Society of Portland.

[2] For information concerning Missionary Societies and early missionary work in the District of Maine, I am indebted to Vol. I of *History of the Congregational Churches in Maine* by the Rev. Calvin Montague Clark of the Bangor Theological Seminary. Portland, 1935.

and were released by their congregations to work for a few weeks or, at most, months among the outlying districts of the New England wilderness. Traveling on horseback, with their saddle-bags stuffed with religious publications, or on foot with far less scrip for their journey, they traversed roads which were but little better than trails or paths through the woods between widely scattered and sparsely settled communities. Bridges were scarce, and fording streams on foot or on horseback or being ferried across in friendly boats or canoes, the order of the day. In 1807 the larger portion of the population of Maine was settled, as it is, in fact, today, in the south and west parts of the Province in what were then the counties of York, Cumberland, and Lincoln, where the people numbered some 120,000 in comparison to the 100,000 scattered over the far greater remainder of a vast area. In 1807, also, most of the cultivated land was in these older counties. The newer, particularly those of Penobscot, Hancock, and Washington, lived primarily by lumbering, fishing, and shipbuilding. In the eastern regions of Hancock County, once one left the Bluehill and Mt. Desert area where, as has already been said, the churches were in a comparatively flourishing condition, and in all of Washington, the few struggling church groups were mostly destitute of any settled pastors; and on the countless and long points of land extending seaward, on the many islands, and in the midst of the forests were hundreds of families "whose children," according to the Rev. David Winthrop, writing in 1816, "at ten and twelve years old cannot yet tell who was their Creator and are, indeed, on the verge of pagan darkness." [1]

It was into this region that the Rev. Jonathan Fisher made his way on foot for more than 300 miles during the full month of September, 1801, on his first missionary journey, of which he gives a long account in his Diary for that year. On the whole, he says, "the five weeks' mission was a pleasant one, although a sinful fear of men often operated to hinder me from using that

[1] From the Trustees' Report of the Maine Missionary Society, 1816.

faithfulness in private conversations with respect to their spiritual conditions which I ought to use." His travels, begun at Union River, extended as far as St. Andrews in what is now New Brunswick. He visited the settlements of Sullivan, Gouldsboro, Steuben, Narragaugus (now Cherryfield), Columbia, Addison, Machias, Dennis Village (now Dennysville), and Robbinston. He plodded "up the Schoodic through wild woods to St. Stephens, St. Davids, and St. Andrews," "calling from house to house" and going even to distant points of land "in search of sinners." At East Machias and Addison he found piety and hospitality to refresh his depressed spirits over "the low state of religion in general found throughout this unchartered region." At Addison he found also .50 "tied up in the corner of his cravat," and at East Machias a certain Mr. Smith generously gave him $3. The weather was mild and pleasant and "the wild country beautiful." His spirits alternately rose and fell throughout his journey, rose, over meeting at Narragaugus a Miss Polly Camel, "truly pious," fell, over an almost angry debate with "young Mr. Godfrey of Gouldsboro, surely a Deist if not an Atheist." "Alas," he writes, "poor is that courage which can be daunted by a great house and gay habits! But I find myself more at home with the simple and the lowly." At Columbia Falls he fell in with Fathers Jotham Sewall and Abijah Wines, with whom he walked to Machias and on to Dennis Village, listening on two evenings to "able discourses" given by these friends. Father Sewall leaving for work among the islands, he and the Rev. Mr. Wines proceeded "through the mire and water of a doleful road" to the Schoodic, where they parted. In these settlements on the Schoodic he found "not one person giving evidence of new birth." "The prospect is dark and gloomy, indeed," he writes, "but yet with God all things are possible. His spirit can work wonders, and in his own time it shall be done." At St. Andrews he says: "The vermin, fleas, were so numerous in the house of Mr. Alexander Greenlaw that I hardly had a wink of sleep during the night"; but at St. Andrews he found also "a giantess" in the wife of a certain Mr. Dority, a woman who apparently afforded him not a little compensating excitement!

At Narragaugus on the long way home Divine Providence lent him "sudden and unexpected assistance" during an evening meeting:

"A few people collected to whom I preached from 2 Peter 3:11 on the importance of being prepared for the Day of Judgment. At the close of my discourse I said to sinners: 'This very night ye may be summoned into Eternity and your state forever fixed. Realize the awful scenes which have been mentioned as though they were just before you, and then dare to continue in sin if ye think best! Whereupon Mr. Bucknam, a ship's carpenter present, fainted away and fell backward across the seat behind him. Being taken up, he was presently seized with severe vomiting. In about 20 mins. he came to himself, comfortable but weak. After the confusion was over, I closed with prayer, referring to the event just passed as a Providential warning to be always ready and as an intimation of our constant dependence upon God."

Father Fisher's missionary journeys continued throughout the next twenty years of his life. Most, if not all, of these were taken under the patronage of the Maine Missionary Society, acting as agent for the Massachusetts Society for the Propagation of the Gospel, the latter society after 1808 employing the former to act in this capacity for its work in Maine, to dispense its books, and to recommend suitable men as missionaries. In August, 1808, Father Fisher takes a trip of 118 miles, this time "on horseback with a load of books," to Union River, Trenton, and the various settlements on Mt. Desert Island, a journey in which he "was much favored by God and enjoyed a good measure of comfort and satisfaction." In February, 1815, in bitter weather he sets out on foot for Corinth by way of Bucksport and Bangor, with Cotton Mather, whom he thinks "very valuable," in his pocket as a companion on the snowy roads. He finds the views of frozen lakes and white forests on this walk of 110 miles "quite sublime in spite of the severe cold." In July, 1817, he spends a week on the Cranberry Islands, a depressing sojourn, since "of the 75 persons on Great Cranberry only 3 are professors of religion, and on Little Cranberry only one soul out of 3 large families settled there indulges any hope." In 1818 he takes four journeys, in June, August, October, and November, of a week each, to Mt. Desert, to Brooksville, to Penobscot, and to Sedgwick. In the last three places, he says, there are now no resident Congregational pastors, and the lack is sadly seen, especially in "the spread of fornication" throughout these villages and their outlying districts. In Penobscot he takes joy in celebrating the Lord's Supper, the first time it has been observed since the British took the town in 1814. For these journeys he employs one text for public sermons and private entreaty alike, *This night thy soul shall be required of thee*. It was quite evidently a favorite of his.

From 1819 to 1823 he is regularly employed in the missionary service at Sedgwick and Brooksville, going several times each year for one week from Monday until Saturday and always on foot. He writes of cold so extreme that he is "frozen some" and comes near "to being frozen exceedingly," of rain and sleet which wets him to the skin and brings on "a distressing hoarseness and loss of voice," of plowing through snow to the tops of his boots and of being compelled "to walk on the tops of fences"; but he writes also of "precious seasons of spiritual comfort." "About the 1st of December, 1819, when I was returning from a short missionary tour, I was indulged with a most precious season of spiritual comfort. My soul, calm and serene, witnessed the sealing of the Spirit in a sweet pledge of the heavenly inheritance. Weighed in the balance against *this* happiness, what is all earthly pleasure? The web of a spider against a talent of gold!"

In 1819 he sums up his journeyings for the year just completed:

"Under the foregoing missionary appointment I have spent 59 days, travelled 278 miles on foot, made 257 family visits, preached 62 sermons, attended 2 conferences, celebrated the

Lord's Supper 3 times, received 1 member to the Congregational Church from the Baptists, and baptized 5 children. I have generally enjoyed myself in the service comfortably, and I have witnessed several times a peculiar manifestation of the Divine Presence. I have sound reason to hope that some of the children of God have been quickened, some strengthened, some refreshed, that some check has been opposed to the progress of immorality, and that impression has been made on the minds of the impenitent which will never be effaced. Generally when I have preached, the attention has been solemn. In private families I have generally been received with the appearance of cordiality, and I have been requested to present thanks to the Society for the notice taken of them to whom I have been sent." [1]

In addition to his missionary ventures Father Fisher fared often abroad to attend upon various church conferences and ministerial associations which were constantly springing up in the early years of the nineteenth century. The Hancock Ministers' Association of 1797 still continued active; and in 1825 the Hancock County Conference was organized, in 1827 being enlarged into the Hancock and Waldo Conference. In 1828 the Congregational ministers of these two counties formed a Bible Society as well, for the purpose of distributing Bibles and other religious publications through regions destitute of such literature. It is difficult to be certain just how often meetings of these various groups were held; but from the parson's Diaries two meetings yearly seems to have been the general rule for each, with more frequent meetings in the case of the more local ministers' associations.[2] From many entries it is clear that Father Fisher was rarely absent from such inspiring get-togethers.

He attended frequently also upon the ordination of brethren

[1] Payment for such missionary service was at this time made on the basis of $50 a month. Hospitality was apparently given without compensation.
[2] The Rev. Calvin Clark corroborates this assumption in his treatment of early Maine County Conferences in Vol. II, Chap. XII, of his *History of the Congregational Churches in Maine*.

to the pastorates of one or another of the frontier churches. He quite clearly loved these journeys, free from responsibility and filled with the assurance of "a blessed time of refreshment with fellow Christians" once he had reached his destination. Among his papers are copies of several "charges" given by him to new ministers, solemn adjurations and fervent counsel; or perhaps his duty was the ordination sermon, or the closing prayer, or the right hand of fellowship. He obviously found profound pleasure upon these occasions in conversation with his friends and colleagues on subjects dear to his heart, conversation for the most part denied him at home for the lack of a companion. He writes touchingly of these hours: "disputations among us concerning the alarming spread of Unitarianism in Boston"; "a pleasant talk on the mysteries of Divine Election"; "the sublime doctrines of our holy faith were reviewed before bed-time." His "old shoes repaired stoutly and set in order," he goes happily to Winthrop, to Bangor, to Brewer, to Foxcroft, to Brooks and Jackson, to Mariaville, to Machias, traversing all manner of roads in all manner of weathers. He sees a woodpecker hammering at a tree; he notes the flight of an eagle; he meets some Passamaquoddy Indians and endeavors to talk with them from what he knows of the language of those on the Penobscot; he comments on the sunrise. Once he walks ten miles before breakfast, "a peaceful morning, all but man free of wickedness and sin." In a letter written in September, 1818, he describes a journey to Robbinston, "130 miles distant on our Eastern boundary to attend the installation of the Rev. Daniel Lovejoy in the ministry there. I was the nearest minister in this region able to attend." And he concludes his paragraph with words which characterize well all his many pilgrimages "for the prize of the high calling of God in Christ Jesus":

"May God ever give me a heart to be ready for every good word and good work to which he may call me; to take up cheerfully every cross in my path of duty."

2

Under the terms of Mr. Fisher's settlement in Bluehill in 1796 he was to be allowed an absence of five weeks each year from his labors without sacrifice of salary. His purse, alas! proved too flat and too empty to permit him such a vacation as often as he would have wished; and yet over a period of thirty-five years, from 1798 to 1833, he managed to give himself eleven journeys to Boston, Dedham, and Cambridge. On only two of these, in 1809 and 1822, does he go alone. Apparently his generous nature chided him against savoring such unparalleled pleasure by himself, for on nine of his vacation tours he is accompanied always by Mrs. Fisher and often by one or more of the children.

He usually chose late September for his departure and was absent throughout October. He, with Mrs. Fisher and the fortunate children selected (in 1803, Jonathan, Sally, and Betsy, in 1807, Betsy only, in 1811, Josiah and Nancy, in 1823, Polly), always traveled by some Bluehill vessel laden for Boston. The voyage with favorable winds usually took two nights with a landing on the third day; the cost per passenger was $1.50 each way, the children carried free of charge. Until 1833, when he and Mrs. Fisher took their last trip together, and he bade "a long farewell to dear and familiar scenes," he does not mention a cook among the ship's hands, which usually numbered three or four, and food was evidently supplied by the few passengers for themselves. Once he mentions the vessel being infested with fleas, "most trying to our sleep," and on two passages he finds it necessary to reprimand both captain and crew "for unseemly language, even deplorable profanity." The family when able, for all were usually seasick, apparently braided hats or strung buttons for sale in Boston or in Dedham, as they sat in the cabin or on the deck. Nor did they go unencumbered by other commodities for possible payment of their expenses. Caraway seeds were always taken, garden seeds as well, bolts of cloth woven by Mrs. Fisher and the girls, picture frames, innumerable strings of buttons, and the parson's own literary works in substantial quantity. Once arrived in Boston, they traveled by coach to Dedham where they were "joyfully received" by Fishers and Averys.

The parson was given to writing poems on board, descriptive of the voyage and the reflections arising therefrom. In 1809, when he is traveling alone and when adverse winds and fog result in fourteen days of delay and anxiety, he writes a long poem of fifty stanzas entitled:

A voyage from Bluehill to Salem,

commencing on the evening of the 24th of September, 1809.

*Written to pass innocently the hours of leisure
on board the schooner Minerva.*

Some of these many verses are not without interest, regardless of their quality as poetry, perhaps, indeed, because of it!

As cool September abdicates his throne,
   And leaves October entering his domain,
I quit my home, my offspring, and my crown
   Of bliss connubial, for the watery plain.

The trading barque, with many a billet stored
   From Bluehill's forests, in the winding bay
Safe moored, receives me with my little hoard
   Of clothes and viands, for the destined way.

Her sides I mount, and over tier on tier
   Of high-piled lumber, bear my chest along;
Down the dark cabin now my course I steer,
   And take my seat amidst the clustered throng.

* * *

Eleven souls compose our little band,
   Each worth a world, but which of all prepared
For sudden death? Great God, in thy kind hand
   Take us in charge, and let our lives be spared.

All night we wait the coy, the lingering breeze,
  By many an insect in our berths beset;
Short, interrupted sleep we scarcely seize
  Till rising day resumes her golden seat.
* * *

We hail another day, our joys renew,
  By favoring winds are borne along our way;
Deer Isle we pass, the Thoroughfare beat through,
  Then lie becalmed in Isle au Haut's wide bay.
* * *

Rent now our sails, alas! Our sheets are strained,
  Our leeway rapid, rocks and shoals abound;
Our cordage in confusion, barque ill manned,
  And gloomy fogs envelope all around.

Dear, heavenly Master, issue thy command;
  Repair this wreck, with comely order grace
Our barque throughout, our sails anew expand,
  Till hope shall anchor in the port of peace.
* * *

Farewell, Mouse Island! Portland light, adieu!
  Come, welcome waves, all hail thou briny main!
Heaven grant us soon the risen lights in view
  To hail with pleasure, and to pass Cape Ann.

Now comes the sickening swell, the vessel rolls,
  The head and back are pained, the stomach heaves.
Yet often thus our heavenly friend controls
  Some latent ill, some long complaint relieves.

Hail! Salem harbor! in thy bosom fair
  This fifteenth night our vessel finds repose;
Thanks to our God, whose kind, indulgent care
  Has brought our voyage to a peaceful close.

Shipmates, adieu! We part, perhaps to meet
  On earth no more; be this our future prize:
Through faith in Christ, to find a calm retreat,
  Each in the Salem of the blissful skies!

These visits to the scenes of his college years, in spite of discomforts on the way, were quite clearly to the Rev. Mr. Fisher wells of refreshment in the Valley of Baca. He went daily from strength to strength during his month's sojourn. He writes of tea with the President of Harvard, of breakfast in the College Hall, of walks about the Yard and visits to his old rooms in Massachusetts and Hollis Halls, of a walk to Beverly where Abiel Abbot lived and of talks with him by his fire. He dines with Levi Hedge, now Professor at Harvard, with "members of the Academy of Arts and Sciences"; he looks upon "pleasant pictures which refresh my soul" in art galleries and museums; he takes tea with John S. Popkin, still unmarried in spite of Mr. Fisher's encouragement to that happy state by several letters through their years of friendship. In 1807 he "collects and packs" his wooden clock, made by him as an undergraduate, and transports it to Bluehill, where it still is. In 1809 he calls upon "her that was Miss Betsy Heath, now Mrs. Howe," with whom "under the entire sanction of Mrs. Fisher," he has kept up "a friendly correspondence" since his marriage. In 1809 also he indulges himself in "two lessons in Hebrew for the sake of receiving helpful answers" to questions evidently unanswerable by his solitary study in Bluehill. And during that same pleasant holiday, perhaps more pleasant because he was unaccompanied by wife and children, he revisits Holden for the first time in fourteen years. He goes there on foot "through the enjoyable weather," recalling as he walks his old days, and after his journey of some forty miles greets once more his Uncle Joseph Avery, still preaching there.

Vacationing again by himself in 1822 and without the restraining hand of Mrs. Fisher, who was apparently always "an economist," he buys himself "a new Beaver." One imagines that upon its purchase he may have recalled the thirtieth anniversary of a similar hat, bought at his Commencement. The price was the same, $8, seemingly a stupendous extravagance, like the first. One imagines, too, in the light of the early sad fate of this new hat, that he may have felt some uneasy qualms of conscience as he donned it to call again upon "her that was Miss Betsy

Heath" and to visit other old friends. For when he returned home and set out a week later on a journey to Brooksville, the Beaver proved an ironic investment. In crossing the Brooksville ferry in a small boat by himself, he lost an oar in the swift tide and "in a floundering attempt to retrieve the oar" (for, according to his own statement, he managed a boat very badly) he lost his hat as well. He recovered it at last, "filled with salt water and in a sorry condition." "I put it on my bald head," he writes, "with fear of the ague as the water ran in streams down my face. Lord, let me never again be proud of anything I possess! Lord, it is well!"

The holiday season of September, 1823, was an especially bountiful one, overflowing with pleasures to be long remembered and re-lived. Perhaps its abundance was, indeed, a compensation for its irritating preparation, which the parson relates with unusual fullness. In the first place, on the morning of September 15th, the day they were to sail, he could not get a stubborn key freed from the lock of his chest. He was finally obliged to take the lock off, which necessity caused delay. Polly added then to the general confusion by losing the key to her trunk, which she finally discovered "at Brother Hewins." Starting on foot down the long hill with Mrs. Fisher and Polly to embark at the village wharf, he was greatly discomfited by the wheelbarrow containing the luggage, which on the steep grade got out of his control and broke, dumping Fisher possessions in the road. Once repairs had been made, which necessitated a trip back to the parsonage, and they had all at last reached the pier, they found the vessel already hauled off and sailing down the bay. There was nothing for it but to await another due to leave on the 19th.

"But," writes the parson, "wonderful, indeed, are the inscrutable ways of Providence!" For, as the disappointed trio turned the wheelbarrow about for the hard trudge homewards, the head of the family heard suspicious voices proceeding from the cabin of another vessel tied up at the wharf. Investigating, he discovered "a circle of youth playing cards in abandon"! He at once delivered to them "a calm and serious lecture on their danger"; and, as he rejoined Mrs. Fisher and the doubtless tearful Polly, he was struck by the irrefutable knowledge that each of the morning mishaps had been ordained from the beginning by that God who knows and determines all and whose plans cannot be set aside by the devices of His children.

Once off on the 19th, however, the month's holiday proved sufficiently pleasurable to compensate for ten vacationless years to come. Mr. Fisher preached several sermons in Dedham, for which he was paid $8 each; he was invited to occupy the pulpits of the Old South and of Park Street churches. The compensation is not recorded; perhaps the honor was sufficient. He attended at Salem with great interest the ordination of six missionaries, one for Bombay, five for frontier posts. He dined with Mr. Hedge and Mr. Popkin and met in addition "9 or 10 others of my classmates"; he visited Dorchester, Milton, Dover, and Roxbury; and to his great satisfaction he managed to induce "not a few persons to give sums of money, considerable at times, small at others" to the support of the Bangor Theological Seminary. He took Polly "to see the treasures in the New England Museum and to watch the swan on Boston Common." And it was on this trip that Mrs. Fisher received the unexpected legacy with which they purchased their second-hand chaise. On their return they broke their journey in Portland to pay a visit to Betsy "in her new and agreeable home." Here to the parson's delight he was invited to preach at the Second Congregational Church, then ably shepherded by the "eloquent Rev. Edward Payson" and to converse with that learned gentleman on subjects close to the heart of each. When they reached home in early November, just before Sally's marriage to Mr. Joshua Wood, Parson Fisher must have felt fortified for whatever God had planned for him.

In 1833, at the age of sixty-four, he and Mrs. Fisher took their last journey together to those places and scenes which had given them both their lives and determined their destinies on this earth. He evidently felt quite certain (although his conjecture proved later to be wrong) that he should never again, "until a brighter day shall dawn," greet his friends of earlier years. "On September 20th," he writes, "I went up to the lantern of the State House, never expecting to ascend those 180 steps again. I took a view on all sides and bade adieu to that beautiful prospect forever! May a more glorious one in the coming world open upon my delighted eyes!" He records on this visit a most pleasant all-night stay with Levi Hedge and a trip with him to the cemetery at Auburn, "where we descended a spacious tomb designed for strangers and unknown wayfarers." He mentions also "tea and pleasurable conversation with Dr. J. S. Popkin," now Eliot Professor of Greek Literature at Harvard.

"In the College," he writes, "my curiosity was gratified and my astonishment excited by the view of the grand library, the ingenious philosophical apparatus, and the almost innumerable specimens of productions from the bowels of the earth in the great Cabinet of Minerals. In this Cabinet we see one part of the great world in miniature, and to the reflecting mind it speaks in powerfully expressive language the wisdom and goodness of God. In my classmates and former friends in Cambridge, I saw as in a glass my own decay and the ripening of my body for the tomb. Harvard, did it equal in correctness of doctrine and purity of morals its external advantages, would be, I suspect, the most noble seminary for literature on all the continent."

He relates his disappointment over his failure to interest several booksellers, Crocker and Brewster, Hillyard and Gray, and others not named, in the manuscript of his recently completed book, *Scripture Animals*. "I showed my mss. to several booksellers, but found no one willing to make an offer for it. The leading objection was that a work somewhat similar had been published in Boston the past summer. I then solicited the assistance of one or two wealthy friends to help me in publishing it; but the demands upon them for other charities were so numerous that they thought they could not help me. Though this is no little disappointment to me, I endeavor to be calm and resigned under it. God is disposing of me and of all that pertains to me in such a way as seems good in his sight."

At the close of this memorable holiday he bought another new hat. It cost $5.25.

3

The years 1811 and 1825 were immensely enlivened for Father Fisher by two hangings in which he took a prominent part in diverse ways: as spiritual adviser to the condemned, as interested onlooker, and as scribe. The first of these momentous occasions took place on October 31, 1811. Ebenezer Ball, a resident of Deer Isle, was on that day hanged in the shire town of Castine for the murder of John Downs, a deputy sheriff, who had gone to Deer Isle to arrest Ball on the charge of passing counterfeit money.

The parson's acquaintance with the criminal began in August preceding the execution. On the 5th of that month he went to Castine and visited Ball in his cell in order to give him spiritual consolation and counsel. He is brief in his Diary account of the interview. "I found Ball very stupid, resting partly upon the hope of a pardon and partly upon his belief in universal salvation." No pardon being granted, the carrying out of the sentence was placed for October 31st; and Father Fisher, rising early on that eventful morning and borrowing Mr. Robert Johnson's horse, rode the sixteen miles to Castine through the October woods in order to be early for this unprecedented experience in his life.

The account which he gives of it under the date of October 31st is the longest entry descriptive of any "temporal concern" throughout his earthly career:

At one o'clock P.M. I went to the prison where sheriff and ministers were assembled. By request of the High Sheriff I prayed with Ball. On first speaking to him before prayer I felt a thrill through every nerve. After prayer Rev. Mr. Blood addressed him. Mr. Bell also, a Methodist elder, addressed him.

Next, a procession was formed. A hollow square was made by

light infantry and artillery companies. First, within the square, rode the High Sheriff; next, on foot, two men in white; next, a negro with a horse and cart containing the prisoner's coffin, not painted except a grey stripe around the edge. After the coffin, a platoon of deputy sheriffs with drawn swords. After this, the prisoner with 4 or 5 ministers on each hand. Behind the prisoner, 2 sheriffs holding handkerchiefs tied into the rope with which he was pinioned. After this, the artillery company. In this order the procession went forward, preceded with drum and fife playing a death march.

The gallows was erected in the center of the old fort on Castine Hill. It was in shape of a sign-post attached to a high stage, which the prisoner, sheriff, and clergy ascended by a flight of stairs. After the sheriff had commanded order, Rev. Mr. Brown addressed the spectators from the stage in a pertinent speech and then addressed the prisoner. Rev. Mr. Blood then prayed. The High Sheriff then demanded of the prisoner whether he was ready for his fate. He wished to speak to Mr. Green of Deer Isle, to whom he gave a bill of sale of his body for burial. The Sheriff called for Green, who came up the stage. Ball whispered with him a few moments and then signified that he was ready.

He was then veiled with a white cap falling over his face, and conducted upon a fall-scaffold under the arm of the gallows, and his rope hitched to a hook over his head. The Sheriff gave him a handkerchief in his hand, bidding him to take his own time and, when he was perfectly ready, to throw it for a signal. He held it about one minute, then dropped it, when by machinery the support of the fall-scaffold was removed, which, dropping from under his feet, launched him suddenly into the World to come.

This criminal from first to last exhibited a striking example of hardness of heart. Through all his confinement, when visited by ministers, he studiously avoided conversing with them upon spiritual subjects, but appeared ready to converse upon the most trifling affairs and to indulge in vulgar, profane wit. From the prison to the gallows he walked with a firm step, was not seen to change his countenance or shed a tear. His look was, rather, fixed and sullen. On the way to the gallows and on the stage the Rev. Mr. Blood asked him whether he had any confession to make, or wished any particular petition to be offered for him at the throne of Grace, but he uniformly answered, No! When turned off, which was about 3 o'clock, he fell about 5 ft. before the rope took him up. The fall probably immediately dislocated his neck, as he expired with hardly a perceivable struggle. When the bell tolled at 12 the night before his execution, he is said to have expressed himself in a profane, blasphemous manner. As he lived, so he died—an example of uncommon hardness of heart.

When I visited him Aug. 5, 1811, he expressed himself in terms of great severity against one of the witnesses who had testified against him on his trial. I asked him if he did not expect that, if this witness had testified falsely against him, with design to take away his life, and should continue impenitent, he would not receive in a future state a full retribution for his conduct? He said he expected he would, but when admonished of the importance of being prepared himself for a solemn futurity and warned of the danger of falling into Hell, he said he believed there was no Hell but what was in this world. Of this, it seems, he has endeavored to persuade himself, and this persuasion has probably assisted him in braving it out against the fear of death.

In the evening I returned from Castine home.

The scenes of Ebenezer Ball's execution and the awful state of his immortal soul evidently remained in Father Fisher's imagination. In his Diary for November 7th, 8th, and 9th he writes that he is composing "some verses on the hanging of Ball"; on November 15th he says he is preparing "a box-wood plate" to accompany them. On November 29th, after attending an ordination at Bangor, he tarries at Buckstown on his way home and contracts with a Mr. A. H. Holland there to print his verses and his engraving in the form of a broadside sheet. Mr. Holland agrees to print 300, of which number the parson is to have 100 for private sale. In case the demand calls for a second printing, the author is to receive 1 copy for every 10 over the original 300.

On December 16th the broadsides are ready. In appearance the single sheet measured 18 x 11 inches. It was bordered in black, and contained an inside border, also in black and in the design of a hangman's rope, which surrounded the poem. The wood-cut at the top of the sheet showed Ball suspended from the gallows above a large gathering of people. The lines in couplet form were 140 in number.

The climactic moment, which appropriately occurs in the middle of the poem, is described thus:

> The prayer is closed. The prisoner now has leave
> Warning to give or counsel to receive,
> A few short moments. With a friend he speaks;
> His eyes are shrouded, in his hand he takes
> A 'kerchief signal; on the scaffold led,
> The fatal cord is fastened on his head.
> —Awful suspense!—The appointed signal given,
> The scaffold drops—Behold—twixt earth and heaven
> He hangs, expiring! Chill'd is every vein
> Thro' the vast crowd; a sudden thrill of pain
> Darts thro' each nerve; a sudden, deep surprize
> Moves the whole host, and mingled moans arise.

Mr. Fisher, returning from Castine via Bucksport on the day of publication, collects his allotment of the broadsides and sets out for home. His walk is a long one, since he stops at every house to read his verses and to sell them if possible. He disposes of 34 on the way home, in quantities, at .05 each, singly at either .06 or .07, the price dependent apparently upon either the interest or the generosity of the purchaser.

Father Fisher did well on his broadside. According to his Diary, he is selling the sheets constantly throughout the winter. He carries them to "the head of the bay" on all errands there, and he sells several at two weddings in February; in fact, he never attends a conference or a ministerial association, or travels to a neighboring village for a "pulpit exchange," or even goes on his pastoral calls without a supply of them in some bag or pocket. He sells them at the wholesale price of .05 each to Jonathan, Sally, Nancy, and Betsy, who, true to parental nurture and practice, carry them to school for sale and pocket the profit for themselves. So well, indeed, did both Mr. Holland and Mr. Fisher do for themselves with their timely and unusual venture that a second edition of 200 copies of *Lines on the Death of* *Ebenezer Ball* was issued on March 18, 1812.

Encouraged by this new source of income, Father Fisher anticipated Time and Chance in the second hanging which he attended. The condemned in this case was Seth Elliot, who, in December, 1824, was tried in Castine for the murder of his child "while he was in a fit of intoxication." Confidently expecting a sentence of death for Elliot and doubtless incited to action by his professed Universalism, Mr. Fisher, a fortnight before the sentence was pronounced, composed some verses in the form of a soliloquy, supposedly uttered by Elliot on the gallows, and accompanied it by yet another wood-cut engraving, this time of Elliot on the scaffold in the place of Ball. These compositions he sent on December 21st to "Mr. Daniel Pike of Bangor," who straightway arranged for the printing of 250 sheets by E. Brewster, Printer, in that town. Probably somewhat to the author's embarrassment, Elliot, condemned to die on the gallows on December 30th, was reprieved until February 3rd. The broadsides already printed, dated, and ready for the earlier date, the parson spends "most of the day" on January 12th emending each of the 250 by inserting the words, "By reprieve, Feb. 3, 1825." In the interim between December 30th and the date of execution, he visits Elliot twice in his cell for prayer and spiritual counsel, but finds him "little disposed to say anything."

On the day of execution Father Fisher again starts early for Castine, laden with his broadsides for sale on the fatal spot. Mingling among "the great concourse gathered around the gallows," he "disposed of 18 doz. copies," the perspicacity of his preparedness for the event yielding him a rich reward. He does not name the cost of the broadside, but, with the price of *Lines on the Death of Ebenezer Ball* in mind, together with the heightened value lent by immediacy, it was probably not less than .08 or .10 a sheet. Upon his return home the next day some $20 at least must have been secure in his pocket. Nor does he anywhere mention further sales or a new edition.

The Seth Elliot broadside is in size identical with the Ebenezer Ball, and the engraving similar. It is printed on a similar sheet, bordered with a black line. The title reads:

Elliot's Soliloquy:
Lines on the Death of Seth Elliot,
Executed at Castine
for the
Murder of One of His Children;
December 30, 1824.

Although the parson has inserted, after the date, in his own handwriting, "By reprieve, Feb. 3, 1825," he does not, however, identify himself on the sheet as the author, an omission unusual with him, for on all other of his productions he is careful to place his name, often accompanied by the letters, A.M., in which he obviously took great pride.

The soliloquy in couplets expresses Elliot's late understanding of the pernicious heresy of Universalism, which has contributed to his crime with its false doctrine of salvation after death even for the most depraved sinners. It also pleads with his survivors to shun "the alluring cup, the inebriating bowl," to banish their unchaste and loose desires, and to observe the Sabbath. Two stanzas will suffice for its quite adequate characterization:

I have been honour'd, and a worthy rank
Held with my neighbours, till my spirit drank
Deep draughts and frequent of that ancient lie,
By Satan forg'd, "Ye shall not surely die."
Pleased with the doctrine, to my lasting shame,
I soon intemperate and unclean became;
To lust and passion gave the loosen'd rein,
Till home was hated, and my peace was slain.

That ancient lie, the universal scheme,
Still lulls ten thousands in a fatal dream,
Persuades its votaries they may live at ease,
Indulge in sin, their fleshly nature please,
Slight God and duty, Christ and truth deny,

And then at death to heaven and glory fly.
Thus I could wish it were, and did;—but no,
God's holy word does not allow it so;
Heaven's declarations make it sure and plain,
To die in sin leads down to endless pain;
The fire of wrath, which gives the sting to sin,
Is never quench'd; the galling worm within,
Corroding conscience, gives perpetual wounds,
While the law's curse, *death, death,* forever sounds.

It is conceivable, since Father Fisher makes no further reference to Elliot in Diaries or letters and says nothing about the few remaining copies of his broadside, that he may have uneasily questioned those conflicting emotions which resulted in his shrewd seizure upon time and occasion. He does not, however, in this matter share with us any possible qualms of conscience or any spiritual diagnosis. Perhaps, indeed, with countless others before and since his day, he embraced the always sinister conclusion that the end justifies the means. Or perhaps he even felt secure in the thought that his inspiration to advanced composition, like all other inspirations of the human mind, had been foreordained by God since the beginning of Creation!

4

From 1815 to 1835, when Parson Fisher stopped keeping his daily Diary, his entries concerning "our infant theological Seminary" are full and fervent; and practically all his letters between those years, regardless of their recipients, show unmistakably his consuming interest in that "school of the prophets." It is clear that none of his journeyings held greater excitement or more vaulting dreams than those which he made at least twice a year and almost always on foot over the steep hills north to Bucksport and along the Penobscot to the town of Bangor, "a pleasant walk" of thirty-five miles, to attend the meetings of its Board of Trustees, to examine its candidates for the ministry, or "to witness its closing exercises at which our young men deported themselves with dignity and honor." This school, known in its beginnings as the Maine Charity School, was especially dear to his heart, and his efforts in its behalf knew no lessening for twenty years and more. To it he gave money which he could ill afford, and for its support and continuation he begged unashamedly from literally everybody he knew, or did not know, from Bluehill to Boston. No one, indeed, with a potential penny was safe from him on land or sea! To him the Seminary was a "spring in our wilderness," its waters, streams of refreshment and cultivation to a dry and thirsty land.

The early years of the nineteenth century brought home to the Congregational ministers of New England, and especially to those in the District of Maine, problems and anxieties concerning the supply of pastors needed in the Province, and also, with their ideals for an educated clergy, equally difficult problems concerning the higher education of young men destined for that profession. The Baptists, permanently established in the Province as early as 1768, were constantly gaining converts; other denominations, particularly the Methodists, were increasingly active; and neither of these sects shared the convictions of the so-called "Established Clergy" as to the necessity for "a literary education" which should precede theological training. Indeed, even the theological training required by them was often slight and sometimes quite negligible. Out of this anxiety there was formed in Portland on July 27, 1811, an association known as the Society for Theological Education, one of the earliest societies of its kind in the United States. Incorporated the following year, on February 27, 1812, under the laws of Massachusetts, its object was "to procure for pious young men a collegiate education in order that they may be prepared for the Gospel ministry." Among its founders were Fathers John Sawyer of Bangor and Jotham Sewall of Chesterville, already known to Parson Fisher as fellow itinerants in the eastern wilderness of the District of Maine.

It was early recognized by the Society that a "literary and theological institution of learning" was essential to its aims and ideals; and a committee of four men, among whom was the Rev.

Mighill Blood of Bucksport, was at once appointed to establish the proposed seminary as soon as possible. By February, 1814, a charter for such a school was granted by the Massachusetts Legislature, to be known as the Maine Charity School "for the purpose of promoting religion and morality and for the education of youth in such languages and in such of the Liberal Arts and Sciences as the Trustees from time to time shall judge most useful." On May 5, 1814, Jonathan Fisher was made a member of the Board of Trustees, who numbered, in all, thirteen men.

The Maine Charity School opened in October, 1816, with six students, at Hampden, near Bangor, an arrangement having been made with the Academy there to unite the two institutions for a period of three years. The first preceptor was Mr. Jehudi Ashmun, a brilliant young graduate of the University of Vermont in that year. Ashmun was not himself a theologian, but acted as head of the combined schools, and in the following year was named also Professor of Classical Literature. In the same year the Rev. Abijah Wines, with whom Jonathan Fisher had traveled in Washington County in 1801, was made Professor of Theology. Mr. Ashmun and Mr. Wines, together with a "Tutor," comprised the first faculty.

The Maine Charity School was modeled "after the Dissenting Colleges in England." Like them it had a two years' Classical Course, which included the study of Virgil, Tacitus, the Orations of Cicero, and the Greek Testament, together with that of "Geography, Mathematics, Natural Philosophy, Rhetoric, Logic, and English Composition." The young men upon entrance, in addition to possessing "good talents and real piety," were required to possess also "a good knowledge of English, Latin and Greek grammar, three books of Virgil, and one of the Evangelists in Greek." After two years of "literary studies" they entered upon their training in theology.

It was early seen that, upon the expiration of these two years, some other provision than that of the Academy at Hampden was advisable, if not necessary; and in 1819 the school was moved to Bangor and began to be known as the Bangor Theological Seminary instead of the Maine Charity School. Several towns, among which were Castine, Brewer, and Bucksport, had competed for the residence of the seminary within their borders, all raising funds for that hope and purpose. Bangor, however, offering more (Mr. Fisher quotes the sum in a Diary entry as $8916) and the gift of a parcel of land there having been offered by Mr. Isaac Davenport of Milton, Mass., the seminary in its new location above the wide Penobscot began its more autonomous existence in the autumn of 1819.[1]

Parson Fisher's Diaries are filled with his zeal and enthusiasm for the new seminary. He records carefully the details of Board Meetings, most of which have for their chief concern the raising of funds. At one meeting in 1817 he gives $20; in 1818, he can spare but $2; in 1820 he proudly carries $60 collected from his parish; in 1822 the Female Cent Society sends by him $3.50 and his church, $17.11; in 1823 he is able to take with him $24.23, the amount of one morning's contribution. And in March, 1824, he proudly announces that he has obtained within the borders of his parish from "297 subscribers the sum of $542.25 for our Infant Seminary." This generous figure, he goes on to say, makes Bluehill the leader of all those communities in eastern Maine which in 1824 contributed together $1100 to Father Jotham Sewall, acting as "collecting agent."

This "drive" for funds for the Bangor Seminary in 1824 seems to have been the result of an impassioned letter written by Parson Fisher to the Rev. Mighill Blood of Bucksport in November, 1823. In it he gives a carefully worked out plan for the encouraging of subscriptions for "shares in the seminary" at $25 each. "In case the Institution *must go down*," he writes, "I shall mourn over it with deep and undissembled sorrow. I pledge myself for

[1] I am indebted for the early history of this Maine Seminary to the Rev. Calvin Montague Clark in his *History of Bangor Theological Seminary*. Pilgrim Press, Boston, New York, and Chicago, 1916. The Fisher Diaries also supply many of the same details.

four shares." His Diary records that his $100 was paid over a period of four years.

He is constantly collecting clothing as well as money for "our pious and needy youths." In March, 1820, he carries "$25 worth of clothing collected for my Charity School" when he sets forth for a meeting of the Board of Trustees. In 1828 he sends, from "Ladies in Bluehill, 1 Feather bed, 1 straw sack, 1 Bedstead and cord, 4 Sheets, 4 Pillow Cases, 4 Blankets, 1 Quilt, 1 Coverlid, 1 fire set, 4 chairs, 1 looking glass, and 2 napkins." In his letters to neighboring clergymen he begs that they "will stir up the hands and hearts of the willing females in their parishes for stockings, shirts, drawers, vests, blankets, handkerchiefs, cravats." Each year, he says, costs each student $75, exclusive of books and clothing. "Whatever female hands can frame or whatever can be found of discarded clothing is a gift to God's work."

In letters to his mother and to other members of his family he explains in detail his beloved institution and his hope for its benevolent influence in Maine. On September 14, 1818, he writes:

The Maine Charity School is an institution for the education of young men of piety for the ministry, and for schoolmasters, upon the plan of the Dissenters' Academies in England. It has now 19 students under its patronage. The object is to furnish them with as good an education as may be obtained by four years' close application. While I was recently present there, there was an examination of the students and an Exhibition which I think would not have dishonored a college. The little vine we have here planted is yet in its infancy, and we cannot expect its fruits will be like the fruits of those come to mature age. But with the blessing of God, and the patronage of friends able to advance its funds, we hope it will grow to much usefulness. I am strongly averse to an unlearned ministry; but if in this District we wait to be supplied from other institutions, I am fully persuaded that the ground will be preoccupied by Sectarians, many of whom will be not only unlearned, but *very* unlearned. Some of these have already set up such a cry against a college education that some societies would hardly receive a minister educated at a College. With respect to such places and persons we must be wise as serpents as well as harmless as doves.

I think our institution will raise the tone of the education in the District of Maine. While we shall be indulged with such instructors as Mr. Ashmun, in particular, who is now one of our professors, what *can* be done by the students in learning, I think *will* be done. Mr. Ashmun is both correct and indefatigable.

In July, 1823, indignant over "certain remarks" of Dr. Leonard Woods of the Andover Theological Seminary concerning that of Bangor, he writes at some length in a letter to a niece his opinions on the products of the two institutions:

Respecting the remarks of my Friend, Dr. Woods, on the Bangor Seminary, I would observe that I think his idea of it is much too low. This may result in part from a strong partiality for the Institution, where he is now placed, and in part from the want of a more full acquaintance with our infant Seminary. I have been acquainted with several from the Andover Institution, who have taught in our Academy in Bluehill, who have come well recommended by Dr. Woods and have appeared worthy of it. I am acquainted with several educated at Bangor and have listened to the preaching of those from each Seminary. I have noticed the reception of both by hearers of various classes. I feel prepared to say that, as practical preachers of the Gospel, suited to the condition of new settlements, those from Bangor do not fall far in the rear of those from Andover. I find that after 8 or 10 years of study and sedentary habits, some young men of deep literary knowledge are greatly disqualified for the privations, sacrifices, and hardships which ministers in many of the settlements in our vicinity are compelled to sustain.

There is a polish of style in the discourses of students from Andover of which ours cannot boast, but upon very many hearers in this region it is more than lost; it is not understood. I do not mean by all this to derogate from the Institution at Andover; it is no doubt of vast importance to our land. It furnishes ministers adapted to the more refined societies, ministers who may skilfully wield the sword of the Spirit against the Unitarians of the Harvard School and other learned Heretics. But on most in this region I find by observation that this higher class of arguments has very little effect; they do not feel their

weight because they do not understand them. I myself sometimes use arguments with some people that I am almost ashamed
of, simply because they appear to have greater influences than
arguments that are, in fact, more solid.

Pioneers may be as necessary to an army in some situations as
the more regular troops which follow them. For the sake of
Christ and his kingdom, I hope that we in this region shall never
disdain the name and the office of Pioneers.

Father Fisher's untiring labor for the "infant Seminary" undoubtedly helped immeasurably to insure its life. He lived to
see it well on its feet, its health and strength assured. That his
faith in it, his constant prayers and work for it, were not forgotten is made evident in the closing words of an address given
in 1870, on the occasion of the fiftieth anniversary of its first
graduating class, by Dr. Enoch Pond, who himself gave fifty
years of his life as a member of its faculty and administration.

"I cannot close . . . without recording our obligations to certain individuals, no longer with us, who loved the Seminary
from the first and who never ceased to pray and to labor for it so
long as they lived. Among these were Fathers Sewall, Sawyer, and
Fisher, whose portraits adorn our chapel and whose memory is
dear to all our hearts."

VII

THE PARSON IN HIS STUDY

SCRIPTURE ANIMALS,

OR

NATURAL HISTORY

OF THE LIVING CREATURES NAMED IN THE BIBLE,

WRITTEN ESPECIALLY FOR YOUTH.

ILLUSTRATED WITH CUTS.

BY JONATHAN FISHER, A. M.

He giveth to the beast his food, and to the young ravens which cry.
Psalm 147: 9.

PORTLAND
PUBLISHED BY WILLIAM HYDE.
1834.

Title Page of *Scripture Animals* with Fisher's Profile

ELCFANT. ELEPHANT.

Fisher Wood Engravings for *Scripture Animals*

IN 1818 Parson Fisher, writing to his mother, proudly says that he has "completed the wainscoting" of his study and that he finds this room of his own "a great solace for retirement to pursue those thoughts and perusings which have ever been my delight." His fireplace, he says, "draws excellently," and by the light of his blazing logs he is able "without a candle" to read his Hebrew every winter morning. He describes the study as a "pleasing room, even though small." It faced the north and west. From its north window he could see beyond trees and fields the green, wooded height of Blue Hill, which he often climbed "to enjoy the pleasant prospect from its summit"; from its west window he looked beyond his own fields and pastures toward "Brother Hewins' " house. His study-table made by him could be easily converted into a work-bench with niches, cut beneath its cover, for small tools; and it was there rather than in his "shop" that he engraved his many woodcuts. Although he obviously possessed a study in his first house, built in 1796, since he often refers to it, he gives no description of it or any hint as to its location.

Jonathan Fisher's study over a period of many years witnessed all manner of intellectual and of manual pursuits. Constant references in the Diaries to "dusting my study and setting my books and papers in order" prove that it was kept in seemly tidiness and apparently by his own hands. Fridays and Saturdays saw him shut within it at work on his two Sabbath discourses. Only twice in the Diaries does he refer to secular pursuits on those days, and on each daring occasion they resulted in dire consequences. In one entry in February, 1810, he ruefully chronicles the breaking of his new pen-knife. This ruin of a cherished possession he ascribes to the Providence of God, who is rightly warning him against the intrusion of the world and especially "against hurrying over my secret prayer in a careless manner." "I received this loss of my pen-knife as a gentle hint of my worldly indulgence." In August, 1833, his hogs break from their sty and start for the fields. It takes him an hour to catch them! "This embarrassment," he writes, "was doubtless sent from God because in the forenoon I had taken more time for worldly affairs than necessary."

But on other days, during the hours unclaimed by manual labor, he was free for those "perusings" and researches always dear to his heart; and from both Diaries and letters it is clear that many evenings, also, if they were fortunately unencumbered by callers, were spent at his study-table or in his chair by the fire. There he heard his various boys construe their Tully, Virgil, and Homer; there he wrote not only his sermons, but his church records, his Family Register of Bluehill, his letters of admonition and excommunication, and the hundreds of personal letters for which he somehow found time; there he prepared the beautiful pages of his Hebrew lexicon; and there he composed his many and various literary works and engraved their accompanying illustrations. He must have worked with amazing rapidity. In March, 1823, he writes that in two years, during his leisure time, he has transcribed "about 15,000 lines of verse and 1000 of prose composed since 1787"; in February, 1824, "in a severe rainstorm," he has in one day sketched "the wolf, scorpion, spider, boar, sow, whale, cachelot, and codfish"; and in February, 1829, he writes in one day "248 lines of my poem on the Millenium." Probably the light from his two study windows was not sufficient for his paintings, which were doubtless done elsewhere in the house; probably, too, his experiments, in 1820 "with pea-coal, pine, and birchbark to obtain gas light for family use," and in 1826 "with sound over wires," were performed within the more spacious boundaries of his "shop." But his study was to him his place of

refuge from the confusion of a large household; and the very
fact that he cared for it himself speaks eloquently of its place
in his affections.

"I set in order my study," he writes upon his return home from
a journey. "I dusted my shelves, rearranged my books, and
bound up my papers. I then swept my hearth and laid my fire.
All is now fresh and ready for my pleasure."

2

Much of the parson's pleasure within his study came from
those hours somehow salvaged for the enjoyment of his books. It
is impossible to ascertain exactly the size of his library. In a small
notebook dated 1830 he lists carefully the books which he has
given to his children. In all, these amount to 156 and were apparently given as wedding presents. Practically all are of a distinctly
religious nature, volumes of sermons or of tracts, or missionary
magazines. Josiah and Willard receive his college texts on
astronomy, arithmetic, and navigation, and Dolly in her portion
gets Parnell's Poems, *The Rambler,* Vol. I., and *The Vicar of
Wakefield.* These lists, together with the remaining books of his
collection, characterize the library itself and suggest that it
probably numbered at least 300 volumes, not an inconsiderable
store for a poor minister in a small village. There is no record
of the actual purchase of books by him during his pastorate;
clearly his budget did not permit such exciting indulgence;
but he writes occasionally of gifts made to him. On one of his
vacation trips to Cambridge his college friend, J. S. Popkin,
presents him with a copy of the Greek Septuagint; on another,
Levi Hedge kindly gives him "several books," which he does not
identify; and in 1822 the Rev. Mighill Blood of Bucksport makes
him the momentous gift of the New Testament in the Malay
language.

In his reading, the enthusiasms of his college days remain
warm and bright within him. He writes often of reading "the
divine lines of *Paradise Lost,*" once "while a winter gale sends

the icy sleet against my window." The poems of Parnell and of Pomfret give him occasional pleasure. Thomson's *Seasons* are a perennial delight; again and again he praises them; and Young's *Night Thoughts* are recorded almost as often. "Not being able to sleep, I arose and read Young on Death." Occasionally he re-reads his Virgil, Cicero, and Homer, perhaps in preparation for his tutoring. Isaac Watts is extolled often; Mrs. Hannah More in both prose and verse is clearly admired; and Cowper is sometimes read and enjoyed.

He makes no mention whatever of the English Romantic poets. Wordsworth and Coleridge were apparently unknown to him. Perhaps their works had not reached the confines of Blue-hill; more probably he was inclined to look askance on the purely literary writings of his own day, unestablished as they were by time. Nor does he make a single reference to those American authors who throughout his life were so widely read. Shakespeare, so enjoyed at Harvard, is not once alluded to, although twice he states that he is reading the tragedies of Corneille.

Most of his reading was along religious and theological lines. He writes of Paley's *Evidences,* Doddridge's *Sermons,* Edwards on *Original Sin,* Bunyan's *Pilgrim's Progress* and the *Holy War,* the last of which he calls "very good." In 1815 he is reading Baxter's *Saints' Everlasting Rest;* in 1821, the *Confessions* of St. Augustine; in 1823, Thomas à Kempis. His copy of Cotton Mather, its title unidentified, fits into his pocket and is carried with him on at least one journey. He was an avid reader and supporter of several missionary magazines of his day, especially of those published in New England, although he lists also the *New York Missionary Magazine.* Throughout his ministry he acted as agent for these periodicals and eagerly collected subscriptions for them in his parish. In 1837 a letter from Mr. Asa Cummings, editor of *The Christian Mirror,* expresses himself as "exceedingly grateful" for Mr. Fisher's labor and lists the names of eighteen subscribers in Bluehill with the receipt of $36 in payment. These publications were carefully bound in leather by the parson's skilful hands, and many of them remain today among the books left by him.

One author demands especial mention because of the numberless references made to him over a period of fifty years. This is the French thinker and theologian, Pascal. From Jonathan Fisher's days at Harvard when, as a divinity student, he began the study of French, Pascal remained until his death his almost daily companion. Morning after morning he translates Pascal, whose name must, indeed, have become a Fisher household word, perhaps even one of amusement among the children. Else why did Nancy Fisher Kittredge, who from her letters was evidently a young woman possessed of a charming and subtle humor, write her father in 1838 that she and Hosea have decided to name their second son *Pascal* Kittredge?

3

From that day, when at six years old Jonathan Fisher saw some Greek characters in a book of his mother's and was "excited by their mystery," to the end of his life, his interest in the study of languages never left him. In all the Diaries there are few entries which do not contain some reference to this study. If he is not translating Pascal, he is reading the Old Testament in the original Hebrew; if he is not amusing himself with "a few words of the Penobscot Indian language," he is bending over Arabic or Malay. Or perhaps he is rendering "the Greek of the Septuagint or of the Evangelists into Latin for an exercise."

The Rev. Swan L. Pomroy, who was for thirty years pastor of the Bangor Congregational Church and who visited the Bluehill parsonage about the year 1825, writes in 1855 to the Rev. William Sprague of Albany of the parson's linguistic adventures:

"He had a decided taste for philological studies and, considering his remote frontier residence with but few books within his reach, he made no small attainments. With the original languages of the Bible he was quite familiar and was accustomed to read from Hebrew and Greek in his family devotions. Sometimes also he read from the Latin and the French. When I was at his house nearly thirty years ago, he was poring over an Arabic New Testament without either lexicon or grammar. The most marvelous achievement of his life was a Hebrew Lexicon, which he found time to make, written with great care and labor, and arranged, in the main, on correct philosophical principles. It was nearly completed when I saw it, and, had it been published, would have been superior to any Hebrew-English Lexicon then in use. But just as it was finished, the learned work of Gesenius, translated by Gibbs, made its appearance, and his manuscript, the work of many years, was laid aside. It is still in being and ought to be deposited in the archives of some public institution as a monument to his untiring industry."

In a notebook, transcribed by the parson in 1825 and 1826 and largely comprised of drawings and descriptions of experiments in geometry, physics, and astronomy, some of them evidently dating from his college days, the concluding pages are given to carefully copied alphabets of Arabic and Malay and to a long list of proper names, mostly Biblical, in Malay.[1] There are also some pages devoted to Hebrew consonant and vowel sounds. How much progress he managed to make by himself in Arabic and Malay, he does not say, although he often writes of studying the New Testament in both. He evidently did not begin their study until around 1822, whereas his reading of Hebrew is recorded regularly from 1798 on. He states in several Diary entries and in letters also that, after he has set the family table at 5 A.M. for breakfast, he repairs to his study for work on that language, and he quite apparently began early in his ministry to read the entire Old Testament in it. He writes his mother that he finds the historical books very easy although the prophets and poets cause him difficulty. In 1815 he translates Habbakuk into English verse; in 1821 he is deep in Isaiah 53 and making a metrical transla-

---

[1] Linguists are probably aware of the fact, heretofore unknown by me, that since the 14th century the Malay language has employed the Arabic alphabet, with the addition of some five letters of its own.

tion of it also; in 1822 he is rendering the book of Jonah into the same form, and in 1826, that of the prophet Zephaniah.

In the Diaries he has nothing to say of the initial plans for his Hebrew lexicon, which, from several of his letters, he evidently considered the most important scholarly labor of his life. The first reference to it occurs in January, 1819, when he writes that he is "selecting Hebrew names for my lexicon." Work on it, however, proceeds apace from that date until 1824. There are few days when he is not choosing words for it or framing definitions. In 1821 he writes his mother that he has completed 70 pages of it and has been very busy upon it, "together with other studies and labors." "Whoever needs be idle," he concludes, "that has a disposition to labor?" In the same year he writes the Rev. Rufus Bailey of Norwich, Vt. (whose "obscure chirography," he says in passing, makes him think of Count Rumford's remark, "Slow mastication promotes nutriment."): "I have at length matured my plan and compiled and transcribed 72 pages towards my contemplated Hebrew Lexicon. This must be to me, if I live, the work of my leisure for 15 or 20 years to come. I have but little expectation of seeing it finished, but the work leads to that critical examination of the Scriptures which rewards me in great measure as I go along."

References to the lexicon cease abruptly after 1824. It was in that year that J. W. Gibbs published from Andover, Mass., his English translation of the Hebrew-German Lexicon of the great German scholar, Heinrich Gesenius. Parson Fisher makes no allusion in the Diary or in his letters to the Gibbs translation. It was characteristic of him that he rarely described his disappointments. But that he was acquainted early with the work of his rival is shown not only by his sudden surrender of his own labor, but also by a comment placed upon a beautiful copy of the first 19 pages of his lexicon which he made six years before his death. On the heavy paper cover of this copy he has written:

> A Fourth and corrected copy of the Commencement of a Hebrew Lexicon, laid by because Superceded by Gibbs's Translation.
>
> Jonathan Fisher
> Dec. 18, 1841

The Rev. Mr. Pomroy was more enthusiastic than accurate in his description of the parson's lexicon. Although his work upon it was considerable, and surely remarkable in view of the relatively few hours which he could devote to it, it was not by any means "finished" as Mr. Pomroy states in his letter to Mr. Sprague. The pages of it, now in Bluehill, number at most but 82, and, as nearly as can be ascertained from remaining parts of the four copies made, it did not, in its words and definitions, extend far beyond the beginning letters of the Hebrew alphabet.

4

When Levi Hedge in 1791 in a letter to his classmate, Jonathan Fisher, remarked that "Fisher's Muse is always with him," he was a prophet as well as a critic. For the parson's Muse continued during all his days to urge him on from creation to creation. It is, indeed, almost impossible to picture the Rev. Mr. Fisher without an "eagle's quill" or a pencil in his hand during the hours spent in his study. His books are lavishly annotated with notes and comments in pencil or in ink; and the extraordinary number of literary works of one sort or another which he left behind him would leave the busiest person today astounded, on the one hand, and, on the other, apologetic for his own relatively idle existence.

Jonathan Fisher's literary ventures were of every conceivable nature as his many notebooks and manuscripts and his published works bear witness. First of all, he quite evidently adored the copying or the composing of stray bits of extraneous information, picked up and garnered from every source under the sun or from no ascertainable source at all. Several hand-bound manuscript volumes are packed with these heterogeneous scraps, all inscribed in his shorthand code; and such odds and ends are also found in hundreds on the blank pages of his sermon booklets. He copies, or composes, countless recipes: for keeping eggs "fresh for 2 years in strong lime water," for pastry, plum pudding, yeast, "cold and hot soap," spruce beer, a dozen different "conserves," "a pleasant cordial made of brown sugar, cinnamon, and rum," currant wine, apple cider, Indian pudding, and for a barley and pea soup "to serve 1200 persons at once," followed by a recipe for the same soup to serve a solitary diner. His remedies are set down by the score: for diarrhoea, "hoopingcough," lockjaw, spasms, bleeding cuts, measles, bruises, insect bites, itch, heartburn, toothache, and sore breasts following childbirth. He gives more household hints than all the present women's magazines, combined in one issue: for mending china, making liquid shoe-blacking, weaving, the care of fur, preserving house-plants, cleaning paint, making glue and ink, dyeing cloth, coloring buttons, killing rats and mice, keeping hands free from chapping, and knitting a "neck handkerchief" in blue and white stripes. On dozens of pages he is lavish with "reminders" for farmers: on pruning apple trees, draining swamps, using "privy manure," sowing wheat, drying winter peas, dressing a harness, fattening hogs, spreading salt on ploughed land, and conquering cut-worms. And all these named, but a small fraction of such output!

He copies "extracts and anecdotes," "brief thoughts and meditations," these in their original languages rather than in his shorthand: from Plato, Aristotle, Homer, Virgil, Ovid, Horace, Quintilian, Tertullian, Montaigne, Pascal, Milton, Addison, Young, John Locke, *and* Jonathan Fisher. He likes to write mottoes:

> *Where hearts agree, no strife can be.*

> *This ring is round and hath no end,*
> *So is my love to thee, my friend.*

> *'Tis love alone, makes two but one.*

A book of no inconsiderable size could be filled with his epitaphs, which he obviously loved to compose. Some of these were written to order, engraved on tombstones, and, we surmise, paid for; others were written for his own satisfaction:

> Full many a year the loom he ply'd,
> Respected lived, lamented dy'd.
> Of him a worthy, numerous train
> Surviv'd his memory to sustain.
>
> From a high scaffold in his barn he fell,
> A speedy exit to his soul was given.
> Calm resignation bids us say, 'tis well,
> And faith pursues the parting saint to heaven.
>
> Fanny, thou lovely saint!
>   Where dwells thy spirit now?
> Above the regions of complaint,
>   And far beyond all sin and woe.

One notebook deals largely with historical accounts. He sketches the reigns of the Roman emperors from Domitian with anecdotes relating to them; he describes the March of the 10,000 Greeks. He gives many brief paragraphs on the Church Fathers, Origen, Ambrose, Chrysostom, Augustine; he sketches early heresies. He describes with evident admiration the training of soldiers in Bavaria with some historical events which have resulted in such military thoroughness and strength. He records in both prose and verse the various incidents in the history of the Jews from the Creation to the Captivity with chronology carefully set down.

According to the Rev. Mr. Pomroy, the parson "was not a born poet, and never could have made one, although this was the point on which, if in anything, he prided himself." No diagnosis could be more accurate. Parson Fisher dearly loved "to tune his lyre"; and there is no indication that he ever realized how tuneless it remained. It is impossible to say exactly how many manuscript volumes of verses he left behind him, copied in his clear and beautiful hand and bound in leather or in cloth as "momentoes" for his children; but from those preserved and those recorded in the Diaries there must have been no less than twenty and probably more. To these he gives titles: *Scraps, Written by Jonathan Fisher: Transcribed for the Amusement of His Surviving Relatives; The Poetic Repository in Five Parts; The Cottage Tablet; The Believer's Column.* The subjects of these hundreds of poems range from those distinctly religious, which comprise the great majority, to those on nature, a winter storm, the lily of the vale, the dove, the snowdrop, the return of rain after drought; from pious adjurations on sobriety in youth, honoring parents, and the training of children, to eloquent patriotic outbursts on the glory of George Washington, the beauties of America, and the evils which threaten the nation from its treatment of the Indian and its injustice to the slave. Interspersed among the poems are occasional prose works, sometimes in essay form, sometimes in dialogue, on dueling, gaming, the theatre, dancing, Universalism, and the evil power of gold. If amusement did not come now and again to the aid of the reader of these innumerable pages, they would be difficult, if not impossible, of perusal.

Occasionally, however, there are helpful gleams of pleasurable humor in the midst of incomparable dullness. In "the early youth" of his youngest daughter, Dolly, he and she once collaborate in creation. He writes as a foreword to a poem that, "as an amusing game," he has written one line and she another on a slate:

> J.F. I have a little, harmless neighbor.
> D.F. It is the ant, so full of labor.
> J. Her industrious life shall be
> D. A good example now for me.
> J. Well the morning hours she prizes,
> D. To her tasks she early rises,
> J. Labors freely all the day
> D. To secure her needful prey.

Again, on a small scrap of paper found among his possessions, he has written alphabetical "distichs for a child's primer," which, although *he* doubtless did not regard them as funny, are lacking neither in charm nor ingenuity:

If Daniel pray,   Queen Esther sues
Lions obey.   And saves the Jews.

Iscariot base   Job feels the rod,
His Lord betrays.   Yet blesses God.

Vashti for pride   Xerxes did die,
Was set aside   .   And so must I.

In the last of his many manuscript volumes, transcribed in 1845, two years before his death, he bids farewell to his "harp," which, he says, "has pled the cause of morals and religion, warned sinners, comforted the mourning, and honored the dead":

Farewell, my harp! No more my pen,
    Beyond this short essay,
Methinks will be resumed again
    In metre to display

My scattered thoughts, for now I find
    The weight of numerous years
Lies heavy on my waning mind
    And much its strength impairs.
            * * * *
Farewell, my harp! I hope in heaven
    A better harp to share,
If, as I hope, by Grace 'tis given
    To find a mansion there.

5

In addition to his countless poems, some turgid and tiresome essays on various doctrines of the Christian faith, and an occasional pious story, usually for children, which appeared now and again in *The Christian Mirror*, mostly between 1825 and 1835, Mr. Fisher published four books: *A Short Essay on*

Baptism, issued by Samuel Armstrong of Boston in 1817, *The Youth's Primer,* under the same imprint and in the same year, *Short Poems,* printed by Arthur Shirley of Portland in 1827, and *Scripture Animals,* published by William Hyde of Portland in 1834. In consideration of the reader's patience one hesitates to describe in any detail these volumes; yet the conception and execution of them all merit some brief attention and the last of them surely a larger space.

The *Essay on Baptism* was begun in 1804 when Parson Fisher was anxiously witnessing the discontent and doubt of several among his flock over this very question as related to themselves. The portion dealing with Infant Baptism, the apparent source of their initial heartsearchings, was completed at once and used as a sermon in the same year. Why it was not published until 1817 is not clear unless, as was the case with Mr. Fisher's other literary wares, he failed to induce a publisher to undertake it. In the summer of 1817 he added other material on the subject of baptism in general and by August had completed its 100 pages of question and answer with some "meditations" and poems added for good measure; and when he left for his vacation in September, he carried the manuscript with him, together with that of *The Youth's Primer,* the work of his "leisure" for some eight years past. One suspects that the prudent and shrewd Mr. Fisher used his *Essay on Baptism* as a kind of rider to accompany his *Youth's Primer;* in other words, that the bestowal of the Primer upon Mr. Armstrong was conditioned by his willingness to print the Essay also; but this perhaps unfair assumption is based only upon imagination, upon lack of evidence to the contrary, *and* upon the dull and deadening pages of the Essay itself. At all events Mr. Armstrong published both in October, 1817. The author himself read the proof sheets and saw his books through the press during his vacation. Once they were ready, he characteristically seized upon time and place and eagerly peddled both volumes among acquaintances, friends, and strangers in the vicinity of Boston.

The business deal with Mr. Armstrong is not entirely clear. He apparently paid the author "about $80 for cuts and copyright" of the Primer and allowed him for private sale 533 copies on an edition of 3000. The $80 seems to have been paid in kind, in other words, in Primers. Since there is no mention of the financial terms governing the publication of the Essay, that inescapable incubus may have been turned over to Mr. Armstrong to do with as he could, the only payment to be a substantial number of copies. The parson writes of packing up his 533 Primers for the voyage homeward, and he must have taken an almost equal number of Essays as well, for in a letter to his mother in 1819 he says that he has sold 468 Essays for which he has received over $115.

One gathers from the pages of his Diary that between 1817 and 1820 he is a busy and ardent purveyor and salesman of his produce. He carries Essays and Primers with him wherever he goes, hawks them from one end of Bluehill to another, carries them on missionary journeys, and to Bangor for Trustee Meetings at the Bangor Seminary. In November, 1827, the supply of both must have still been ample, for in that month he leaves for sale in Bangor 90 Essays and 50 Primers. It is clear, also, that he left them for sale in most shops and stores in Hancock County, sent them to his daughters to sell in the places where they were teaching, and confidently assumed that the obliging Mr. Andrew Witham would accept them, at least now and then, in payment for foodstuffs and other commodities. Each sold at .25 a copy, or at .20 in quantities of a dozen or more.

It is difficult to understand today how the most fervent minds, even in 1817, could have enjoyed, or *endured,* the *Essay on Baptism. The Youth's Primer,* however, is a rather engaging little volume, in the composition of which the parson quite clearly took delight. He began it in April, 1807, and, according to his Diaries, worked on it "in leisure moments" until its completion in 1815. It is dedicated

To the American Youth of both Sexes
With a sincere desire to please them with what is
profitable, to entertain them with what is good, to instruct them in religion, and to promote their temporal
interest and their eternal happiness.

It is based on a series of short verses, arranged in alphabetical
order and in the form of the "distichs" quoted earlier:

By Adam came   Our parents fell
Our sin and shame.   And we rebel.

Amidst our cheer   All shortly must
Death may be near.   Be laid in dust.

Moses with awe   While Sinai quakes
Receives the Law.   With God he speaks.

Good Nehemiah   For Israel pleads
With warm desire   And well succeeds.

Each pair of verses is accompanied by undeniably solemn reflections and explanations; but the woodcuts accompanying them
are often odd and interesting, and there are interspersed as well
occasional stories: of a Black Prince and how he loved to read
the Bible; of Xenophon's March of the 10,000; and of Cyrus and
his conquest of Babylon. Now and again a poem, not too somber,
lights up the pages:

The Lions ask their meat of God,
On him the Ravens wait for food.
The beasts of every name
And fowl of every wing
That chatter, croak, or sing
Present their humble claim.

The parson's love for imparting information, always incurable,
prompts him to give his young readers a sketch of "Scripture
chronology" from the creation of Adam in 4004 B.C., whose
name, he tells them, means "red earth," to the kings of Israel
and Judah. And when he reaches U, which, of course, stands for

Uriah, the Hittite, he cannot resist writing them a brief letter on "the fleeing of youthful lusts":

To preserve chastity, let marriage come to your aid in due season; to this end let early industry and careful economy provide for the charges of the marriage state. When connected, live joyfully with your partner. . . . Such is the desire of your sincere friend,

Benevolus.

Nevertheless, *The Youth's Primer* has more than a little appeal, even after 130 years. For it possesses that rare and intangible quality, born of the author's own enthusiasm and affection not only for his subject, but for his readers as well, which lifts any book above the dull level of the lifeless and the commonplace.

Mr. Fisher's next, and without doubt dearest, publishing venture, that of seeing his poems within commercial covers, was long-deferred, but his hope sprang eternal from 1805 onward. In Boston in that year he tried in vain to interest various firms and persons in them; in 1807 he tried again; and in 1823 he carried three fat volumes of manuscript to Mr. Armstrong, only to be disappointed a third time. Early in 1827 he determines to undertake their publication on his own; and in March he writes Mr. Arthur Shirley of Portland of his conclusion. He describes his poems not too inaptly in the following words: "The style of my verses is doubtless calculated for the fireside of the cottage than for the shelves of genius, but the hope that they will be useful induces me to think of publishing a few of them." He states that he is able to pay $60 and has "the encouragement of a loan of equal amount." He orders 1000 copies and at the same time 100 subscription sheets, and he straightway launches a selling campaign far and wide. He sends his subscription sheets to Portland, N. Yarmouth, Waldoboro, Bath, Albion, Bangor, Belfast, Hampden, Frankfort, Prospect, Sullivan, Ellsworth, Penobscot, Bucksport, Orland, and Castine, the postage costing him $3.04. Evidently some altruistic "Brother in Christ" in each town was entrusted with the circulation of these and urged to ferret out as many subscribers as possible. Young Hosea Kittredge, then in his third year at Amherst College, receives sheets for Amherst and Conway and manages to dispose of 42 copies, we trust at the cost of not too great embarrassment to himself!

Short Poems, including A Sketch of the Scriptures to the Book of Ruth, Satan's Great Device, or Lines on Intemperance, I and Conscience, or A Dialogue on Universalism, and a few Others on Various Subjects, which is the long title to this short book of 143 pages, appeared in September, 1827. In December the parson writes his mother that he has sold "672 copies to subscribers at .25 each, 51 at the retail price of .35, and given away 57." The selling continues up to the year 1833 when, in a small notebook, which includes the names of all subscribers and the recipients of gift copies, he assesses his accounts and discovers that he has made $23.04 as the total gain on his enterprise.

A sufficient number of lines have been quoted in preceding pages to prove easily that the Rev. Mr. Pomroy was quite accurate in his opinion of the Rev. Mr. Fisher as a poet. He was accurate likewise in his statement that the parson prided himself on his poetry more than on his other accomplishments. In spite of rebuffs from publishers, he continued until two years before his death to transcribe his verses and to add hundreds of lines to their superabundance. Even his admission to Mr. Shirley that his poems are not meant for the shelves of genius suggests a seemly humility rather than sound self-appraisal. Tenacious to the end, he persevered with his Miltonic conventions, his apostrophes to Hymen, Solitude, and the Sacred Nine, his *Aves and Vales,* and his endless hackneyed and overworked rhymes and figures. And he is seemingly so convinced that his own accents are harmonious that in 1840 he writes to Mr. Cummings of the *Mirror* a letter severely criticising its current poetry for the "lack of musical appeal." Young poets, he says, should return to the Immortals for their models, to Milton, Thomson, Watts, Cowper, and Young, who from the beginning have formed his own verses. For surely those "inharmonies," which he is forced reluctantly to peruse in the pages of the *Mirror,* "cannot be pleasing to a refined taste"—like his own!

Mr. Fisher's last book, *Scripture Animals,* was his major literary accomplishment and, in fact, no small achievement. There is a liveliness about it quickly sensed by one who turns its pages today, for its author, consciously or unconsciously, is more clearly within it than in any other of his books. Its genesis was early. Even during his years at Harvard, one remembers, he was writing and illustrating with watercolors a "Natural History Book"; he was composing also a "Dictionary of Natural History"; and in 1793 during his vacations at Dedham he began his woodcut engravings of birds and animals. His college notebooks are freely interspersed with watercolor paintings of various creatures.

One book, now owned by a great-great-granddaughter, is worthy of especial mention. Bound in leather apparently late in his life, since some of the pictures in it are dated 1840 and 1841, it is comprised for the most part of paintings done during his last years at Harvard. The pages of very heavy paper, in size 17 x 11 inches, contain large and beautifully colored representations of birds, animals, and flowers. Of beasts, there are the zebra, bear, wolf, rhinoceros, elephant, ant-eater, catamount, and others; of birds, the hawk, eagle, butcher bird, Brazilian macaw, the "great horned owl from Athens," and the "little owl"; of flowers, a strawberry plant, a spray of blue larkspur, and a lovely arrangement of garden peas, with blossoms, pod, and fruit. At the close is a page given to the painting of many shells in delicate colors. Most of the paintings are copied from books on natural history known to him, largely from the work of George Edwards, which he owned; but the bear and the catamount, painted in 1795, are taken from those beasts seen in Bluehill in that year, and the lion is modeled from one brought "from Africa to New York in 1794 and in the winter following exhibited in Boston, being between 4 and 5 years old." (Jonathan Fisher paid .50 to see him and says he was "upwards of 3 ft. high and measured 7 ft. from nostrils to tail.") Below the figures are their names in English, Hebrew, Greek, Latin, and French, and many of the pages below the pictures contain in parallel columns long descriptions of the beast presented, one column in phonetic spelling, the other in French. All are carefully dated and signed, often with the words: *Jonathan Fisher delin. et pinx.* The flower paintings are made from specimens in his Bluehill garden.

The observation and study of nature was quite clearly a passion with Jonathan Fisher all his days; and this delight through which he might glorify God, instruct the young, and at the same time give himself intense enjoyment, was capable of easy and inevitable rationalization. Since the Bible contained numberless references to animals and since his pen must be dedicated only and always to the blessed purposes of God in the salvation of souls, this combination of duty and pleasure early engaged his mind and energies.

He began seriously to write his *Natural History of the Bible,* the original title of *Scripture Animals,* in 1819, and, according to his Diary entries, he is constantly at work upon it until 1832, when he decides upon its final title. In 1833 he has finished the text and the engraving of its many cuts and in September of that year carries manuscripts and blocks with him to Boston in the eager hope of interesting one among "several booksellers" in its publication. His disappointment over the refusal of all to undertake this has already been recorded.

In November, 1833, he arranged with William Hyde of Portland to publish 1000 copies of his book, and it appeared in the spring of 1834. The entire cost of the edition was $600. Of the 1000 copies issued by Mr. Hyde, Mr. Fisher bought 625 for private sale, and his son-in-law, Capt. Jeremiah Stevens, rallying nobly to the Fisher standard, purchased 125 copies. The remaining 250 are listed by Mr. Hyde in his account to the author as sold at .60 each to various shops and individuals in the neighborhood of Portland. The parson obviously paid his bill to Mr. Hyde, which for printing and binding amounted to $375, by the later sale of his 625 copies, although he was allowed $130 of that sum for the use of his cuts. Neither Mr. Hyde nor Mr. Fisher made much money on their undertaking, but perhaps the pride of the latter in his book compensated for the loss of monetary gain. Whether or not he disposed of all his copies is not stated, for, since his Diaries closed in 1835, we have only his letters to depend upon for information. In two of these, descriptive of his "western tour" in 1839, he says he sold "while away" 111 copies at .90 each, and, without doubt, in view of his talents as a salesman, he managed to dispose of many more within and without his parish. What Capt. Jeremiah Stevens did with his 125, clearly bought for the honor of the family, remains a subject of amusing conjecture. Perhaps he carried them on his ship and distributed them about his West Indian ports of call!

Jonathan Fisher's evident satisfaction and pride in this last of his books are justified by an examination of it. It consists of 347 pages and is illustrated throughout by woodcuts of the animals described in alphabetical order. Its title page,

Scripture Animals
or
Natural History
Of the Living Creatures Named in the Bible
Written Especially for Youth
Illustrated with Cuts
By Jonathan Fisher, A.M.

is stamped by an illustration which ingeniously combines the branches of trees in order to reveal the profile of the Rev. Mr. Fisher himself. A foreword explains that most of the cuts are copied from the work of various engravers, "Bewick, Mavor, the Cabinet, several Lexicons, and some other works," although a few of them are "from nature." "Of the execution," he says, "I may remark that, not being able to hire them engraved, I have engraved them myself, and having no instruction in the art and but little practice, I can lay no claim to elegance in their appearance." The foreword also justifies the naming of most of the animals in Hebrew and Greek, and some of them in Latin and French as well, by some words descriptive of his own love of languages; and he expresses his hope that the sight of these strange words may "raise a desire in the bosoms of some young persons of natural genius to seek an education."

The charm of *Scripture Animals* (and its charm is undeniable) lies, first of all, in the author's eager and personal description of certain of his subjects. These begin with the *adder,* the *ant,* and the *ass,* and continue through the alphabet in so far as the Bible provides creatures of the initial letters. He is careful to list the number of times each beast is mentioned therein and, unless these are too many as in the case of the *lion* and the *sheep,* the scriptural passages pertaining to it. Once this is done, he proceeds to comment upon the habits of each creature, and now and again he relates personal experiences as the source of his knowledge. When he is writing of the *owl,* which he has drawn from the one found in his woodhouse in February, 1832, he describes the hoots and the sudden screams which have many times startled him on his solitary wayfarings through the woods at night; when he is dealing with the *mouse,* he tells of the great number of field mice in the District of Maine and in Massachusetts in the year 1809, so many that a fox once threw thirteen of them out of his mouth in one gulp! The *pigeon* brings to mind the huge flocks he has seen in Bluehill, which fly at the rate of a mile a minute and which have been killed by thousands. The *caterpillar,* also drawn from nature, recalls one which, while he was in college, he placed in a little box and fed daily with leaves. He watched it spin its cocoon with fascinated eyes and after some weeks saw it emerge as a beautiful moth.

There is charm also in the short poems which follow most

of the descriptions. Here, for once, his pleasure in his task
softens his moral and religious reflections and results occasionally in some rather captivating lines:

On Behemoth, the Elephant, "a paraphrase from Job":

> He sinks the river, which his thirst supplies,
>   With fearless leisure; and believes he may
> Drink Jordan dry; 'tis little in his eyes,
>   While with his trunk he clears his cumbered way.

On the patient Ox, from Isaiah 1:

> He knows his master; ready to obey,
> Is mild and docile, does not often stray.
> Though oft he labors with attending pain,
> How rare to hear him in his toil complain!

On the Bittern:

> The Bittern loves a lone abode,
>   And hides from human view.
> And we, to think of Heaven and God,
>   Should love retirement, too.

Indeed, he takes such evident joy in this book that he cannot
forbear adding an Appendix of animals and fish not, as a matter
of fact, found in the Bible, but interesting in themselves: the
haddock, for instance, and the *rattlesnake,* to which rum is a
fatal poison as it should likewise be to mankind! And lastly, in
an essay on Man and his tragic Fall, he finds excuse to write
of the Laplanders and the Tartars, who, although they are, of
course, depraved and fallen like the rest of us, nevertheless
possess odd habits of life worthy of description.

Even the somber design of death on the final page—a tomb-
stone with skull and bones, which may have seemed to him a
fitting bit of solemnity to offset any possible suggestion of too
much delight in his book—cannot dim the life within it. Or
the Latin words with which he takes farewell of his young
readers:

Occumbit Sol, veniunt umbrae.

The sun sets; the shadows gather.[1]

6

Jonathan Fisher's painting of pictures was, like his trout fishing, an indulgence and, perhaps, not so easy of rationalization; yet just as the one provided food for family mouths, so the other yielded, from time to time, at least a little money for the family budget. The parson's work as an artist was carried on throughout his life, the best of it, his copy of his self-portrait shown in this book, not accomplished until 1838.

Perhaps his ability in drawing, design, and painting was inherited, together with her other gifts to him, from his mother, Katharine Avery Fisher. A small notebook of hers, inscribed on its cover

Katharine Fisher
Her Writeing, Drawing
and Painting

New Braintree, March $\frac{e}{Y}$ 19:1767

contains, in addition to some facts of Fisher genealogy and the copy of some poems by the Rev. Mr. Haven of Dedham, three drawings done by her. Two are of floral sprays in watercolor, still bright, the other, an intricate and charming design of leaves, flowers, and berries in black and white. It is interesting to note also that in his many letters to his mother, he writes in detail of his painting, evidently being sure of her eagerness to hear of it.

In addition to his wood engravings and his watercolors of birds and animals painted at Harvard, he also accomplished there several still-life studies of fruit and flowers: some apples

---

[1] For those who may be interested in examining copies of *The Youth's Primer* and *Scripture Animals,* the names of certain libraries containing one or both may be welcome. The *Primer* is in the Harvard Library, the Boston Athenaeum, and the Boston Public. *Scripture Animals* is at Harvard, the New York Public, Swarthmore College, and the Grosvenor Library in Buffalo, N. Y.

on a pewter plate, some ripening plums in shades of green, yellow, and red, some butterflies' wings in delicate and lovely tones. His larger pictures, painted in Bluehill from 1798 on, were mostly done in oils which he obviously mixed himself, as frequent Diary entries note the purchase of white and red lead, carmine, vermillion, and ochre. In April, 1798, he is painting a view of Dedham and one of Cambridge; in the same year he completes "6 Natural History Paintings" which he sells at Buckstown for $7.50; in June, 1803, while he is on his vacation, he paints the Avery house in Dedham, a canvas now owned by his great-grandson, Samuel Fisher; in July, 1805, he does an unidentified "Painting," which he sells to Capt. Buck of Buckstown for $3.

In the ante-room of the President's office at Princeton there is a large painting, in size some 59 x 26 inches, which bears at the bottom the following inscription:

A North West Prospect of Nassau Hall
with a Front View of the President's House in
New Jersey. J. Fisher Pinxit from an Old
Print. Feb. 1807.

The painting of this picture, acquired by Princeton in 1930 from a Bluehill descendant of the artist, is described at some length in his Diary. He began it in December, 1806, in response to a request from Esq. John Peters "for a picture." He worked on it in January and February, 1807, made a frame for it, and on March 1st carried it to Esq. Peters, who paid him $12 for it. The "old print" from which it was copied and enlarged has been identified as an engraving by Henry Dawkins, which had appeared in *A True Account of the College of New Jersey*, published in 1764. Since Esq. Peters had no connection whatsoever with the New Jersey college, the painting was evidently done only to provide him with a picture for one of the walls of his large and beautiful red brick house in Bluehill. Perhaps its subject in its arrangement of buildings was of especial interest to Mr. Peters, since in addition to other pursuits, he was himself a surveyor and something of an architect.[1]

Between 1806 and 1824 the parson seems to have been too busy on his many woodcuts for *The Youth's Primer* and *Scripture Animals* to work much with canvas and colors. At least his Diaries and letters for those years say little concerning his painting, although one must always keep in mind that he may have looked upon this dabbling in paints as too much of a pleasant pastime, too little of a contribution to his labor for God, and hence was reluctant to record it. In the Howard Collection in Bluehill there are some twelve canvases, most of which are undated and some of which may have been done between these years. These are, for the most part, copies of unidentified pictures and range from studies in still life to "The Descent from the Cross" and a scene from *Paul and Virginia*. Most are of little value except for the interesting scope of their subjects; but among them is a fine sketch in watercolor of Harvard College and a large picture of Bluehill in 1824. The picture of Harvard is one of several such watercolors depicting the college buildings of Fisher's sojourn there. Most of these were done early and probably originated at least from the "exercises in Mathematical Parts," of which he writes in his undergraduate Diary.

The painting of Bluehill in 1824 was sketched in the autumn of that year and completed in May, 1825. He writes his mother about it with some enthusiasm, saying, however, that he thinks it the last large picture he will paint. He sketched the village from a hill to the northeast and placed in the foreground a fat and quiet horse, three persons, two of whom gaze upon the scene before them, and a long stone wall. Although the colors in blues, greens, and white are, of course, dingy and faded from the dust and wear of more than a century, the picture with its homes and meeting-house, its trees, fields, and pastures, still holds charm and interest.

[1] A full description of this painting is given by Janet S. Byrne in *The Princeton University Library Chronicle*, June, 1945.

The most valuable and noteworthy of all the Fisher paintings is the self-portrait of the parson. The original of this was begun on the 19th of April, 1824, and completed on the 28th; and it was accomplished through the study of himself before a mirror. Upon this, according to his Diary, he worked every one of the eight days devoted to it "except Sunday." Apparently he allowed his eagerness to encroach upon his Friday and Saturday always dedicated to the composition of his Sunday sermon. Perhaps he explained, if he did not excuse, this daring act, at least to himself, as the irresistible claim upon him of "that last infirmity of noble minds." At all events, Divine Providence for once does not seem either to have reprimanded or punished him!

He comments on the "likeness" as "not so good as I should have wished," and in the following year made a second portrait from the first. In 1838 he made two other copies, desiring, he says, to leave one for each of his four surviving daughters. One of these now hangs in the Congregational Church in Bluehill; one, in the Bangor Theological Seminary; the third, from which the copy in this book is made, is in Litchfield, Conn.; and the fourth is owned by a great-great-granddaughter in New York City.

Jonathan Fisher's self-portrait is not unknown in Maine beyond the confines of Bluehill and Bangor, for it was recently shown at Colby College in an exhibition of early Maine art. Nor is it unfamiliar to the students of American art at Smith College where a slide made from it is often thrown upon a screen. One's imagination takes delight and satisfaction in the thought of how the parson would relish this surviving interest in him and in the work of his never idle hands and his always teeming mind. Of the portrait and of his other work with brush and pencil and engraving tools, his fellow artists of another age can speak with greater authority than can his scribe.

Oliver Larkin, Professor of Art at Smith College, writes of him:

At a time when few American artists practised still life paint-ing, Fisher made his exquisite small watercolor of apples on a pewter plate, rounding them off with patient gradations and set-ting them firmly in space. With something of Audubon's thor-oughness he laid each small feather on a bird's breast or wing, and his placing of a pea vine on a sheet of paper reveals a de-lightful sense of pattern. When Fisher limned his own portrait, he revealed the whole man. This is not the customary "prim-itive" likeness, so often a flat, maplike presentation. The shad-ing of the head gives it a startling and solid reality against the dark background; and on this firm structure Jonathan has traced every wrinkle and crease which age and character produce. One can believe that these eyes missed nothing in the world around him; that this strong hand could carve wood and metal; that this forefinger could stab the consciences of his parishioners.

And Karl Kup, Curator of Prints of the New York Public Library, says of his woodcuts:

Fisher's style of engraving, in the manner of the typical *primitive,* shows the lack of training. But it is made up by a most fervent desire to please, and by an almost childlike per-sistence to get that animal upon the wood block, come what may. His modeling is poor, that we must admit; . . . his proportions of drawing are not always right. But in the handling of the tool. . . . Fisher shows real feeling for the wood block and real craftsmanship in the execution of his engraving. He knows no fear in flicking out small bits to get the texture of either fur or feathers. He engraves the most enchanting landscapes around and behind his animals.

7

The memory of the Fisher children, in their later years, of their father's study and his many labors therein is echoed by some sentences of a letter written in 1838 by Nancy Fisher Kittredge. It is addressed to her "Honored and Beloved Parents" and concludes with these words:

O had I the wings of a dove and power to use them, I would

soon be seated with you, dear father, in that little room, consecrated to Learning and Devotion, and perhaps sometimes even to the Muses! It is doubtless best for you that I cannot. I should be worse than a buzzing Fly about your ears. But if we meet not again there, may we meet together where no sin can alloy. Till then, ever pray for your unworthy, but affectionate and grateful daughter,

Nancy Fisher Kittredge.

VIII

MR. FISHER AND HIS TIMES

1

THE Rev. Mr. Fisher during his declining years was destined and privileged alike to live in one of the most stirring and important periods of American history. The 1830's and 1840's were years of great and widespread social and intellectual ferment, when zeal for political, social, and humanitarian reform affected virtually every phase of American life. The political reforms of the new Jacksonian democracy, the organization of labor and the improvements in its conditions, the reforms in debtors' laws, in prisons and asylums, and in the curricula of schools, the growth of the temperance movement, and the agitation over the question of slavery—all combined to make this period one of tremendous social progress and importance. The discussion of these matters in the growing number of newspapers, on lecture platforms, and in pulpits stirred up the minds and the emotions of all intelligent Americans. It was both natural and inevitable that such questions and problems should have made an indelible impression upon such a man as Jonathan Fisher.

It is not until the late 1820's and early 1830's that the parson's interest in national and in State reforms finds any extensive expression in his Diaries and letters. This is partly explained, of course, by the fact that the earlier years themselves were not so rife with reform movements; but it without doubt more specifically resulted from the nature and the needs of the environment in which he lived. One must always remember that the subject of most engrossing and vital interest to the members of any young and vigorous frontier community was the harsh reality of maintaining an existence and of striving to obtain material security. The town of Bluehill, like many others in the District of Maine, as well as like those along the new Western frontier, was such a community during Mr. Fisher's early residence there; and he, like his rural ministerial colleagues elsewhere, had little time for reflection on matters other than those relating to the spiritual well-being of his busy and often hard-headed parishioners. Not until the growth and relative consolidation of the community, and of the country at large, had brought release from the ever-present struggle for existence and material well-being, did he have more time for the wider interests of his fellowmen wherever they might be. Yet even in these early years he managed to keep remarkably well-informed on both national and world affairs, and occasionally he makes pertinent comment upon such matters.

At the beginning of the nineteenth century Mr. Fisher's views, as we should expect, accurately reflected those of the still staunchly Federalist New England in which he lived. On January 25, 1808, he records in his Diary his profound anxiety over the effects of the embargo, which in December, 1807, Mr. Jefferson had "inflicted" upon the country to the indignation, even the despair, of commercial and seafaring New England. "Deeply affected, so as to be deprived of sleep, with a view to the threatening situation in our land." He was a member of the committee empowered to draw up Bluehill's resolution of bitter protest, one of the many such resolutions adopted by the town-meetings of most seafaring towns along the New England coastline.

On June 27, 1812, after he has learned of the declaration of war against England, he writes:

"First received direct news of a declaration of war on the part of our government with Great Britain, a war which I believe to be unjust on our part and greatly impolitic, a war which I fear will issue in the subjection of America to Bonaparte, the despot of Europe, a war which, if prosecuted, must lead us into many serious trials and sufferings; a war in which I have for several years expected the majority of our rulers would

Garden Study by Jonathan Fisher

A Study in Still Life by Jonathan Fisher

involve us through the measures they have been pursuing, but which I most sincerely deprecate, and against which I have endeavored to use my feeble influence. I am now exceedingly at a stand to know the path of duty in many respects. We deserve to be chastised; but may God in his mercy alleviate these sufferings which, without his favorable interposition, must be severe. Wrote sermons on the subject of the proclaimed war."

These sermons, two in number, were delivered on August 20th, the day, a Wednesday, being observed as a "Continental Fast." In them he "gave a brief history of the leading events of the nation from the commencement of our Revolution to the present, particularly with respect to the sources of our present division and danger." They describe in great detail the background of the war, show a rather thorough knowledge of the issues involved, and certainly reflect the prevailing attitude of the great majority of New Englanders. One could hardly expect the conservative and Calvinistic Mr. Fisher to view with much sympathy the reputedly atheistical Thomas Jefferson and his Republican administration; and yet, in justice to the parson, his indignation in these sermons seems to be based on no religious grounds, but rather to stem from the conventional Federalist political and economic position. The larger part of his audience was undoubtedly strongly with him, although "during the afternoon discourse two hearers left the meeting-house on account of political views."

With his always meager salary, his meticulous honesty in business dealings, and his constant struggle against finding himself involved in debt, Parson Fisher was naturally concerned with economic questions, especially with those of his own environment. During the war years of 1813 and 1814 he writes of the scarcity of food. "Hunger prevails in some sections of our District. A woman and two children have died of it in Frankfort. Our own bread allowance is but ⅓ of our usual supply, and, therefore, we eat with particular relish what we have." In 1819 he writes of "bad times among us, resulting, in my opinion, from the unwise and unsafe policies of our rulers." A rueful Diary entry for April 25, 1826, clearly shows his displeasure and concern over the unsound system of state and local banks, which was such a trial to that period and which was to become within a few years a burning national issue.

"Found among my money a $10 bill of the Passamaquoddy Bank, which is now gone down, making $15 I have lost within about 6 months by the failing of banks. My daughter Nancy has a $5 bill of the same bank. The failing of banks appears to me to be the effect of a wicked course of swindling. How long must the Christian public endure it?"

The bitterness against Mr. Jefferson and his Republican successors was repeated several years later in Mr. Fisher's reactions to certain of the Jacksonian policies, markedly to the law requiring the transportation of the mails on Sunday. This government-inspired profanation of the Sabbath aroused his wrath, and he covered many miles on foot throughout his scattered parish in order to obtain signatures to a petition urging its repeal. "I obtained," he writes, "56 names to the petition." This petition, composed by him and carefully copied and preserved among his papers, reads as follows:

Bluehill, Maine. Nov. 19, 1829.

To the Honorable, the Senate, and the House of Representatives in Congress assembled, the Petition of the undersigned humbly showeth,

That, whereas we believe the Sabbath was made for man in a peculiar sense, that the seventh day of the week at the Creation was sanctified and set apart by the Creator himself to be kept holy for the temporal, and especially for the spiritual and eternal good of man; and that it might be a fit season in which to attend to that spiritual meditation and devotion which promote the relief of the body from secular toil and a preparation of the soul for immortal joys; and a fit season also in which man, laying aside his temporal concerns, may meet with his fellowman and join in social and public prayer and praise to God and in receiving religious instruction; and whereas we believe that at the resurrection of Jesus Christ the sacredness of the seventh day of the week was transferred to the first, so that it has become the Sabbath, or Lord's day, that while by its recurrence once in seven days it should still commemorate the finishing of the more glorious work of Redemption and the triumph of the Savior over death and the grave; and whereas the transportation of the mail on the Sabbath, the Lord's day, obliges many conscientious persons to relinquish an occupation in which they are obtaining their temporal support, or to profane the holy day and deny themselves the privilege of public worship; and whereas we also believe that the profanation of the Sabbath exposes a nation to the judgment of God: We, the undersigned, inhabitants of Bluehill, in the County of Hancock and State of Maine, earnestly request that the law requiring the transportation of the Mail and the opening of post-offices on the Sabbath may be repealed.

The defeat of this campaign against the Sunday mails, which was carried on by thousands of zealous clergymen in countless small towns and villages, only added strength to the parson's conviction that the servants of God throughout the nation must not only rise, but *unite,* to rescue their country from faithlessness to Laws incomparably higher and more binding than those of man's making; and, true to St. Paul's charge, he girded up his loins and polished his armor for the battle against the rulers of the darkness of this world, against spiritual wickedness in high places. In a poem published on December 20, 1831, in *The Christian Mirror* of Portland, he foresees a day of awful reckoning before the country for its treatment of the slave, the Indian, and the holy Sabbath:

> . . . . While the Black-man toils,
> Enslaved unjustly; and the Redman mourns,
> Deni'd his rights; and while the holy day
> Of sacred rest, which God himself has claim'd
> For his own worship and the needful care
> Of souls immortal, is with daring hand
> Thro' all our coasts incessantly profan'd—
> I see a gathering cloud; dreary and dark
> It hangs portentous; in its bosom hid
> Are slumb'ring lightnings.

. . . . Plead we still—for what?
That God would move our rulers to repeal
Whatever laws in operation tend
The Sabbath to dishonor.

Mr. Fisher was particularly distressed by his government's
policy toward the Indians. In a Diary entry for December 19,
1831, composed after he has read President Jackson's message
to Congress, he writes:

"Read the *Mirror*. The President's message is a well-composed
document as far as respects language, but as respects the Indians
within the limits of the United States, it holds a main principle
in the operation of which the poor Indians must suffer the greatest cruelties. It is a principle subversive of the faith of treaties,
a principle which, if carried into effect, will ruin them. Oh,
that God would interpose and deliver these oppressed sufferers
from the arm of oppression! The course pursued by the dominant part of the nation toward the Indians is an awful demon-
stration that the nation as such is selfish and that no confidence
can be placed in obtaining justice where selfishness reigns, any
farther than present self-interest may seem to prompt."

Parson Fisher's interest in these matters and his opinions concerning them were primarily those of an intelligent and thoughtful citizen; nor can it be assumed from any evidence at hand
that his influence upon men's minds concerning them extended
much beyond the boundaries of his parish. In the two great and
growing questions of his time, however, the questions of temperance and of slavery, he not only played a leading local part,
but he made also a not inconsiderable contribution to their
development on an even larger scale. His attitude toward these
problems and his efforts on their behalf are interesting and
significant, both because they were typical of many New England
Congregational clergymen of that period and because they reflect the early development of the temperance and the abolition
movements in New England.

2

Parson Fisher, as has been suggested earlier in these pages, was not in his early years in Bluehill deeply distressed over the common use of spiritous liquors; in fact, he frankly states that he has "always had a fondness" for them. In the first quarter of the nineteenth century most Maine men drank alcoholic beverages as a matter of course, the parson among them, although his use of them was without doubt confined to infrequent social occasions and to their employment as medicine. He states quite frankly in the Diaries up to 1826 his customary purchase of rum and brandy; in 1813, for example, he buys rum at Mr. Witham's store four times during that year, twice, one quart, twice, one pint. One of these purchases is carefully marked "on trust, a pint of rum, .25." It is quite clear that neither he nor his parishioners, of whom Mr. Witham was one, regarded such purchases as in any way unusual. Wine was made in the parsonage from fruits and berries and obviously consumed there during the first twenty-five years of his ministry. His notebooks contain any number of recipes for various "cordials, wines, and liquers" with careful rules for their successful concoction. It is clear, also, that the cases of church discipline arising from intemperance had to do, not with the use in itself of intoxicating liquors, but with the often deplorable behavior resulting from that use, a fact already enlarged upon in a previous chapter. As Neal Dow, the principal advocate of the temperance movement in Maine, himself makes clear: "Elders, deacons, and Sabbath School teachers competed with each other for customers for liquor as well as for dry goods and other family supplies, and cheerfully donated generously of profits thus obtained." [1]

It was not until Mr. Fisher, through his own observation and experience, became aware of the baneful effects on human conduct of such indulgence that he began to take the matter of

[1] Louis Clinton Hatch, ed., *Maine, A History* (New York: American Historical Society, 1919), Vol. I, p. 296.

temperance seriously. From 1812 to 1823 the number of entries in his Diary descriptive of these effects increases. A man is drowned through intoxication; another is "deranged with fits"; a third is "running to destruction with open eyes." "Old Bryant came to my house in a state of intoxication. I made him lie in the barn. Miserable, miserable creature!" On his missionary journeys to Mt. Desert, Sedgwick, and Brooksville in 1818 and the years immediately following, he is alarmed over the spread of fornication, obviously in many cases the result of intemperance, and over poverty and destitution stemming from the same cause. By 1814 he is preaching in Bluehill a sermon against the sins arising from intemperance and himself reading tracts upon the subject; by 1826 he has determined against the use of spirits in his home, even as medicine. By 1826 also he is "arguing" with individuals, not only against intemperance, but against the sale of "ardent spirits."

"Nov. 10, 1828. At Mr. McIntyre's today I inquired if he did not intend, after the manner of some others, to quit selling ardent spirits. He replied that he did not know but he ought to do it, but for certain reasons he could not at present. 'But,' said he, 'I think I have not made much by selling them, for, in looking over my books, I find that most of my bad debts have been contracted for ardent spirits.' "

It cannot be claimed, however, that Mr. Fisher, like many of his Congregational brethren, was one of the pioneers in this movement within the District, and later within the State, of Maine, for which its Protestant clergymen of all sects were in large measure responsible. He was familiar with the earliest temperance society in Maine, organized in Portland on April 24, 1812, as the Society for Suppressing Immorality and Vice; for he read from his pulpit in 1814 an address published by this society, and in his Diary for May, 1815, he mentions making a copy of its constitution. He must also have known of Father Jotham Sewall's adherence to it, since Father Sewall was a frequent visitor to the parsonage and in his own diary makes clear that his attitude is identical with that of "many other ministers of the Gospel": "That we will ourselves and in our families abstain from the use of strong drink, except as a medicine, and will use our influence to have others renounce the practice and to have it understood that civility does not require and expediency does not permit the offering of it as part of hospitable entertainment in social visits." Mr. Fisher's own whole-hearted interest in the movement and his determination to labor in its cause probably began in earnest in 1826, when, at a meeting of the Hancock Church Conference, of which his church was a leading member and he himself a founder, the following resolution was passed: "Resolved, that the Churches of this Conference view the traffic in and the common use of intoxicating liquors as sinful, and ought, therefore, to be immediately abandoned." His zeal may well have been further kindled through two visits to Portland in 1823 and 1827, where he saw a good deal of the Rev. Edward Payson, one of the early and most important pioneers in the Maine Temperance Movement. At all events, in 1829, when the Bluehill Temperance Society was organized, one of some sixty such organizations in the new State of Maine, Parson Fisher, convinced at last of his duty as a Christian and a clergyman, threw in his lot unreservedly for the cause. Indeed, it was at the parsonage that Mr. Asa Mead, who came to Bluehill on September 30, 1829, for the purpose of organizing such a society, drew up, together with Mr. Fisher, its initial resolutions.

Once enlisted in the growing army, signed and sealed under its banner, the parson with characteristic vigor gave his all. For eight years until his retirement in 1837, he is constantly battling against the enemy. He preaches in his own pulpit, holds meetings in the Academy "for the youth there," speaks in various schoolhouses, joins with the Baptists in the common cause, and is a constant attendant at the meetings of the new Bluehill Temperance Society, at which, he writes in 1834, "the attendance is very small, only 6 or 8 persons, though it numbers 268." He writes reports of the local organization to the Maine Temperance Society, travels to neighboring towns to hold temperance meetings, and writes poems, essays, and stories on the subject for *The Christian Mirror*. One of these poems, *Satan's Great Device*, written as early as 1823 and included in his volume, *Short Poems*, is prefaced by an eloquent foreword:

To the Reader

The march of intemperance during a few years past has been so rapid, and with such gigantic steps, that every true friend of the nation must, upon serious reflection, tremble for the consequences. Millions of Dollars are annually wasted for millions of gallons of poison, which is swallowed by the inconsiderate, and thousands are made occasional maniacs by the fatal potion; thousands more are hurried to an untimely grave, and their souls sink down into an awful, irretrievable ruin. Every Christian and even every true patriot, in the view of this, should feel himself bound by the strongest ties to apply the weight of his influence to check the spreading infection. The case of habitual sots is nearly hopeless; but those just entering upon the pernicious career may be induced to stop, and reform, and the temperate may take warning and beware. One mode of attack may have the better effect upon one, another upon another, for the turns of mind are infinitely various. I feel constrained to attempt something; the circle of my acquaintance has my example; the following lines, perhaps, may reach beyond that circle, and will have, I would hope, some good effect where my example cannot be seen.

Mr. Fisher paid dearly for his zeal in an evident loss of prestige and affection among his parishioners. On November 28, 1831, he writes in his Diary: "Had yesterday but a thin audience. The affection of the people of my charge seems to have grown cold against me, partly, I believe, on account of the exertion I have made for the temperance cause." Evidently the flames, lighted in 1829 by the eloquence of Mr. Mead and of other speakers who went to and fro along the coast, died to embers or even to ashes, once the kindling was withdrawn. Many persons who had momentarily been fired under the urge of enthusiasm to renounce their former pleasures quite clearly repented of their fervor and turned against the new society, although the editor of the short-lived *Bluehill Beacon and Journal* states in 1830 that, between 1828 and 1830, when the population numbered 1362, the quantity of liquor sold in that town, which before 1828 had been "annually between 25 and 28 hogsheads," had been reduced by ⅓ and that within these years he had not noted "an immoderate use of ardent spirits." The parson, however, in spite of opposition from many in his parish (for in his Diary he not only refers to criticism in general, but also to calls from various parishioners who take him to task for his stand), continued firm and unyielding in his labors for temperance at home and abroad; and it was doubtless through such activities of his own and of others like him, even in small fields, that Maine later became the leader in the national temperance and prohibition movement.

Jonathan Fisher's work for the temperance cause, relatively late as had been his entire conversion to it, was in one significant sense particularly noteworthy and commendable. Quite evidently he did not espouse the cause because of any conviction that the use of spirits was unscriptural, that it had been forbidden by God in His holy and irrefutable Word. Such conviction on his part, as his life constantly reveals even in the smallest matters, would have left no room for human judgment or free will. His position was grounded simply on the assumption that any practice or example which caused one's brother to offend must needs be sacrificed by all true Christians for the common good. He makes this position entirely clear in a letter, written on December 21, 1835, to the editor of *The Christian Mirror,* in which he gives his opinions upon both "the wine question and the slave question." Upon the first of these he writes:

Mr. Cummings:

While my younger Brethren in the ministry around me have occupied their pens upon the wine question and the slave question, I have hitherto withheld mine from both these subjects.

But if days should speak, it may not be unsuitable that I should give my opinion. In this I do not intend to enter into any dispute with any individual:

I will say a word upon the wine question. Respecting this, my conviction is full and settled, that the only true ground of urging its disuse is that suggested by the holy Apostle when he says in Romans 14:21: *It is good neither to eat flesh, nor to drink wine, nor anything whereby thy brother stumbleth, or is made weak.* I do not believe that I could draw any true argument from Scripture against the temperate use of fermented wine, or unfermented, rising out of the nature of either. I believe that in ten thousands of instances it has been used as a drink in both states, with the full approbation of our benevolent Creator. But, if in any place the use of wine appears to have become mischievous, and there seems to be any probability that by wholly disusing it as a drink we may prevent our brothers' stumbling, or, in other words, promote the cause of temperance, then I think we ought to disuse it. On this principle I have myself abstained from it these six or eight years, or more. I should have done the same if I had never heard the name of *alcohol,* or had never heard of the distinction between fermented and unfermented wine.

3

Mr. Fisher's interest in the question of slavery was inseparably connected with his deep and even passionate devotion to an organization related to that question, The American Society for Colonizing the Free People of Color of the United States, or The American Colonization Society, as it was more commonly called. To this Society from its founding in Washington in 1816 he gave his unqualified support, his faith, his labor, his pen— *and* his money.

His interest in it may well have been stimulated by the early connection with the Society of Mr. Jehudi Ashmun, who, it will be recalled, had in 1816 become preceptor of the new Maine Charity School at Hampden and a year later its Professor of Classical Literature. Mr. Ashmun, an extremely gifted young man, had left the Theological Seminary because of unkind and seemingly unjust rumours concerning his character in connection

with an unhappy love affair. He had in 1822 sailed from Baltimore to Liberia as the principal agent of the Colonization
Society to supervise and, in fact, to save the colony of American
Negroes there which had been transported by the society. Unable
to endure the sickly climate, he returned after six years of heroic
labor to die in New Haven in 1826, a martyr to a plan, noble
perhaps in conception, but thoroughly impracticable in execution.[1] Mr. Fisher was throughout Mr. Ashmun's career his loyal
champion and friend; and he often in both Diaries and letters
refers to him with admiration.

Not that Mr. Fisher was in the least unaware of what the dark
and forboding institution of slavery meant in itself to the nation.
Long before the year 1820, when the entrance of Maine into the
Union as a free state together with Missouri as a slave state
brought the issue of slavery to the foreground and began to stir
the minds of Maine people over a problem heretofore of relatively little concern to them, the parson in his study had quite
apparently thought upon this condition of injustice and cruelty
to his fellowmen. Indeed, even during his undergraduate days
at Harvard he had been so impressed by a tragic story from
the South that on June 30, 1792, he had written a poem called,
*Lines Occasioned by the Murder of a Young Negro Woman
Whipped to Death by Her Master.* Its last lines are peculiarly
prophetic of the future:

> Sons of pity, let your bosoms
> Warn'd, with indignation flow,
> Rouse with spirit worthy freemen,
> Save the tortured slaves from woe.

In 1812 he compares his weariness at the close of a long, hot day
spent in haying with that "of the black men toiling under the
whips of their masters in the far hotter cotton fields of the South.
May God have mercy upon them!" In December, 1813, he writes

[1] By 1835 the Society had returned during eighteen years to Africa only
some 3000 Negroes, which number was less than the natural increase in the
United States during one month.

in his Diary that he is painting a picture of an African slave. And in the years following 1816 he is constantly referring to the American Colonization Society and its plans for transporting freed slaves to Liberia.

Between 1820 and 1831 his Diaries, his letters, and his literary work show an increasing awareness and concern over this question of slavery which was threatening to rend his nation, and, as well, an ever-growing interest in the plans and aims of the Liberian Colonization scheme. Throughout these years on July 4th, which was evidently observed in Bluehill by religious exercises, he preaches a sermon on the subject of Colonization and donates the contribution of his congregation on that day to its cause. Three times during these years he preaches on Sunday against the sin of holding "our black brothers in cruel bondage," and, once, a visiting clergyman, the Rev. Eliphalet Gillet of Hallowell, gives a discourse on the same subject. The tone of Mr. Fisher's sermons is purely humanitarian and Christian with almost no mention of any political issues involved. In March, 1829, he publishes in *The Christian Mirror* a poem of 65 lines entitled *Oppression*. Although the greater part of it is devoted to the treatment of the Indians, the closing lines concern slavery:

> Nor to these alone
> Our neighboring Red Men should we give the hand
> Of kind regard, but to the darker race
> Who dwell enslaved among us. That foul blot,
> The name of *Slavery*, from a land so free
> In civil institutions, we should strive
> With one consent to cancel and erase
> And banish it forever.

Again in November, 1829, he publishes, also in the *Mirror,* a still longer poem, *My Native Land.* In this he deals eloquently with the beauty of America, her stirring history, her gift of freedom, and at the close, as in the former, he assails his country for the blackest of her crimes:

But, O my native Land,
Thou hast thy crimes; degenerate is the race
Of thy once noble sons; a foul disgrace
Has rested on thee long, the galling yoke
Of blasting Slavery.

These poems surely prove that Mr. Fisher had long been opposed on moral and religious grounds to the institution of slavery, that it caused him both personal suffering and grave realization of the dangers threatening the country because of it. But two events which happened in 1831 caused him even greater consternation and alarm and without question threw him still further into the ranks of the American Colonization Society with its plan for gradual emancipation of the slaves through the deportation of those already freed. One of these events was the publication of William Lloyd Garrison's *Liberator,* the famous abolitionist organ which urged immediate emancipation and the violence of which seemingly made impossible any peaceable solution of the question. The other, occurring some months later, was the Nat Turner Slave Insurrection, in which over fifty white persons were killed and the blame for which was placed at once by leading Southerners upon *The Liberator.* These events, when combined with the nullification controversy with South Carolina, caused tremendous schism between North and South, and from this time the extremists of both sections led the way to its inevitable conclusion.

Mr. Fisher was by nature no extremist. He hated and suspected violence of all sorts. He believed firmly in those rules laid down in the First Epistle General of St. Peter which command men to submit themselves to the ordinance of their rulers and which condemn those foolish ones who use their liberty "for a cloak of maliciousness." To him Garrison was among those to be condemned because of his uncompromising radicalism, unbound by those safeguards of tradition and conservatism always reverenced by the parson and those of his school of thought. To him, a man then of sixty-three, Garrison was a young upstart, incendiary and dangerous, whose early criticism of the Liberian Colonization scheme in his pages only increased Mr. Fisher's dismay and suspicion. That he feared from the start the indiscretions and misplaced zeal of the abolitionists and their methods is made abundantly clear from his writings between 1831 and 1839.

In December, 1831, at the close of the fateful year which saw both the establishment of *The Liberator* and the horrors of the Nat Turner uprising, he wrote for the *Mirror* a poem entitled *An Alarming Prospect.* In this in no uncertain words he expresses his feelings against slavery and his vision of the future:

> Far to the south of my abode I view
> No narrow space of our luxuriant soil
> Till'd by the labor of a sable race
> In Hopeless bondage, stripp'd of all that's dear,
> Their native freedom, like the tribes of old
> Of Israel's sons, the haughty Pharaoh's slaves.
> The more oppressed, they multiply the more.
> E'en now their masters tremble at the thought
> Of scenes before them, lest some burning spark,
> Wafted by winds, ill-boding, should alight
> Amidst the rubbish, and enkindle flames
> Fierce and terrific, wasting as they spread,
> Till streams of blood shall quench them.

And yet, in the same poem, he offers a solution which to him is the only safe and sane way out of a perilous situation:

> Plead we for what?
> That God would bless the Colony commenc'd
> On Afric's coast, and move the nation's heart
> With all the speed that prudence can advise
> To free the slaves, and send them to the land
> Of their fore-fathers. 'Tis a work sublime,
> But hard in execution,—not too fast—
> For this the cause would ruin—not too slow—
> For then the cause would languish.

In February, 1834, he reiterates his faith in this solution, regardless of its magnitude, in a letter written to the Rev. Randolph Gurley, director of the American Colonization Society and during its existence its foremost figure:

There are some good men, literary men, and men of talents in Maine, who are for immediate emancipation. I cannot think with them. I am for emancipation as soon as it can take place with safety, and I think duty does not require it sooner. To the Colonization Society I feel a strong attachment, and I suspect the greater part of men of intelligence and good principles in Maine are its friends. I have thought that God in his Providence has suffered the Abolitionists to spring up to prevent a too rapid growth of the Colony for its moral and spiritual health, and to excite a more close inspection of it on the part of its friends. I do think the Colony will prove a blessing in some degree to this nation and a great blessing to Africa. I can do but little more than pray for it, but what I can do, I feel disposed to do. I hope the friends of the Colony will move on steadily and firmly and not answer railing with railing if they should be reproached. I think it of vital importance that measures should be encouraged in this nation for the education of Africans of good mind to send to the Colony. There must be intelligence to guide and defend a nation especially in its infancy. Let the foundation of the Colony be well laid, let schools and religious institutions be well supported in it, and I doubt not but its growth will by and by be in a sort of geometrical progression.

I believe the Colonization plan will encourage many masters to emancipate their slaves, who otherwise would not, and that the example of these will encourage others; but that a trial of immediate emancipation, if there were no such plan, would long defeat its own object.

That the Colony may finally prosper, it must be reared on a foundation of pure religious principles. The pure principles of Christianity are destined ere long to leaven all nations, except such as shall be destroyed for the rejection of them. My prayer is that you, Dear Sir, may prosper in your work, and the Society prosper, and the Colony at length become a great Christian nation.

On August 23, 1835, he delivers a sermon to his church in Bluehill which expresses his sentiments against radicalism and violence:

In times of extensive public excitement and ill-boding agitation, like the present, the serious, thoughtful mind looks for a resting-place where it may repose in peace. It is the object of the following discourse to endeavor to guide my dear hearers to such a place of rest.

When evils to be deprecated become widespread and deep-rooted in a nation, if these are to be assailed with a view to their removal, it should be done with the greatest caution and prudence. Indiscreet zeal in the case is exceedingly dangerous. There is no well-informed Christian who does not contemplate slavery, as it generally exists, as a great evil and who would not only gladly see it removed from the land, but also banished from the world. The slavery which exists in a great part of this nation is a serious evil, and never will the happy suns of the millennial period shine upon it until this evil is removed. It is an evil deeply felt by very many slaveholders themselves, but it is so circumstanced that for the present they know not what to do to relieve themselves of it.

By the constitution of the United States the management of the concern of slavery within its own limits is left to the legislature of each state itself. Any individual has a right to treat upon the subject of slavery and to point out its nature and tendency, if it be done in a discreet and becoming manner; but he has no right to interfere, directly, with the proceedings of the slave-holding states. Individuals of the non-slave-holding states have of late been pointing out freely what they consider to be the evils of slavery. In some cases it has been well done; but in many other cases I am satisfied that there has been indiscreet zeal on the part of persons, whose motives I would by no means impeach. Without looking far enough forward, however, and without intending evil, they have been the occasion of an excitement which to me appears already to endanger the peace and unity of the nation and to threaten us with the horrors of a civil war.

Should the flames of such a contest be enkindled, they will not be easily extinguished; should they rage furiously and extensively, our repose, our property, and our lives would be in jeopardy. By reason of the influx of unprincipled foreigners and by reason of abundance of wickedness of native growth, I see, or I *think* I see, in our land a vast deal of combustible matter, which, if once inflamed, is likely to burn furiously . . . In this view of dismaying prospects, I would urge upon my dear hearers to lay as strong a restraint as may be over their passions, and to use as calm and pacific language as possible in their discussions, and this with a desire to avert the evils which threaten us.

In December, 1835, in the same letter in which he gives his stand on the wine question, he expresses his opinions on slavery to Mr. Cummings of *The Christian Mirror,* again professing his faith in African colonization:

I will now say a word upon the slave question. I will begin with the words of Solomon, Proverbs 15:1: *A soft answer turneth away wrath, but grievous words stir up anger:* If we at the North, all of us, who have written, had addressed the slaveholders with mild persuasives, I think some of them might have been won over to the cause of emancipation; but we have, some of us at least, used such grievous words that we have stirred up their anger; and now I believe all we can do in the way of debate will avail nothing towards the liberation of the enslaved. What can be done to this end I think must be done chiefly by colonizing; and from the first to this day I have been the unshaken friend of colonization. To say nothing of the abstract question of slavery, I believe it is no person's duty to emancipate his slaves till he can see a probability of their being in as favorable a condition as before emancipation. I believe, however, that it is the duty of all slaveholders to be seeking for the opportunity to set their slaves at liberty in such manner as shall be for their advantage.

I can readily conceive of a nominal freedom of Africans, much worse than the bondage they generally experience. Let covetous masters liberate their slaves immediately; what would be the result? If not reformed from their covetousness, they may soon so manage as to bring these emancipated ones into a state much more abject than they have yet endured, and still let them be nominally free. As for emancipation upon the soil, I have not yet been able to see how it can be effected to the profit of the emancipated, till the great mass of the slaveholders shall become pious.

Meanwhile the abolitionist doctrines, which at first had met with considerable opposition in the New England States because of their long-standing commercial ties with the Southern planters, were gaining ever-increasing adherents even in Maine. The first anti-slavery society in that state was formed in Hallowell in November, 1833, and was followed in 1835 by a State Anti-Slavery Society under Samuel Pond of Bucksport as president. In 1835, also, the short-lived Maine Union in Behalf of the Colored Race, a middle-of-the-road organization which urged the final extinction of slavery, but decried excitement and violence, was founded in Portland under William Ladd of Minot. A scrap of paper found among Mr. Fisher's documents and dated June 25, 1835, records that, together with "30 other ministers," he had attended the meeting at "the Widow Billings in Bangor to consult what to do for the benefit of the colored population of this nation." This was the preliminary meeting to the founding of the Maine Union. Mr. Fisher apparently was not present at the actual founding three months later.

In spite, however, of these centers of agitation, the Maine Legislature in 1836 issued the following statement: "Slavery is a question in which we as a State have no interest; it is unknown in Maine, and those States who recognize its existence have the exclusive control of the subject within their borders. . . . It is not for Maine, or the citizens of Maine, to interfere with the internal regulations of any other independent State; no possible good can result from such an interference with affairs over which they can exercise no control." [1] That this statement, which seemingly not only defined the policy of the State, but also expressed its lack of interest in the question of slavery, was, nevertheless, not supported in general by its people, particularly by those in the rural areas, is shown by the resolutions against slavery adopted by most of the County Conferences of Churches, whose clergy were in many cases staunch supporters of the anti-slavery cause.

The Kennebec Conference of Churches was the first to take this stand in September, 1833, two months before the formation of the Hallowell Anti-Slavery Society. The Hancock and Waldo

[1] L. C. Hatch, ed., *Maine, A History*, Vol. I., p. 293.

Conference followed in October, 1834, and the next few years saw the Conferences of Penobscot, York, Somerset, and Washington in the same camp. By the middle of the year 1839 nine of the eleven Church Conferences, in varying degrees of vigor, it is true, had announced their condemnation of slavery. It is significant to note that the Conferences of Cumberland and Lincoln Counties, which possessed respectively the centers of Portland and of Bath with close business connections with the slave-holders and cotton growers of the South, did not join with their Christian brethren of the other counties. Not until the year 1854 with the passage of the Kansas-Nebraska Bill did Cumberland throw in its forces; and Lincoln, from 1842 on, only mildly deprecated "any attempt to justify slavery by the Bible" and asserted that the cause of the slaves demands "sympathies and prayers." [1]

The Hancock and Waldo Conference of October 7 and 8, 1834, is, of course, of especial interest because of the important membership within it of Mr. Fisher and his church; and its resolutions against slavery, taken on those eventful days in October, assume even larger interest when we realize that the meetings which passed them were held in Bluehill with Mr. Fisher and his church as hosts to the other churches of the two counties. The resolutions, introduced by the Rev. Silas McKeen of Belfast, were four in number. The two most noteworthy read as follows:

Resolved: That the act of holding human beings as property to be bought and sold is absolutely unjustifiable and highly criminal and ought, therefore, to be abandoned.

Resolved: That we approve of all wise and prudent measures tending to deliver our country from the guilt, disgrace, and danger of slaveholding; and to raise up our oppressed brethren of color to a full participation in all the privileges, both civil and religious, which we ourselves enjoy.

It is strange that Mr. Fisher in his Diary for these days neither

[1] For this account of the action taken against slavery by the various Church Conferences I am indebted to the Rev. Calvin Clark in his book, *Anti-Slavery and Maine Congregationalists.* Portland, 1940.

records these resolutions nor, indeed, even mentions them as being passed. He names the visiting ministers, from Bucksport, Prospect (now Searsport), Deer Isle, Castine, and Belfast, together with "several others accompanied by delegates," and says he "assigned them to their places of entertainment." Although in earlier portions of the Diary he is given to recording such conference meetings in detail, he is silent upon this most important one; nor does he in a letter to Mr. Cummings, supposedly descriptive of the Conference, refer to the resolutions passed or, in fact, relate any details other than the texts of the sermons preached, none of which would seem to bear on the subject of slavery, the reports given, and the fact that the Rev. Mr. Blood tarried for a few days after the Conference to assist him in his church. It is impossible, of course, to assign any entirely plausible reason for such silence. His Diary entries, it is true, are much more brief in 1834 than in preceding years and, as has been noted, were completely discontinued in January, 1835. At the time of the Conference, and earlier, he has been greatly cheered by a long-awaited revival in his church, which, perhaps in his mind, takes precedence for the moment even over the affairs of his country. But yet he finds time and space to thank God for his sixty-sixth birthday, which fell on October 7th, and to record that his crop of apples was "36 bushels." Was he, perhaps, unable and unwilling to go to the length traveled by his fellow churches? This he does not say.

Two years later in 1836 the Hancock and Waldo Conference, meeting in Ellsworth, passed even more drastic resolutions against slavery as "an outrage on human rights," the agitator at this meeting being the Rev. Stephen Thurston of Prospect. Mr. Fisher had a deep personal interest in young Mr. Thurston, who had been brought up in Sedgwick, lived and studied as a boy for some months with Parson Fisher, and was at one time a member of his church. Perhaps for the parson's peace of mind it was not unfortunate that he was prevented by illness from attending this conference meeting, as he writes in a letter to its clerk. In October, 1839, two years after his retirement, the Hancock and Waldo Conference at its autumn session on Mt. Desert, again apparently prompted by the zealous Mr. Thurston, adopted another resolution, which must have brought bitter grief to Mr. Fisher:

Resolved: That we regard any system of expatriation, without expressing any opinion as to its justice, as a totally inadequate remedy for slavery. Passed, *nemine contradicente.*

The last two words seem sufficient to prove that Mr. Fisher was again not present, for, even as a retired clergyman, he could hardly have kept silent had he heard his dream of many years thus assailed and derogated. Let us hope that he was bending over his beloved Hebrew in his study in Bluehill!

In January, 1838, he writes a letter to Mr. Cummings which clearly states his views on abolition and yet again reaffirms his faith in colonization:

I confess I sometimes feel almost weary of seeing so much in the *Mirror* about war and abolition; but for peace sake I endeavor to bear with it. I am sometimes ready to think that the idea of some persons about free discussion is the privilege of having all that is said, said *on their own side;* but we are all the subjects of *poor human nature.*

I am an unshaken friend of African Colonization, and I should be glad to see more in the *Mirror* in favor of it; but perhaps it will go on silently increasing, while the rushing sound of Abolition will be dying on the ear like the last sighing of a tempestuous wind, which bears over us a black, but rainless cloud.

I indeed wish for the emancipation of slaves, but not until religion so prevails in the slave-holding States that it can take place to the safety and advantage of both the slaves and their Masters.

And, finally, on March 18, 1839, he writes what was apparently his last letter to the *Mirror* on the subject dear to his heart:

Mr. Cummings:

In the *Mirror* of the 14th instant I met with a sketch of the doings of the late annual meeting of the Maine Anti-slavery Society, including 16 or 17 resolutions. I commenced the piece and read on with tolerably quiet feelings till I came to the following,

"Resolved, that at each successive development of the spirit and movements of the Colonization scheme, we are only re-assured that it originated in prejudice against the colored man, and that, in its entire action upon him, it cuts the sinews of effort, kills hope, and damps the upward aspirations of the soul."

When I read this, I confess my heart burned within me with displeasure at such an unkind slander and unmerited reproach of a cause that is to me very dear. I am so far advanced in life that I do not expect long to have much to do with abolition, or colonization, nor have I of late expected till now to make any further communication in public respecting them. But since reading the above resolution, I have felt constrained to let the world know something of what my views of the Colonization scheme are, and this I shall do in brief particulars.

1. In view of the amiable and venerable characters of most of those who brought forward and matured the Colonization scheme, I believe that it originated in sentiments of Christian benevolence, pure philanthropy, and sound patriotism.

2. I believe that it is calculated to meliorate the condition, elevate the character, and rouse the energies of those colored persons in general who embrace its offers.

3. I believe that hitherto it has been the occasion of the emancipation of more slaves, ten for one, than any other scheme that has been devised.

4. I believe that the colonies planted in Liberia are destin'd to be the germ of a future extended and prosperous Christian nation.

5. I believe that these colonies open a door for the introduction of Christian missions into the interior of Africa more favorably than any other plan that could be set on foot.

6. I believe that if the slave trade on the western coast of Africa is ever to be terminated, colonies along the coast will have a great share in bringing it to a close.

7. I believe the several checks and disasters which have been

experienced by the colonies are designed, in the wise providence of God, to be as the beating of storms upon a tree standing in the open field; if it sustain the shock, they make its roots the firmer.

8. I believe that, though colonization should never remove from this nation a hundredth part of the colored population, it will in time future provide a peaceful and happy asylum for thousands of emancipated slaves, who otherwise would see little before them but hopeless bondage.

9. I believe that the colonization scheme, in its general features, tendencies, and aim, is worthy of the approbation, esteem, and support of the great body of Christians, and true patriots in the nation.

These in brief are some of my leading sentiments upon this subject, whether I shall stand alone in them or have many associates. Such they are and such I expect they will continue to be, and I am not ashamed to own them.

My motive in the above declarations is to cast in my two mites for the encouragement of a cause which I believe to be very good and very cruelly aspersed. As for pecuniary assistance, small is the amount that my circumstances enable me to contribute; but what I can, I will cheerfully bestow.

Mr. Fisher never relinquished his faith in the Colonization Society or his labors in its behalf. His devotion to it was constant and unyielding. He was an ardent reader of *The African Repository and Colonial Journal,* the publication of the Society between 1829 and 1844; and he left among his possessions an almost complete file, bound carefully in leather by himself and interpolated by many marginal notes of comment and enthusiasm. If one is inclined to question the wisdom of his long and firm adherence to an organization pledged to such a hopeless task, one must admire his tenacity to his principles even in the face of growing opposition against its complete inadequacy to meet the magnitude of its problem. One must recognize also his early awareness and keen foresight of what the question of slavery must finally mean to a united nation, nor criticise too severely his staunch and unwavering stand against immediate emancipation. Perhaps, indeed, he foresaw more clearly than many others what proved to be the tragic and even, in many cases, the disastrous consequences of an Act so inevitable and in itself so just and imperative—consequences which, had he lived to see them, would have wrung with pity his always warm and humane heart.

IX

THE LAST YEARS OF THE
REV. JONATHAN FISHER, A.M.

I N his Diaries from 1830 to January, 1835, when he discontinued them, the Rev. Mr. Fisher gives ample evidence that all is not well between him and his "beloved people." On January 3, 1830, he preaches a sermon on the necessity of strict obedience to the commands of God in order to enjoy "true rather than false prosperity," in which sermon he presents a careful, but rather discouraging survey of the spiritual condition of his church and town. There are, he states, 1362 inhabitants of Bluehill, males 696, females 666, under age 777. There are in the entire parish only 666 Bibles and Testaments; there are but 73 members of the Congregational Church, although of the Baptist there are 152. Within the village there are 7 Methodists; and, he is deeply sorry to say, there is indisputable proof that Arminianism, yea, even Universalism, Unitarianism, and Deism have their dangerous, deluded, and imperilled followers even among the members of his own flock.

Perhaps such a sermon did not add to the popularity of Parson Fisher; yet he continued, with his customary adherence to the truth as he saw it, to preach others which unmistakably widened the rift between him and his parishioners. In November, 1831, he is discoursing from Isaiah 1: *I have nourished and brought up children, and they have rebelled against me*; in August, 1832, he announces as his text, also inspired by Isaiah: *I have spread out my hands all day to a rebellious people*. His letters to his children and to others during these years describe his dismay and anxiety. "Alas," he writes, "what a falling off in the church and society under my care. I am borne down in spirit because of it." In a letter to his son Josiah he says that the

Roxana Ray controversy, settled, one remembers, in 1829 by the
calling of a Church Council to the disastrous advantage of Col.
Matthew Ray and his recalcitrant wife, has never lost its dire
effects and that he is distressed over the voluble distaste of many
among his flock, not only toward church discipline, but also
toward his own unchanging doctrines. He, however, states his
position with fervor: "The doctrines of divine foreordination;
entire human depravity; predestination, or eternal election; free
justification and the perseverance of saints are all precious to
me, notwithstanding all that in these days is said against them.
So long as the Scriptures live, these doctrines will live; and so
will the doctrine of man's free, voluntary agency and his ac-
countability to God for his conduct."

In the autumn of 1834 he is immensely cheered by signs of an
approaching revival. His Diary for these months is almost wholly
concerned with the hope that his last years in the Bluehill church
may be thus justified, that God has hearkened to his prayers for
a renewing of His spirit among the erring children of his charge.
Day by day, as "the healing streams continue to flow," he names
and counts the souls who are "indulging faint hopes," who are
"entertaining hopes," and who have "attained to a blessed hope."
"Oct. 13. Mary Dodge entertaining a hope. Several others under
serious impression." "Oct. 15. Julia Dodge and Elvira Stevens
indulging hope. In all=5." "Oct. 27. Abigail and Dolly Powers,
Mrs. Asa Clough, Abigail Johnson, and Lois Kimball. In all=
13." By November 24th the number has mounted to 44; by
November 30th it has reached 50!

One feels his anxiety in these brief entries. In one he writes
of his concern that "37 of the 50 are females," that "40 out of
the 50 are unmarried," and that "25 are under 20 years of age."
"How many of them will endure to the end," he says, "is not
for me to know." Such comments suggest that even *his* knowledge of human psychology leads him to question their "future
stability." In late November he is hurt by a request from several
in his church that a minister from Bangor be called to preach

for several weeks in the hope that more souls may be gathered in. "I have hints," he writes, "that my preaching is not fashionable enough and that I am too strenuous for the doctrine of Election." He compromises by inviting the Rev. Mighill Blood of Bucksport to return to Bluehill, after a sojourn there in October, to add his help and eloquence. The Rev. Wooster Parker of Castine also comes "for two discourses," and Hosea Kittredge, still preceptor of the Academy, proffers "very assiduous labors in the divine cause." In January, 1835, he writes in the last entries of his Diary that 12 more have been added to the 50 presumably saved, and rejoices that among these are "my son Willard and his wife, Mary"; and in a letter dated March 30, 1835, he records that 34 of the 62 have united with his church.

But although this "progressive, still reformation" without doubt brought a measure of healing and comfort to his injured pride and anxious mind, it is evident from his letters that early in the year 1836 he is considering his resignation and the establishment of a successor to his pulpit and pastorate. "What will become of the Church in this place," he writes in a letter to his children, "I know not, but as for the true Church in the world, God will take care of it. Of this I have no doubt. I have been generally calm in my mind; I wish I may continue so; but I shall not know my strength until it has been more tried. My attachment to the world has been, and still is, too strong. God's purpose may be to attenuate the ties that hold me to it. Were I in everything more submissive to his will, I might be more happy and more useful. I do desire that whenever I shall drop my mantle, some good Elisha will take it up."

His decision to drop his mantle was hastened by a serious illness which attacked him in April, 1836. He does not name the illness, but, in a letter written after his recovery, says that from April to August he was "reduced almost to a skeleton" and that his life "for several weeks hung in doubt." He speaks of severe pain in his head, back, and right side, of a painful cough, and of an itching from head to feet, which, especially at night, caused him to long to tear his flesh from his bones and from which for months he had "no surcease." He is grateful for the kindness of his doctors who "gave" him their bills and for the calmness of mind which, after his headache had abated, stayed with him throughout his sickness.

"I generally enjoyed spiritual comfort in my sickness," he writes, "but in the extremity of my suffering I was constrained to plead almost constantly for patience. My first concern, once the pain had left my head, was to examine the ground of my religious hope. This issued in satisfying evidence that my hope was well-grounded. I next meditated upon all the doctrines usually termed evangelical and orthodox. I found great delight in them all; and I could not leave out one of them without breaking a golden chain, no, not even personal, absolute, eternal Election. I hope I shall derive lasting benefit from the chastisement which God in his wisdom has inflicted upon me."

On September 12, 1836, he writes the following letter to his church and his parish in Bluehill:

My Dear Friends,

Having spent a long period in ministerial labors among you, I have become strongly attached to the Church and Society in this place; and it will not be without a measure of grief, and reluctance, in some respects, that I shall witness the dissolving of the relation I sustain towards you. But having been visited with painful and long protracted sickness, and being still unable to perform the duties of Pastor and teacher, and my constitution having received a severe shock, I think it may be expedient that a Successor should be settled in my room. Should you, my friends, conclude in favor of such a measure, I feel willing to have the Pastoral relation dissolved upon the following conditions:

1. That my stated salary cease from the 13th of last July.
2. Having spent the best part of my days laboring among you for the space of forty years, with not a large salary, and having been able to lay up no money, that I have secured to me by the Parish the sum of $2 per week, during my natural life, for the support in part of me and my family.

3. Should my Successor desire to spend some weeks in each year in missionary labors, relinquishing during such time his Salary, if the Parish desire it and my health permit, I will supply his place for the addition of $3 per week to the $2 above stated.

4. Should I at any time receive a missionary appointment, and labor on usual conditions, during the time of such service, I will give up the aforesaid $2 per week.

Should these conditions prove acceptable, and a worthy Successor be settled among you, I shall freely consent to retire from the office of Pastor and teacher, which I now sustain; but in the meantime I will stand ready occasionally to assist my Successor for a sabbath or two, when out of health or on a journey.

And now I will just add that I have long desired to see a faithful Pastor and Teacher settled over this Church and Society before my departure; and should your deliberations issue in such an event, I pray that it may please God to bless his labors among you, that he may be long spared to minister to you, and that you may be well united in him, and among yourselves, and live in peace one with another, and that for Christ's sake you may be received in succession to the heavenly mansions, when called to bid adieu to this transitory state.

With much affection, yours in the bonds of the Gospel of peace,

Jonathan Fisher.

A town-meeting held on September 24, 1836, acted somewhat summarily upon Mr. Fisher's letter. It voted to call a Successor in his place and to accord him $2 a week for one year, but for no longer. Subsequent meetings in the spring of 1837 name a committee "to see what subscriptions can be raised for Mr. Fisher" and set plans in order for the calling of an Ecclesiastical Council to convene on October 25, 1837, both "to attend to the subject of dissolving the Pastoral relation between the Church and the Rev. Jonathan Fisher and to ordain the Rev. Albert Cole as the Pastor and Spiritual Teacher of the said Church and Society."

Concerning these matters so close to him, Mr. Fisher's correspondence reveals little either of disappointment or of undue anxiety. In a letter written to his children in November, 1837, and filled with village news, the weather, a report on the year's farm produce, and accounts of family health and doings, he states briefly that the Rev. Mr. Cole is to receive $600 per annum (in place of his own $280), that Mr. Cole has himself "privately pledged" to employ him "6 Sabbaths a year at $6 a Sabbath, which may help me a little," and that he believes Mr. Cole "not only sound in doctrine, but truly pious." "All this I have sustained," he concludes, "not without some depth of feeling, but with calmness, and, I trust, unfeigned submission. I am now thrown upon the kind hand of God, and the avails of my own industry. I think it probable that for the present I shall work on the farm and at mechanics, and preach now and then a Sabbath and a lecture in Bluehill and vicinity; and I desire that I may not fail to give good private religious instruction whenever I have opportunity. . . . As respects my temporal concerns, I may remark that I have at present a competency. I owe but little, and I have about $200 due to me. I raised this year about 50 bushels of potatoes, some other sauce, such as beets, beans, and peas, and probably 5 bushels of wheat. The crops of wheat, barley, and oats in Maine this summer have been very good. This is a great mercy. Oh, if the fruits of righteousness were as abundant, we should be a happy State!"

Nor does he write at length concerning the Council, which, with pastors and delegates from eight churches, sat on October 23rd and 24th. He was evidently present at least at one session, for he speaks briefly of "taking an unconditional dismission from my beloved charge"; he refers also to "the very flattering recommendation" given him by the Council, although he nowhere records it. The town records, however, which up to the year 1850 include all parish records having to do with the business aspects of the "Established Church," give this recommendation in full. It reads as follows:

We are happy to state that no feelings but those of Respect and Kindness have been exhibited towards the Rev. Mr. Fisher and that, after a Ministry of more than forty Years in this place, he retires, venerable for his years, for his attainments in Learn-